The Voyage of The Aegre

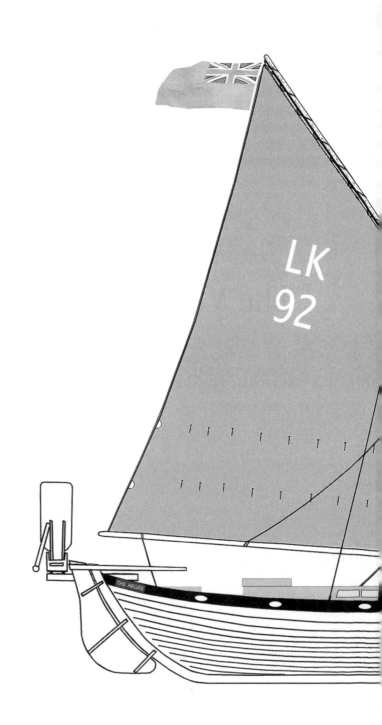

The Voyage
of
The Aegre

From Scotland to the South Seas
in a Shetland boat

NICHOLAS GRAINGER

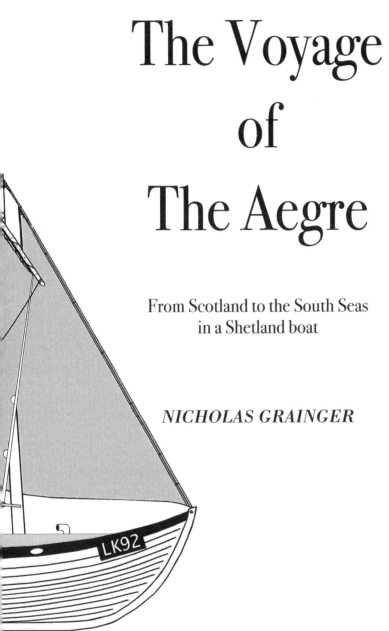

Vinycomb Press
MELBOURNE
2023

Published by Vinycomb Press
PO Box 2440, Brighton Nth, Victoria 3186, Australia

Email info@vinycombpress.com

In association with Left Field Editions, Ludlow

ISBN 978–0–6457639–0–4

E-ISBN 978–0–6457639–1–1

A catalogue record for this book is available from the National Library of Australia

Cover Design: Gene Carl Feldman

Front cover: *The Aegre* departs Ardmore, NW Sutherland, during sailing trials, July 1973. Photo: Jim Archer-Burton

Back cover: A pair of wandering albatrosses. Photo: Nicholas Grainger

Line drawing of Shetland boat under construction on the cover flap and on page 35 used with permission of Dr. A Osler, reproduced from *The Shetland Boat: Mainland and Fair Isle*, 1983 and 2016, A. Osler, Pub. The Shetland Heritage Trust in association with the National Maritime Museum.

Distances: At sea distances are expressed in nautical miles (nm), where 100 nm = 115 land miles and 185 kilometres.

For Tomoko

With thanks for her love, encouragement, insight and support

Foreword

This is an epic sailing tale. They had no experience, no money and an unsuitable boat. Yet they made the voyage of a lifetime.

It's not just the wind that propels boats, it's the determination of the people who sail them. And this couple had more than enough to get themselves halfway round the world.

Your boat is a wreck and sinking, your sextant has gone over the side and you are lost. Oh, and you're hundreds of miles from land. What do you do now? You dig deep and show what true seamanship you possess.

The voyage started as a dream, but when it became a nightmare they showed what true seamanship is.

From a simpler age of sailing when you were led across oceans by the sun and the stars, this book deserves to join the classics. It is simply a top class read.

Paul Heiney
Royal Cruising Club

Foreword

Contents

Maps

Drawings

Photographs

Prologue

'Do you think we're all right?' Julie shouted, emerging from the little cabin of *The Aegre* for her watch and feeling the growing strength of the wind. A nearby breaking wave top roared behind us in the pitch darkness, surrounding the stern in white phosphorescence, then slowly fading in our wake. The wind and sea had been rising since we'd left Tahiti, and no light was needed to show how rough it was.

I shouted back that I thought we should be OK. We'd had weather as bad as this before with no real problem. The boat would swoop and dive, in and out, up and over every wave, but unlike bigger boats, we rarely got any solid water on deck. Our little boat seemed as safe as could be. I gave her a smile and ducked down into the cabin, sliding the hatch shut behind me.

Out of the wind and into the haven of our cosy cabin, its small oil light giving a sense of security and calm. I crawled forward and sprawled onto our damp but comfortable bunk. Sliding out of my thermal underwear, I pulled the duvet up, checked the time, about 00:30, and quickly fell asleep …

I could hear roaring, then I was turning head over heels. My eyes were clenched shut. I managed to open them, but it made no difference to the blackness. Where was I? I'd been asleep in the oil-lamp-lit cabin. Now I was lying in water, but breathing air. What the hell was going on? Were we sinking? Where was Julie?

'Julie! Julie!' I shouted.

There was no reply.

Chapter 1
Learning to live

'The proper function of man is to live, not to exist. I shall not waste my days in trying to prolong them. I shall use my time.' — Jack London

My uncle went to sea in a boat with a calico skin. Yes, they still use them for fishing in south-west Ireland. But he wasn't a fisherman, although as a churchman he was a fisher of souls. The boat was a traditional 30ft open curragh comprising a light oak and larch frame over which was stretched a tarred skin of two thicknesses of cheap calico. He and his pals built it to re-enact the voyage of St Columba from Northern Ireland to Iona, a small island off the west coast of Scotland, 1,400 years before. It was 1963, I was 13, living in England, and I followed their adventure through my mother. It got me thinking.

In those days, my only connections with the sea were the heavy oak beams in our old thatched cottage in the village of Cottenham, near Cambridge. Strangely shaped with unused dowel holes, salvaged from wrecked ships, they said. They were massive. I wondered what sort of ships they'd been part of, to be so big and strong. Where had they been? What stories could they tell?

My mother was a bit like her brother, talkative, energetic, imaginative, and full of grand passions. She loved telling stories. My favourites were about growing up in Ireland and her adventures with her sister Douglas (yes, that was her name). They would go youth hosteling in the nearby Mourne mountains. Ridge walking by day, ceilidhs by night; the hearts they must have broken. They were quite a pair.

'What fun we had!' she would say as she told me one story after another, her eyes sparkling. She was full of energy, and every day she set me an example of how to live a full life. 'Wear out, don't rust out', she would say.

I was doing my best.

I started sailing when I was seven with a friend on the River Cam, not far from Cambridge. The Cam isn't wide, and a Moth is an unstable one-person dinghy, but we two seven-year-olds would tack upwind, run back down to a bridge, tack back upwind, until it was too dark to see the shore. We became pretty good at it. But then my friend's family moved away, taking the Moth with them.

I took to cycling. Encouraged by my mother, I cycled further and further. Every weekend, every back road, every lane, old Roman roads, distant towpaths, disused bridges, old gravel pits and decommissioned WWII airfields. Cycling alone, I loved exploring them all. 'You are now leaving Cambridgeshire', a road sign would say. I'd smile and pedal harder.

When I was seven, my parents sent me to King's College Choir School in Cambridge. This private prep school for boys is famous for its choir. With some of my generation's most outstanding musical talent as classmates, I quickly realised I had no musical talent, nor was I much better in the classroom or out on the playing field.

But I learned something different through going to King's. Most of the boys were boarders, their time day and night largely organised. I was a 'day-boy' living at home and travelling daily to school. It took about an hour each way, a bus ride to Cambridge, then a long walk across town. In the mornings, I would hurry so as not to be late for school but would dawdle back, exploring the laneways of the town that only a curious seven-year would notice. It could take me hours to get home, free time to fill as I pleased. I became independent, enjoying my adventures and the uncertainty of discovering new places. I wanted to be an explorer when I grew up.

King's wasn't a school for explorers, and interest or abilities in such things went largely unrecognized, but then, in my final year, my good friend Tim and I applied for and won a school travel scholarship to cycle and camp around Devon and Cornwall on the far side of Britain. Carrying heavy loads on our bikes, camping in torrential rain, and running out of money, the two-week trip had all the challenges of a grown-up adventure. We had to be hardy and resourceful, and I loved it. We were 12.

My independence was encouraged by my parents, who were adventurous for their time. Every summer we took off on a two-week family camping trip; my parents, my sister Diana and I in an 850cc Austin Mini with a tent on the roof rack, off to look for some sun. To the coast of East Anglia, then to Cornwall and Devon, then to France, Belgium, Holland, Germany, and Switzerland's mountains and valleys.

But sitting in the back of a Mini for hours isn't so much fun when you're ten or twelve. I would read, discovering how a good story could take me into another world. I was Ishmael aboard the *Pequod* with Captain Ahab, sailing the South Seas and the only survivor of the fatal encounter with the great white whale (in an illustrated edition for younger readers). It held me enthralled, not just for a car ride but for years.

On other days I was Joshua Slocum sailing single-handed around the world on the boat I'd built with my own hands. I was Shackleton sailing the *James Caird* to save my crew from Antarctic disaster. I was Bombard crossing the Atlantic in a rubber dinghy to show that seawater could be safely drunk. Well, I had a vivid imagination, and it was more interesting than watching the passing hedgerows of northern France. Books became my friends, and their stories stayed with me long after the holidays were done.

From those casually arranged camping trips with my parents, I realised that travelling is better if it isn't planned too much, and that the freedom to follow a whim can lead to unexpected delights. I learned that the journey can be as much fun as the destination, or more. By the time I was fourteen, I thought the world of the 1960s was a happy and safe place to be explored, full of adventures to be had. Of course, I was naïve; the cold war was becoming even colder, and the first US troops were being sent to Vietnam.

But of more interest to me were growing newspaper stories about a certain yachtsman called Francis Chichester.

Singlehanded sailing captured my father's attention. He'd never shown any interest in boats or sailing before, but the first singlehanded yacht race across the Atlantic in the summer of 1960 caught his imagination. I started to share his attention.

Neither of us knew much about sailing, but there were many apparent challenges. How could one person steer the yacht and make sail changes to suit the wind while also navigating and keeping a lookout for other ships all the time? Wouldn't the sailor have to stop sailing so they could sleep? And how would they cope with being alone at sea for weeks? Would they go a bit mad? Moreover, a single person would have to master all the knowledge and skills needed to sail a yacht across an ocean, particularly coastal and celestial navigation, how the weather works, tides and currents, and how to maintain all the yacht's equipment. Add to that the knowledge and skill to plan such a voyage and fund it.

It wasn't surprising that only five were on the start line for that inaugural race in 1960. Amid great excitement, the first yacht to finish was *Gipsy Moth III*, skippered by Francis Chichester. Chichester had the tuned media sense of today's celebrities. Riding the publicity of that first transatlantic win, he innovatively secured sponsorship to have a much larger yacht designed and built which he sailed non-stop from Plymouth to Sydney, Australia, and back.

It was a pioneering voyage for the reporting of progress by radio from the yacht at sea to a newspaper, and millions of readers, including me, followed his subsequent singlehanded voyage around the world in 1966/7. Suddenly we could all be there vicariously, sharing the highs and lows, getting an insight into what was involved in sailing singlehanded around the world. It was just the most exciting thing I could imagine.

I wondered if ocean voyaging on a small yacht was feasible without good connections, sponsorship, and the ensuing demands and expectations. Alec Rose, an ex-market gardener and grocer, showed just a year later that it was, completing a single-handed around-the-world voyage that was the antithesis of Chichester's, because Rose had no sponsorship and was using just a simple traditional cruising yacht,

More stories about crossing oceans in small boats gripped me. They kept coming up in the newspapers, such as in the late summer of 1966 when John Ridgway and Chay Blyth landed on the west coast of Ireland. Having rowed west to east across the North Atlantic in 92 days, the first time it had been rowed in the 20th century.

But sailing, rowing and adventuring on the ocean seemed no more accessible to me than going to the moon. My childhood friend with the Moth dinghy had moved away, and my father's interest in sailing only extended to reading about it. We lived fifty miles from the sea.

At 13, I moved to Soham Grammar School out in the flat fens near Ely with my friend Tim as weekly boarders, furthering a sense of independence. Tim and I shared a room for five years. Too easily distracted to study any subject seriously, we knew we were unlikely to win any academic awards. Instead, with our independent minds, we cooked up a plan to win the school's annual travel scholarship. We studied the post-trip accounts of all the previous winners for tips. How could we make our entry stand out and be a sure winner?

Others had gone south; we'd go north. Others had borrowed Mum's car or hitchhiked, one had cycled, we'd ride a tandem, and so on. We briefly considered Iceland but then settled on travelling to eastern Lapland, the wild, desolate Lake Inari region in northern Finland on the border with north-west Russia, hundreds of miles north of the Arctic Circle. In summer, the snow melted, and our 'Study of the Flora and Fauna of Eastern Lapland', loosely linked to our A-Level Biology studies, looked feasible, if slightly mad.

Come the school's Prize Giving Day, the academic winners came away with a new edition of the Oxford Dictionary, but it was the Henry Morris Travel Scholarship for Tim and me — 50 UK pounds (1,072 UK pounds, US$1,300, in 2022) in used notes. And then we were off. A wild idea that came to fruition.

Like any decent expedition, half the plan went out of the window before we even left home. In this case, the Soviet Government refused our request to go into the Lake Inari region. We thought it was Finnish territory anyway. No matter, we thought. We'll head in that direction and see what happens.

Tim borrowed a 1920s Royal Enfield tandem, painted pink, it had belonged to the great-aunt of a friend. We called her Samantha. She was more used to being taken for a romantic spin in Cambridge's Grantchester Meadows than along the coarse gravel tracks of sub-Arctic Lapland.

We badly underestimated everything, from how rough the roads were and their effect on poor Samantha, the price of food, the persistence of the little black flies and, on a positive note, the friendliness and support of people along the way.

It was a long hard climb up from the coast to the central plateau. Once there, it was a bleak place. The only signs of people were occasional Lapp camps. Approaching one and caught in heavy rain, we were waved into a tent to shelter. A kettle was boiling on the fire in the middle, and they gave us a warm drink and dried reindeer meat to chew on. We shared our lunch too, crispbread and cheese. They were so warm and welcoming.

A couple of weeks into the trip, in Enontikeo, a small remote town in northern Finland, Samantha finally said enough was enough. After repairing countless punctures, Tim, our self-appointed mechanic, announced that something or other was bent and unrepairable there, and she could carry us no further. But as she was on loan, we somehow had to get her (and ourselves) back to Cambridge, over 2000 miles away. And we were almost out of money.

We found an occasional bus that went north-west to Tromsø on the coast and bought a ticket there for Samantha. Then, as the bus disappeared into the distance, we set out to walk and hitchhike the 335 kilometres (208 miles) to Tromsø. In 1967 there was little traffic on the gravel tracks across Lapland, but the drivers that did appear were generous, and we made it to Tromsø within a day or two. We found Samantha leaning against a wall at the bus depot, waiting for us. Fortunately, nobody else had taken a fancy to her.

Our plan was to take the mailboat with Samantha back to Bergen, 1,750 km (1,070 miles) to the south, but a quick count of our expedition finances left us with a serious dilemma. If we took the mailboat, we'd have no money left for food. Being 17-year-old boys, food was definitely a priority. We resolved the issue by buying a ticket for Samantha, saw her safely aboard, then went back ashore ourselves, headed out walking south to hitchhike the whole length of Norway to Bergen. At least we could eat along the way.

Quite a few adventures later, we made it to Bergen. Samantha did too, and we met up in time to catch our booked ferry back to England. And then we were home.

Did I learn anything from the experience? Yes, lots, but something like 'Things can always get better' stuck with me. For instance, the day up on the central plateau when we came upon a Lapp camp in sheeting rain, and they took us in.

I like to think that Samantha is still tootling around Cambridge, taking romantic rides out to the Grantchester Meadows, nobody but her knowing the places she's been, the stories she could tell.

Back to school for our final year. Ocean sailing, though unreachable, still fascinated me, but I'd developed another interest, in ham radio, and in an unlikely way, this led to my first yachting opportunity. When I became known to my friends as a budding 'ham', a school friend, Pip, asked if I would rewire a yacht his parents had bought and were refitting. *Mollyhawk* was an ageing 14.3 m (47 ft) wooden centreboard sloop which they had brought up the river Cam to Cambridge. She was in the river alongside Banhams boatyard, better known for their ultra-light racing rowing shells. I'd never seen a yacht close up before, and this led to me spending all my spare time one summer aboard her. I loved every minute.

Later I joined her to sail down the bleak east coast of Norfolk and Suffolk. But bad weather rolled in, and soon we were shipping waves over the bow, the white and green water sweeping aft all the way to the cockpit. Hardly able to contain my excitement, I couldn't sleep for two days. Seasickness decimated the crew, but I was on watch with one other, having the time of my life. In the end the bad weather prevailed, and it was all a bit much for poor *Mollyhawk,* who creaked and groaned in protest. Soon the consensus (of wiser heads than mine) was to head for nearby Lowestoft's small, sheltered harbour. But I was changed. I'd glimpsed another world, another life, a new future.

Then reality intruded. My parents expected me to go to university, but radio, photography, an old motorbike and young women were filling my mind. Well, one young woman in particular: Julie Brannan.

With her wavy long blond hair, sheepskin Afghan coat, and left-wing views, Julie was sixties cool, interesting and top of her class, with little apparent effort. She knew all about politics and went on marches and demonstrations. She was the middle one of five sisters, and political debate raged around her mum's big kitchen table, where the teapot never got cold. Her LPs were all quite different from mine. She wasn't at all like me, or anyone I knew. I loved how different she was from me. I was fascinated by her. And she seemed to quite like me, though I didn't know why.

My final school years became a bit of a blur. I should have been studying for university entrance but the temptations of Julie, the first open-air music festivals in Cambridge and hitchhiking around England, France, Germany, Switzerland and Italy were much too attractive. I travelled all over the UK and Europe. The world seemed wonderful, but I failed to get a university place. However, I qualified to study Dispensing Optics at the City College in East London. It would have to do. I would learn about lens design and how to make and fit people's glasses. It didn't sound appealing, but no matter, I was moving to London, it was 1969, and a new world beckoned. And besides, Julie and her family had moved to London the year before.

Living in London and studying optics full-time left much time for other things. It probably shouldn't have, but I filled it with photography, competitive rowing and Julie Brannan. Julie was in her final year of school and still excelling. What would she major in at university? Maths, English, Law, Political Philosophy? Not many have such a choice. Meanwhile we strolled in Kensington Gardens among the beautiful people and saw Simon and Garfunkel in the Albert Hall. Life together was good.

One of my ambitions for London was to join a rowing club. In Cambridge, I'd enviously watched the university crews as they stroked their wonderfully long, sleek, rowing shells over the water in a masterfully controlled way, with an intoxicating sense of elegance and brooding power.

Now I joined Furnivall Sculling Club near Hammersmith Bridge and was soon part of a new crew of four. Suddenly every weekend and a few nights a week were spoken for. Of course, I was too skinny and light at 154lb (70 kg), but I discovered that whilst I wasn't overly strong, I had good stamina and could pull my weight in any boat and keep pulling it to the end. The training and racing were more demanding than anything I'd done before. Having to dig so deep, I discovered strength in myself I didn't know I had. The experience and knowledge would serve me well.

While in London and mainly rowing, my memory of *Mollyhawk* and sailing was far from my thinking, but strangely my mother was instrumental in rekindling it in 1971. I was twenty-one and soon to graduate from London's City College as a Dispensing Optician, but moving to an optician's practice somewhere in the suburbs didn't appeal to me. It seemed I had one last summer holiday of freedom before taking on a proper job.

'Why don't you go to John Ridgway's Adventure School in Scotland?' my mother suggested, 'You remember, the Atlantic rower fellow? I saw it advertised in *The Times*.'

'Huh!' I snorted, having just returned from a weekend hitchhiking expedition to the other side of Britain. 'Maybe I could get a job there!'

'Well, why don't you?' She challenged me.

'I will, I will,' I told her. 'You just watch.'

Chapter 2
Ardmore adventure

*'I wanted freedom, open air and adventure. I
found it on the sea.' — Alain Gerbault*

'I will, you just watch,' I'd half shouted at my mother with the exasperation
of a 21-year-old irritated by a mother who not infrequently beat him to
the draw with disarmingly good ideas. I remembered that about five
years before, John Ridgway and Chay Blyth, had rowed across the Atlantic —
the first to do so in the 20th century. It was big news at the time in England. In
the library, I soon found the book they'd written about it, *A Fighting Chance*.
It was a stirring tale.

Later I read in the papers that they had both individually gained sponsorship
to enter the 1968 inaugural single-handed non-stop around the world yacht
race, sponsored by the *Sunday Times* newspaper. They were each loaned a
small yacht. But these turned out to be inadequate for sailing around the
world, and both Ridgway and Blyth retired before leaving the South Atlantic.

Now it seemed Ridgway had set up an adventure school in Scotland. The
ads were for early summer week-long courses for businessmen — sailing,
kayaking and walking in the mountains of north-west Scotland, and then in
midsummer two-week courses of the same activities for high school students.

An opportunity to meet and work face-to-face with the sailing and rowing
adventurer John Ridgway himself was beyond my dreams. I'd never imagined
such a chance. But my two days sailing on *Mollyhawk*, zero kayaking
experience and growing up in the flattest part of Britain hardly qualified me
to even wash the dishes. Could I actually get a job there?

Full of bravado and a certain independence and resilience fostered in
Lapland, hitchhiking across Europe and in a winning rowing four on the

Thames, I boldly wrote to Ridgway, asking for a summer job. It was early summer 1971.

An answer came more quickly than expected. Excitedly I tore open the envelope.

'Why don't you come up for a couple of weeks to see how we get on? Maybe read my book *Journey to Ardmore* for a bit of background.'

Astonished, I quickly accepted Ridgway's invitation and borrowed the book from the library. In it, Ridgway told his story. Boarding school, Merchant Navy, British Army, SAS, the row, the non-stop round-the-world yacht race and the adventure school. It was a story of endurance and persistence. I learnt how he and his wife Marie Christine had found an empty croft (small stone cottage) on the remote and sparsely populated north-west coast of Scotland just south of Cape Wrath and based the school nearby. The mountains of Foinaven, Arkle and Ben Stack ringed the north-western rim of the view from their croft. In the early summer, they ran week-long courses for middle-aged men and women, by day walking in the hills and sailing the ex-round the world race yacht out to the screaming sea bird colonies of nearby Handa island. At night Marie Christine served gourmet meals with fine wine. During the August summer holidays, they filled the adventure school with secondary school students. A demanding program of hill walking, kayaking, rock climbing, and sailing filled the days.

The Ridgways' plan was to run the school only over the summer each year and go off on their own adventure each winter, and the summer was already half over. Clearly I would be helping with the secondary school student program, which ran until early September.

As soon as the City College term ended, I farewelled Julie and was off up north on the train, firstly to Edinburgh, then on to Inverness and Lairg. I'd never been so far north in Scotland. Finally, I caught the little mail bus that ran out to the far north-west coast. The only passenger, I sat beside Michael, the driver, and an hour and 50 miles later, he pulled up in the middle of nowhere by a lonely signpost to Skerrika. Beneath it was a freshly painted sign: 'John Ridgway School of Adventure.' This pointed up a deserted track along a narrow valley. Soon I was helping Michael unload boxes and boxes of provisions into a small shed by the sign.

Then the mail bus noisily pulled away, leaving me in silence. John had said someone would pick me up from the mailbox. Around me in the heather were outcrops of lichen-covered rock and a small-stream trickling down beside the

Skerrika track. I settled down to wait on a comfy rock, enjoying the peace and quiet. To the north-east a long mountain ridge defined the skyline. It wasn't like the flat fenlands of Cottenham at all.

Soon I heard a distant engine revving in high gear and labouring slowly closer. Then it appeared at the top of the distant hill on the side road, slowly descending towards me. It was a battered green four-wheel drive, and it wheezed to a stop in front of the mailbox. Out stepped a fair-haired youngish man, with a wispy moustache wearing a red ski-style jersey and rough woollen walking breeches to just below the knee, long thick woollen socks and huge old climbing boots, worn like slippers, laces loosely tied. He introduced himself as Richard Shuff, Chief Instructor.

I helped him load the mailbox's contents into the back of the vehicle: sacks of flour, sugar, boxes of canned meat, butter, and sliced bread. Then we headed back up the hill on the rough road. At the top of the rise, the view suddenly opened, and for the first time, I saw Loch a' Chad-Fi. Its blue water was flecked with foam and a dark yellow-brown strip of exposed kelp around its edge. On the southern shore, perhaps a kilometre ahead of us, were the low brown buildings of the School. Then the road seal ended, and the track rose sharply. Richard lurched the vehicle into four-wheel drive, and we staggered on.

In that second full year of operation, John and Marie Christine ran the school with a small team of about eight young instructors and two cooks. Together, I discovered, they formed a close-knit team. I felt like an outsider and rather inadequate but, at the same time, unexpectedly welcome.

Ridgway himself looked the part, a big man with a badly broken nose. Meeting him for the first time, I was a bit in awe. He sat me down and explained how he wanted his instructors to live by three principles. He went on:

'This is a hard place to live; it can rain a lot, and it's often cold and windy. Working here, we all get exhausted sometimes and possibly short-tempered. To work here successfully, I want you to think positively. Not to complain about the weather, food, or others, but to be positive. To think about how you can make the most of what we have, how you can help others. To be a positive, not a negative person.

'I need you to be self-reliant. To be able to look after yourself, to remember to bring all the kit you need, and get the needed knowledge. There is no place here for the whining person asking, 'Who can I borrow a spoon from?'

'I want you to leave things better than you find them (including places and people). So, whether it's a boat you've been using or the bathroom, make sure it's a little better for the next person. Maybe a little cleaner, the boat fuelled up, the mooring lines coiled carefully. And the same goes for people around you.'

Today, business consultants try to sell such hype to cynical employees, but back in 1971, on the windswept shores of Loch a' Chad-Fi beneath the brooding slopes of Foinaven and Arkle, it was all new to me. Twenty-one years old, I was inspired. Moreover, most instructors demonstrated these behaviours, and I saw them working. John was right. It was a demanding environment. We all needed to share equipment, such as the boats, often used in dark and stormy conditions. They needed to be constantly secured the same way, left with fuel tanks full, bilges dry and oars correctly stowed. Our safety depended on it. Even our lives might one day. They seemed to make life a little easier for us all and became a way of life for me.

Standing beside John in the school venture was his wife, Marie Christine. Slim, pretty, usually laughing with her eyes sparkling, she hadn't been long out of a Swiss finishing school when she had met John at a roulette party at a wealthy country home north-west of London. Dressed in a dinner jacket with a hefty pile of chips, she thought he was a secret agent, her very own James Bond. At the time he was in the British Army's SAS, so she may have been more right than wrong. He said she brought him luck. Perhaps she did. Now at the adventure school, far from the casino, she handled all the bookings, travel, food, the bills, the licences, pretty much everything. A sort of Superwoman. She even wore gumboots with flair and style. But most importantly, she kept John in good spirits. Without her, the place might have been a bit grim at times because, as I came to learn, John did the worrying for both of them. For him, disaster was only a step away. The row lived on in his mind.

And then there was their daughter Rebecca, four, already skilled at charming her way into the hearts of us all.

I arrived early in the school holidays. Groups of school students were staying at the school, and I was assigned to look after a group of the eldest. With another instructor, I took them on overnight hikes up the rugged north-west coast, kayaking on Loch Dughail and sailing dinghies on Loch a' Chad-Fi and Loch Laxford. Of course, I wasn't an expert at any of these activities and spent the first few days on a crash course with Richard and some other instructors.

But the highlight for me every week was a day sailing with John and half a dozen students aboard *English Rose IV*. This was the yacht he had sailed single-handed as far as the South Atlantic in the Round the World Race a few years before.

We sailed her out through Loch Laxford into the open sea, then turned south to sail under the soaring cliffs of Handa Island amidst thousands of milling seabirds, the boat lifting to the long swell rolling in from the Atlantic. I willed the wind to freshen so we'd have to tuck in a reef and we'd start to ship water over the bow. I'd imagine we were headed south for the Cape Verde Islands, a thousand miles over the horizon. But we would turn, John would put the kettle on in the cabin for a cup of tea and we'd sail back into the calm of Loch Laxford and our mooring. I just wanted to keep going.

John's transatlantic rowboat was kept near the water's edge in a shed. Curious, I asked him to show me. Standing beside it, I imagined him and Blyth living for three months in the small area between the two decked-in ends full of buoyancy. It was spartan, with two bench seats and no cabin. The boat occupied most of the shed, but I knew it would feel small out on the water. Every move would have to be planned to avoid tipping it.

John explained how they had kept everything simple, but then, in 1966, little technology was available anyway. This was long before satellite phones and compact portable radio transceivers. Their absence led to issues modern adventurers give little thought to. They had no way of contacting the outside world, no way of seeking help if they needed it and no way of receiving weather information. Pre-GPS, they plotted their position using a sextant and chronometer to measure latitude and longitude, but to do that they needed to see the sun, and for any accuracy, they needed relatively calm weather. Both are in short supply in the North Atlantic.

So picture it: taking turns to row and sleep night and day, they pulled the heavy, ungainly boat along, averaging between 1 and 2 knots (1.8–3.7 kph), perpetually wet, unsure of their position and actual progress due to rare sun sights of questionable accuracy. They worried if they had enough food and water to last the (largely guessed) distance to go. They were probably perpetually worried that the weather would get worse and not only make rowing impossible but blow them back the way they had come or, even worse, overturn their boat. They were aware that no one knew where they were. If they needed help, it would never come. It must have played on their minds over the first month, then the second, then the third. Would it ever end? Had they been consigned to their own never-ending version of hell? With all that wind around, they must have wished for a sail. *Phew, rather them than me*, was all I could think.

The experience had profoundly affected John. 'Since the row, every day has been a bonus,' he often said. With death seemingly so close for so long, he'd thought much about life and how he wanted to live it should he survive. Over the endless hours alone heaving on the oars, he refined his ideas into the three principles he decided to try and live by. And the idea of the adventure school came to him. This would be a place where people of all ages could escape to, where they could face the challenges of nature rather than those of the next business meeting, sales targets or sheer employment boredom. Where young people could discover a new world of deserted mountains, lochs, the sea and themselves, finding strength they had never imagined.

All of which had led to the school he and Marie Christine had established at Ardmore.

I was in heaven: sailing, hiking, kayaking, guiding a small bunch of teenagers and doing everything to ensure they just had the best adventure ever. It was challenging for them and for me, but the spirit and sense of care amongst the instructors were unlike anything I'd experienced. At its heart were John and Marie Christine.

One sunny afternoon in my second week, I sat on a stool outside the Ridgways' croft high up on the hill above the loch, and Marie Christine gave me one of her famous haircuts. My late 60s London-style shoulder-length blonde hair was shorn to stubble, the hair blown away in the wind together with my old life. And John invited me to stay on for the rest of the summer.

John had a small library of sailing books. I'd never heard of most of these books, yachts or places, but now I studied them. Stories like that of Robin Knox-Johnston, the only finisher in the 1968 Single Handed Round the World Race. Knox-Johnston demonstrated the value of a small, uncomplicated, seaworthy wooden vessel and the importance of being a jack of all trades, highly resourceful and good at fixing things, because just about everything that could wear out or break on his yacht did.

I also read the terrible story of Donald Crowhurst and his high-tech trimaran entry in the same round-the-world race, a sobering tale for any yachtsman tempted to take on sponsorship for a yacht or voyage. Crowhurst keenly felt the pressure of disappointing his sponsors and took his own life mid-Atlantic.

Much earlier writings about solo voyages in small boats were just as fascinating and almost more relevant to me. Slocum, of course, but others are less well known today, such as *The Cruise of The Kate* by E E Middleton. Middleton was a notable eccentric, who despite making a passage to Australia and back aboard a sailing ship, the *Albermale*, did not believe the Earth was round. Aboard the 23ft *Kate*, Middleton sailed singlehanded around England in 1869. This was the first such recorded voyage and a hazardous undertaking with the constantly changing weather, tides, and shifting sandbanks, but more so for Middleton, for rather than taking an offshore route well away from coastal dangers, he stopped at almost every possible little harbour along the way. His only auxiliary power was an oar. I loved his flush-decked boat; *The Kate* just looked so strong.

There seemed to be many hard lessons in these and the other books in John's sailing library, but the most important to me was a thick book, *Cruising under Sail* by Eric and Susan Hiscock, a compendium of their decades of knowledge gained sailing a small yacht worldwide, with whole chapters on hull form, fitting out, safety at sea, ropes and ropework, spars, sails, accommodation, living onboard, practical navigation, maneuvering under sail, and management in heavy weather. I knew I'd found the bible. It was all I could think about. 'You've got to be keen on sailing to talk with Nick,' John said of me.

At the same time, I was getting a pressure cooker education on coping with sailing, kayaking and camping expeditions in the remote lochs and mountains with the changeable weather of north-west Scotland. Wind and rain, high tides, darkness and the biting midges were all in a day's work, but sailing came as easily to me as if I'd been doing it all my life. In my head, I had. As often as possible, I was out sailing. Out on the water, I felt truly alive, as if the boat was an extension of my body.

As we moved through that August of 1971, I knew that sailing was what I wanted to do. Racing didn't appeal to me, but rather the life on a small yacht at sea; the sense of freedom, harnessing the wind, relentlessly moving forward. I dreamt that one day I would sail the Atlantic. But I had so much to learn, and so much experience to gain. Finding a yacht was also going to be difficult, as I had no money.

Meanwhile, I got on well with the Ridgways. Marie Christine's outstanding competence in everything and John's relaxed style and humour entertained and inspired me as I came to know them better. While the school only ran over the summer, he encouraged me to use the winter back in London to study coastal navigation and offered to pay my fees for a Yachtmaster's coastal navigation correspondence course. He signed himself up too, and soon we both received a welcome package including brass dividers and a special ruler for measuring angles on charts. I determined to study hard and make the most of the autumn and winter. It was as if I was already on my way to a new life. I had so much to thank John and Marie Christine for.

Too soon, it was September, and the school was winding down. The holidays were over. A job as a dispensing optician in West London awaited me. Most reluctantly, on September 22nd 1971, I turned my back on the north of Scotland, the adventurous life, and hitchhiked south, wondering how I could possibly cope with returning to life indoors in London.

Chapter 3
A London winter and Scottish summer

'The only way to get a good crew is to marry one.' — Eric Hiscock

Back in London, it was time for another haircut. My sun and rain-bleached hair littered the floor, like my dream of sailing. Now my wind-burnt face was all that was left of my summer, and that would soon fade too.

I hoped to see Julie when I got back to London. I'd missed her over the summer, but she had already left London and gone to Warwick University to study mathematics.

I started working 9–5 in a small room interpreting eye correction prescriptions into optimised lenses, helping people choose frames, measuring faces, and fitting glasses. To keep sane, I kept going outside to look up at the sky between the buildings. I would squint into the sun, wondering about the purpose of life. At the end of each day, I would rush back to the room I'd rented, eat quickly, and then get out the charts to work on my latest navigation assignment. Usually, this was in the heavily tidal and shallow Thames estuary. I would calculate a yacht's true, magnetic and compass course to sail from one port to another. The yacht's course would need to allow for changing tides and winds. I'd work out when lighthouses would appear and disappear, where the tide, wind and shallows might meet and create a dangerous sea. And I'd calculate the best time to depart for the fastest course. I was a model student and studied harder than I ever had at school.

With my first month's pay I bought an old 650cc Triumph Bonneville motorbike and then on the weekends I'd roar up the motorway to visit Julie in Warwick. She seemed to be enjoying her new university life. But like it or not, she learnt a lot about sailing and my dream of going coastal and ocean cruising. But how could I fund a small yacht for coastal cruising and build my sailing experience?

One idea was to join up with another keen person, to share the work and our earnings. A few spells on oil rigs looked a better bet than optics. Sometime in the next three years, we'd buy a small yacht. Along the way, we'd build our sailing experience. Julie? I didn't think so, having just started her mathematics degree at a good university. But one of the Adventure School instructors, Krister Nylund, seemed ideal. We'd got on well. He was ever cheerful, resourceful, and a strong hard worker. I thought he'd be a great companion.

'Sailing is the answer!' I wrote to him with my idea of an ocean voyage together. He slowly replied, saying no, sorry, this was not for him. I was hugely disappointed.

I settled into working at the opticians in Feltham, SW London. I was boarding with an elderly widow, Mrs. Harrington, a tall, white-haired, rather elegant woman. She might have been austere, but she wasn't. She owned a toyshop and as I came to know her better she would bring back the latest novelties to test on me over dinner. We laughed and laughed. I would often share my adventure ambitions too. We got on well. One evening, I explained my frustrations with working at the opticians, my escape plan, and my difficulty finding a partner. 'Why don't you ask Julie?' she said. Well, I couldn't imagine Julie wanting to do it. She'd never even been on a boat. 'And she's just starting a mathematics degree. There's no way she'd drop out to go off to sail the world,' I said. 'If you were Julie, would you?'

She turned to me, smiling broadly. 'Like a shot', she replied.

Her answer shocked me, but I suddenly wondered if Julie was a possibility. Sure, she had no sailing experience, but she was one of those people that could pick up pretty much anything if she wanted to. She was a wonderful partner, but we'd never really talked about the future, we were young, it was 1971, the world seemed full of opportunities. But was it fair to distract her from her university studies?

Another trip back to Warwick, where I found Julie becoming bored with studying, already disillusioned with the university. Nervously I asked her if she would join me in my dream to go ocean sailing. To go forward together, to try and work at John Ridgway's School next summer, and maybe the next, harden ourselves up a bit, develop our sailing skills and experience. Spend the winters in the most lucrative temporary jobs we could find back in London.

Save and save. Look for a moderate-sized open sailing boat or small yacht. Do some coastal cruising. Possibly look for crewing positions on a charter yacht. One day, sail the world aboard our own.

Surely Julie would say no. But it was 1971, and there was a great sense of freedom in the air. And Mrs. Harrington was right, for Julie smiled, looked me in the eye and said, 'Yes, let's do it.'

I was stunned, and wondered where all this would lead.

The next step was to ask John and Marie Christine if they would employ us both for the 1972 spring and summer seasons. They responded to my letter with little enthusiasm. We met them one winter's day in York. They had reservations about Julie and me coming up together. I could continue as an instructor for sure, and Julie could become part of the small catering team, which she was quite amenable to. But to live together, we would have to be married.

'We can't have our school students going home and telling Mum and Dad that a couple of the staff were just shacked up together', said John. 'Sorry, you'd need to be married.'

Well, it was 1971, and the north of Scotland was a long way from the liberated London we knew.

By then, we had been together for about three years. Julie was 18, and I was 21. I don't think we'd ever talked of marrying before, any more than we had of sailing the Atlantic. In those days in oh-so-emancipated London, couples just lived together as we had. Marriage didn't seem important. But our dream of ocean sailing seemed important and if we needed to be married to advance that, so be it we agreed. It seemed almost a formality. But it felt good too. I loved Julie, she was a beautiful person. I thought she'd be a wonderful partner on this grand life-adventure, highly capable, adaptable, resourceful, loyal and well able to cope with me.

We married in mid-February 1972. It was just a small wedding, our parents, sisters and a few friends, with drinks and nibbles back at Julie's parents' house near Putney. Julie wore a long blue dress, matching her eyes, her long blonde hair falling to her shoulders. She looked stunning. We were so happy. That night Julie and I caught the overnight sleeper train to Inverness, then the branch line to Lairg and finally the little bus to the Skerrika mailbox on the far north-west coast. From there, we walked. It was deep winter and icy cold at the remote, deserted school buildings on the edge of Loch a 'Chad-Fi. We found a key to one of the huts and moved in, lighting a paraffin lamp in the cold stale air. No-one had lived there for months. Our honeymoon? For us the beginning of a new life.

A few days later, Chief Instructor Richard Shuff arrived to plan a training course for new instructors. Meanwhile there were new drains to be dug, paths to be laid, and endless painting, all supervised by maintenance man extraordinaire Lance Bell, a taciturn retired foundry foreman from Teesside. Lance had a pragmatic view on most things. He seemed able to make or repair just about anything and was an invaluable resource to the school. Underlying his work was a simple philosophy that has served me well: Do things just the once, right, and never fight the weather.

Julie started working under the guidance of Marie Christine learning all about the practical side of running the adventure school, ensuring the food supplies were ordered and stocks maintained, cooking for the growing band of instructors, and soon to be joined by two other catering staff. Then under John's firm eye she learnt all about handling small boats, a critical skill for everyday life at the Adventure School. 'Pretend you're a cat' he would say to her, moving his own considerable bulk around a small clinker dinghy, without tipping it. And then onto teaching her all about Seagull outboard motors, how the running moorings worked and the knots to be always used. But she was quick learner, and this young London woman from Southfields soon mastered it all.

A small group of new instructors arrived a few weeks before the first course, and one turned out to be a sailing soulmate. Brian King was from Cold Spring Harbour, Long Island, a fashionable hamlet where his father had an exclusive men's clothes shop an hour out of New York City. Brian was expected to take it over, but he had other ideas. He was about my age, lived in a faded blue salt-stained sailing smock, and had short dark curly hair above an already receding hairline. A wispy chevron-shaped moustache gave him the look of a Mexican bandit from a silent movie. He was midway through a BA degree, which required travelling the world working at things that caught his interest. 'That's the sort of degree I could do,' John was heard to say.

The sea, sailing and sailing boats were Brian's passion. His enthusiasm was infectious. He was the first person I'd met outside of a book committed to going ocean sailing. He was more experienced and knowledgeable than me, but I was catching up fast. We spent as much time as we could out on the water. Ashore we would practice sailing skills together, such as tying a multitude of knots and splicing lines together. Could we tie the knots in the dark, with one hand, with two hands but behind our backs, and who was the quickest?

Working for the Ridgways at the school, I was busy all summer hiking, kayaking and sailing. Julie became expert in handling small boats, troubleshooting Seagull outboards, cooking for seventy and a member of the Green Water club (after falling into the icy loch). We moved into our first home, a single-room hut Lance built on a rocky knoll above the school, looking out over Loch a 'Chad-Fi. Idyllic, except that it caught the wind and would violently shake in the gales that swept in from the North Atlantic. On many a night, I feared it would be blown flat. It was eventually, but we were long gone by then.

I spent all my free time aboard the 16ft double-ender *Kirsty*, sailing out through Loch a 'Chad-Fi to Loch Laxford, and even to Handa island a few times. *Kirsty's* light timber hull had just seven frames, a centreboard and a Gunter rig. She seemed to go so well on every point of sail, in light airs and strong, with one crew or five. She would almost steer herself on some points of sail. I practised sailing her without any rudder at all. Asking around, I learnt she was similar to a Shetland Fourern design, whatever that was. She seemed wonderful to me, and I thought that if I could find a bigger one and deck her over, I would have an excellent little boat that I could sail almost anywhere. Visions came to me of Julie and I camping aboard, cruising down the west coast of Scotland, mostly finding a little sheltered harbour or nook for the night, but with maybe an occasional night at sea. The boat would be uncomplicated, with no engine, no electrics and an easy rig. It should be possible to row it a short way if there was no wind. It would draw little and could be pulled up on a beach if needed. And most importantly, it would be affordable for us.

Back in reality, or what passed for it at the Ridgway's adventure school, I would sometimes take a few moments to revisit the small wooden building just above the rocky shore beneath John and Marie Christine's croft. Inside was *English Rose III*, the 20ft dory that John and Chay Blyth had rowed across the North Atlantic five years before. She was as she had been when they landed on the Aran Islands. I'd looked at her with John the previous summer. Now I studied her with more understanding.

English Rose III was so simple. She was open except for buoyancy compartments built into either end, making her unsinkable. But what if she had rolled over? Could they have survived? It seemed that any small vessel could eventually turn over at sea, and the question is, what happens then?

Can the boat be righted? What has been broken? Can it be repaired? Can the crew continue? Have they the will and the knowledge, and the resources? These seemed like critical factors as I looked at the simple lines of *English Rose III* and her basic equipment.

But these men's resilience must have been outstanding as well. Both were ex-British Army Parachute Regiment and ex-SAS. They were used to thinking through scenarios, planning to survive, and readying themselves to do just whatever it took. I knew we had to be like that. But to me, the lesson of *English Rose III* was simplicity. This was why the idea of a little decked-over Shetland boat with an uncomplicated rig and no engine or electrics appealed to me.

We started to ask around. Did anyone know of any small Shetland boats for sale? We asked the locals in the Rhiconich pub, Willie the Post, who walked the four miles out to Ardmore every day, and every visitor to Ardmore or the school. Some of these visitors came by sea. Over the summer, about five or six yachts, far from their usual haunts, would come sailing into Loch Laxford. Occasionally, smaller yachts would come further into the loch to anchor in front of the school buildings.

It was one such small yacht in late August that changed everything. A little yacht with tan sails came tacking up the loch and anchored in front of the school. With so few sailing visitors. I grabbed a loaf of fresh bread as a welcoming present, jumped into a dinghy and rowed out to greet the newcomer.

'Welcome aboard,' the sole sailor said.

Which is how I met Hugh Eaglesfield aboard his boat *Tammie Nellie*. He'd sailed around the north coast of Scotland. Of course, I eventually asked him about any Shetland boats he knew of, and this time I struck gold.

'Aye, a friend of mine has one, about 21ft overall. She's over in Scrabster, near Thurso on the north coast. He has her set up for day sailing. She was built just a few years ago. He's been talking about possibly selling her. Here, let me give you his phone number.'

Had we discovered our Shetland boat?

Chapter 4
The perfect boat

'*He laid a good plank*' someone said of Tom Edwardson, the boatbuilder from the island of Yell in the Shetlands, who built *The Aegre* in 1966. One of his rules of thumb was that it should be possible to stand a bottle upright on the third strake from the keel. The bottle being full or not wasn't specified.

John Ridgway gave Julie and me a couple of days off and the loan of a long-wheelbase Land Rover pickup. We headed off to Scrabster, 85 miles away on a single-track road along Scotland's desolate north coast.

There was only one Shetland-style boat in Scrabster's small, protected harbour. Glistening varnished topsides reflected the ripple of the waves. She had a tan tent cover stretched over the boom and was decked in forward of her short, varnished mast, with narrow side decks aft around her large open cockpit. She looked beautiful. Her nameplate on her quarter said '*THE AEGRE*.'

Her owner, Andy Bryce, soon showed up. Slightly built and wearing a rough turtle-neck jersey and salt-stained navy trousers, he looked more like a fisherman than the nuclear engineer he turned out to be, his serious black framed glasses and Welsh accent the only giveaway.

Andy pulled the stern of *The Aegre* in close to the stone steps, and we jumped aboard. She was stable and smelt of linseed oil and varnish. Andy busied himself, preparing the boat to cast off. I helped him fold up the tent cover, which had been over the boom. With the cover gone, the beautifully varnished mast and spars were revealed. These were of Oregon pine, light but strong.

'She's got a standing lug rig,' Andy said, busying himself around the mast. I had no idea what that was, but it looked complicated.

Earlier, looking out to Thurso Bay, I had seen a few lazy whitecaps developing, the tops of waves breaking in a freshening wind. But there was just a light breeze in the shelter of the small harbour behind the high seawall. Andy clambered up onto the foredeck and hanked the small tan Dacron jib to the forestay and halyard. Then he busied himself with the large tan mainsail. Hauling on a halyard, he raised a slim wooden spar (the lug) to which the top of the almost square mainsail was laced. The sail unfolded beneath the lug. The bottom of the sail was attached at both corners to a long, varnished boom. I'd never seen such a sail before. It seemed awfully complicated. I wondered how it would sail and how it might be simplified.

With the jib raised and backed in the light breeze, we fell off on the starboard tack, heading for the narrow harbour entrance. Andy let go of the mooring and tightened the mainsheet. The large sail quickly filled, and with hardly a ripple, *The Aegre* surged forward, heeling gently. All I could think was 'Oh wow!'

'Stand by to go about,' Andy called.

We needed to make one tack through the wind to give the harbour walls at the entrance more clearance. Andy was on the helm, steering. As he swung the tiller over, *The Aegre* easily turned, and I switched the jib-sheets over as we came onto the other tack with the wind on the other side of the boat.

In moments we were out through the harbour entrance, *The Aegre* now lifting to the swell in the bay. With a gentle swoosh from the bow, we were on our way.

Julie and I sat out on the windward side deck, but the boat was just gently heeled. She was holding up to the wind well and seemed relatively stiff. We were soon flying along as we picked up more breeze. The sails pulling us along strongly.

Now heading out across Thurso Bay, we could settle down. Andy told us he grew up in Porthmadog in Wales and had moved to Thurso in the early 1960s, ten years before, to work at the nearby nuclear power station. In 1965 he married Elizabeth Inkster from the Shetland Islands. In 1966 he commissioned a boatbuilder from Yell (one of the Shetland Islands), Tom Edwardson, to build a Shetland model boat 21'6" 'over the stems.' During the spring of 1966, Bryce had often gone over to Wick to see her grow from when the keel and stems were set up on blocks until she was fully built. Her lines

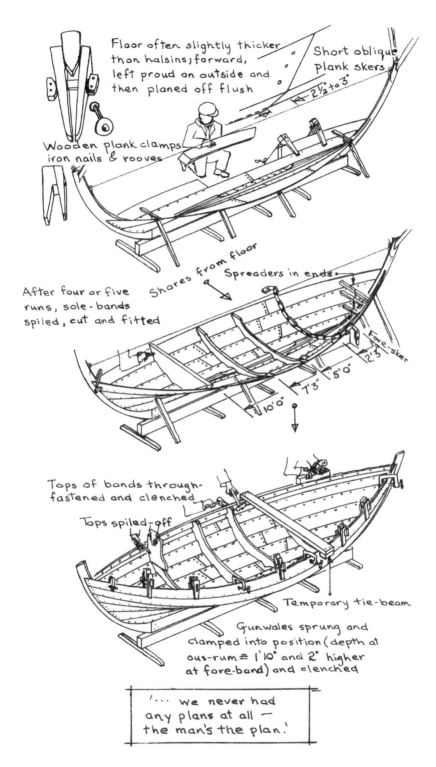

Floor often slightly thicker than halsins; forward, left proud on outside and then planed off flush

Short oblique plank skers

2½ to 3"

Wooden plank clamps iron nails & rooves

After four or five runs, sole-bands spiled, cut and fitted

Shores from floor

Spreaders in ends

Fore-sker

2'3"

5'0"

7'3"

10'0"

Tops of bands through-fastened and clenched

Tops spiled-off

Temporary tie-beam

Gunwales sprung and clamped into position (depth at ous-rum ± 1'10" and 2" higher at fore-band) and clenched

'... we never had any plans at all — the man's the plan.'

Building a Shetland boat (Dr A Osler)

developed purely from Tom Edwardson's eye, without the use of any moulds. As Shetland boat builders said, 'Edwardson laid a good plank.'

I took the helm and the mainsheet from Andy. Now in control of the boat, I could feel she was almost steering herself. I had wondered if the large mainsail would make her difficult to steer, but not at all. Just light, constant pressure to windward was all that was needed to hold a straight course.

As Scrabster harbour receded astern the wind was freshening, and *The Aegre* was speeding along, spray from the bow flying high.

'Let's reduce sail, tuck in a reef,' Andy called. He lowered the mainsail to the deck, and we quickly tied in the reef and reset the sail. Now under her reduced rig, *The Aegre* was sailing just as fast as before but feeling much less pressed. Andy told me that beneath the floor, he had ten cwt (508kg) of cut Caithness slate, which he thought gave her stability, and the weight didn't seem to slow her down at all.

'She's built of half-inch overlapping mahogany planks with copper fastenings. Sawn Oregon frames added later,' he explained. 'All the strength is in the planking.'

And where did her name, *The Aegre*, come from, I asked? Andy explained that he had wanted a Norse word to reflect the boat's heritage. The only one he knew was 'aegre', a name given to a tidal bore in a river. Andy possibly didn't know the word's origin, which is believed to be Aegir, the Norse god of the sea, a river's tidal bore enabling a Norse ship to travel far upstream, being a gift from their god. It was a more fitting choice for his boat than he may have imagined. He had registered her as a fishing boat in Lerwick, Shetland, where she was assigned the register number LK92, now prominently displayed on each side of her bow.

The more we sailed, the more I liked her. I imagined extending the decking aft to give somewhere sheltered to sleep. She was big enough but small enough. The rig? Well, I would have to think about that, but it certainly worked well. I could see she was meticulously maintained, too, without the fussiness of a showboat.

'How much will you take for her?' I yelled above the wind.

'Three hundred pounds, that's what I paid to have her built and rigged. You can have her for that.'

Three hundred! It was 1972, I was just 22, Julie 18, and that was all the money we had. But she seemed just what we wanted. I thought we would never find a more suitable boat for less, and we agreed to buy her.

The next morning Julie and I took everything we could off *The Aegre* and loaded it all onto the tray of the Land Rover: mast and spars, sails, rudder, floorboards, fenders, mooring lines, anchor and chain, half a ton (500kg) of Caithness slate ballast, everything. Andy would bring the hull to the Adventure School on a trailer in a week or two.

Excitedly we headed out on the long drive back to the School. We needed to make good speed, as Julie's parents were arriving that night to visit and stay a few days.

In 1972 the main road along the north coast of Scotland was just a single lane with occasional passing places for when two cars met. Fortunately, there was little traffic. We sped along until I took one of the narrow passing bays a little too widely to avoid another vehicle. Suddenly the grass verge crumbled under the weight of our little truck. The half a ton of slate ballast in the back probably didn't help. Almost in slow motion, the Land Rover rolled onto its left side, slid down into a narrow rocky stream and came to a halt. A little shocked but unhurt, we gingerly climbed out of the driver's door, now above us, and waded to the bank. The Land Rover seemed OK, except that the left side was now partly underwater. There was duckweed on the windows.

Fortunately, all *The Aegre* kit in the back seemed undamaged, but the vehicle was stuck. We would have to get help to haul her out. We thought Julie might have more luck than I in persuading a tow truck driver to come out on a Sunday morning, so she accepted a lift from a stopped car to the nearest village.

It was silent as I sat in the weak sunshine on the side of the upturned 4WD. I chuckled as I remembered John telling us about his driving record: 'I've been in 12 car crashes, every one of them my fault.'

It was ages before I eventually heard the distant sound of a diesel truck. The driver stopped a bit ahead of us, and he and Julie got out. He surveyed the scene without a word. I guessed he had seen it all before. Then he attached his big tow hook to the towing point on the front of the Land Rover. Back in his cab, I thought I saw him adjust his mirror so that he couldn't see anything behind. Then he revved his engine and graunched forward. The Land Rover slowly came upright and emerged back onto the road, water draining out of it. Unhooking the towline, he climbed into it and started the engine, checked the brakes and steering, then turned to us.

'Aye, you're lucky. A normal car would have been a write off.'

Driving a little more cautiously, we made it back just in time to meet Julie's parents.

'You're looking tired,' Julie's mum said to her, 'have you had a busy day?'

Later that night, we returned the Land Rover to the school. It seemed fine. We may have forgotten to mention our little misadventure to anyone, but it eventually came to light. It was a few weeks later that I saw the Land Rover in maintenance man Lance Bell's workshop.

'Bloody wheel bearing on the front left side has gone,' he said. 'One of you young buggers has had this thing in a river. There's duckweed up the back of the dashboard.'

Oops.

A week or so later, on August 26th 1972, Julie's 19th birthday, Andy Bryce arrived, towing a trailer loaded with *The Aegre*. We quickly gathered a small team of instructors to ease her off the trailer and across the kelp-covered rocks at the head of the loch to the water's edge. The incoming tide soon floated her. She was so light and buoyant with no ballast that she lay over on one side as we towed her up Loch a 'Chad-Fi to a safe mooring beneath the wood at Ardmore. Within a few days, we had the ballast loaded back into her and the rig set up. Then we were off, out for a sail on our first free day.

Released from the mooring, *The Aegre* took off quickly in the light wind. We soon passed a group of students in the Mirror dinghies and an instructor in *Kirsty* as we headed out into Loch Laxford under the big tan mainsail and jib. How wonderful it was to be on our boat!

She was smoothly sailing a straight course and needing little effort from me. I looked up and studied the sails, which had seemed such a tangle of lines back in Scrabster. Now I was starting to see order, practicality and even a certain elegance in the rig.

When we turned off the wind and let out the mainsheet, the large, almost rectangular mainsail was like an open barn door. *The Aegre* was quickly up to her maximum hull speed. No need here for a tricky spinnaker. The old-style standing lug rig showed it was much more capable than it looked. My only reservation was that the long spar would still be aloft in the second reef position, and much of the sail would be roughly tied up with the reefing lines above the boom. Acceptable perhaps when out for a day sail, but offshore we had to be prepared for extended periods of strong winds and high seas. We surely needed a smaller, more easily handled sail for such extreme conditions. But for now, sailing around Loch Laxford in light winds, we wondered what else we should do before sailing her south down the coast to England at the end of the summer. We thought we might extend the decking from the mast all the way aft, leaving just a small cockpit for the helmsman. There would only be crawling headroom below, but we could work out some way of sleeping underneath it. At the same time, we could build buoyancy into both ends, as John and Chay Blyth had done with the rowing boat. Then she would float even if badly holed or full of water after a capsize.

But overall, we wanted to keep the boat simple. There would be no engine, no Bermuda rig, no toilet, no shower, no freezer, no electrics, no holes in the hull, but she would be seaworthy, unsinkable, able to survive a complete capsize, inexpensive, probably uncomfortable, but practical too. She would be almost a sailing version of *English Rose III*, the transatlantic rowing dory. We could surely go far in her.

But how long would it take to make the improvements? We quickly realised we couldn't sail her south that autumn. We had neither enough time nor money for the work needed. Our rather vague plan became to try and complete the improvements within the next twelve months. Then, when the school closed in autumn the next year, we might sail to the south of England rather than hitchhike.

Soon we were into September, the days were shortening and the courses ending. Everyone was heading off in different directions. John and Marie Christine, Richard Shuff and Krister were going to Patagonia, Julie and I back to London. And we had not even started work on *The Aegre*.

Then John intervened. 'Why don't we ask my mate Bob Macinnes to do the decking during the winter while you two go south?' Bob was an elderly, highly respected local boat builder in the nearby village of Scourie. 'Find yourselves some lucrative jobs, then come back to fit her out in the spring. He could make a proper job of it. Then next winter, when you sail south, you wouldn't need to stop in the south of England — you could carry straight on for Madeira. Or even go on across the Atlantic to the West Indies!'

Madeira? The West Indies? What was he talking about? Julie and I were shocked by the idea. John knew the size of our boat, he knew us, and he certainly knew something of the sea. But perhaps he was right? After all, smaller boats had sailed the Atlantic. Well, maybe not from the north of Scotland.

I knew John was talking about following the so-called southern route across the Atlantic, taken by sailing vessels for centuries. Ships starting from the islands off the north-west coast of Africa, such as Madeira or the Canary Islands, sailed west-south-west, being blown along in front of the warm and steady north-east trade winds, 2,400 miles (3,860 kilometres) to the West Indies. It was the route that Columbus had taken, followed by countless other voyagers.

But first, we would need to get from Scotland to Madeira and the Canary Islands off North Africa. That seemed like step one, but if we could manage that, then, well, maybe carry on? It seemed like the beginning of a plan.

But first, we had to modify the boat so that she was unsinkable and self-righting, and to give us somewhere to sleep and cook. Some sort of deck was needed. I had heard of Macinnes. He could surely do a much better job than I.

'I'll get him on the blower,' John said, picking up the phone.

Bob Macinnes probably didn't get many calls like that one, but somehow John persuaded him to take a look at the boat. A few days later, John, Julie and I drove south down the coast to Bob's boat shed high on a hill above Scourie. Behind us on a trailer was *The Aegre*.

Bob was a big man in old blue overalls and cap, with enormous, hardened hands and a weather-beaten face. He hardly raised an eyebrow as John leant on the gunwale of *The Aegre* outside Bob's battered old Nissen hut boatshed and sketched the idea for the decking on a piece of scrap paper.

'The West Indies eh? Heh heh heh!' Bob chuckled to himself, taking in the lines of the boat, his eyes sparkling.

Bob agreed he would finish his current work and then build a curved whaleback deck over the whole boat with just a small square hatch and cockpit, and buoyancy chambers at each end so she was unsinkable. We would return to Scotland in the spring. Meanwhile, we would go to London for the winter and earn money to pay Bob and fund the trip.

Nodding his agreement to take on the work, Bob looked up at me over his scratched old glasses. 'The West Indies Eh. Heh heh heh, I wouldn't mind coming with you, that would fix my arthritis!'

Chapter 5
Another London winter

'Empty pockets never held anyone back. Only empty heads and empty hearts can do that.' — Norman Vincent Peale

Lond
L ondon: Orange sodium lights reflected in cold, wet streets. Our summer life in Scotland, our Shetland boat and sailing to the West Indies was like a dream.

We moved in with Julie's mum and went out to look for work. Rumour had it that building sites in the City paid the best for me, and the first one I came to, on the site of the Royal Exchange, employed me on a demolition gang. Julie had similar good luck. She went to Oxford Street, and came back with a job in a department store.

Jobs with regular hours were new to us and gave us spare time to research, think and plan our coming voyage. We are both systematic people, so research came first.

Our initial thinking of a coastal camping cruise from Scotland to the South of England via the Irish Sea between England and Ireland, was still there. The idea was loosely based on E E Middleton's *Cruise of The Kate* solo voyage around England in 1869. Middleton had stopped most nights in small harbours along the way, sailing northwards through the Irish Sea, with the prevailing wind behind him. We'd be going south, against it, but if we took our time and just sailed when the weather and tides were favourable, we'd be fine, wouldn't we?

Ridgway's suggestion not to stop in the south of England but to keep going to Madeira, the island to the west of Portugal, added a new dimension. Our geography wasn't very good, but from looking at a map and reading the accounts of other sailors, we could see that once you were south of England, the coast of France was inhospitable, with its infamous Bay of Biscay. There

41

would be no camping ashore, and we'd be better to go out to sea and sail non-stop to Madeira, a whopping 1,400 miles.

And then Ridgway had said that if all went well to Madeira, we could sail on across the Atlantic to the West Indies, a further 2,400 miles. Wow. Could we do it?

With London's libraries and bookshops nearby, we read everything about ocean sailing on small boats. Our understanding of geography, weather patterns, winds and currents grew. We learned that once we got south of Britain, if we stayed offshore, the wind and current would swing around behind us, making the final off-shore passage to Madeira easier. And from Madeira onwards, we could follow a course that curved south to pick up the warm NE trade wind that would blow us all the way to the West Indies.

It seemed ambitious, but like so many big things, once we divided it into little individual problems and progressively solved them, the voyage started to seem possible.

However, to take on this expanded plan meant equipping *The Aegre* from the start for an ocean passage. No more would we be essentially day sailing, with little need to carry much food, water or spares. Now we'd have to equip the boat to spend days, weeks, and perhaps more than a month at sea.

We started to make lists. Julie was very methodical and soon we had lists of what we needed to do to the boat, the equipment we'd need, and what we needed to learn. And then put a cost against each item. The decking, the flotation, new rigging, anchors, chain, bilge pump, water tanks, navigation charts, compass, sextant, chronometer, nautical almanac, storm sails, sea anchor, a radio receiver, food, self-steering system, waterproof torches, foam mattresses, duvets, wet weather clothing, thermal underwear, barometer, stove, binoculars. Our lists grew every day, and with them, the cost. Could we earn enough in a single winter working in London?

And then there was the thinking. How much buoyancy would we need to float the boat? How much space would it occupy? We calculated we could fit 16 cubic feet of buoyancy into each end of the boat, which would float about 930 kilograms (2,050 lbs), more than enough to float the ballast in the boat. Everything else would float, more or less. So the boat wouldn't sink even if full of water.

How much food and water should we take? We estimated the longest passage would be the 2,500 miles across the Atlantic. How long might it take? What speed might we average? Two knots was the slowest average we could imagine, considering possible headwinds, calms and stormy weather. So the 2,500 miles might take 50 days. We decided to double that to allow for any eventuality, so 100 days. From our research, we learnt we should allow a minimum of one litre of water each per day. We would consume it all—no washing of anything in freshwater. So, we'd need a minimum of 200 litres of water.

Two hundred litres of water would weigh 200 kilograms, a significant amount on a very small boat, and we wondered if we could reduce the Caithness slate ballast. An even better idea was to remove the slate altogether and replace it with a combination of fresh water in tanks and lead ingots. Being denser than the slate, the ingots would allow us to lower the floor and give more headroom beneath the curved deck.

What about food for 100 days? Along with everything else in the boat, we decided our food supplies needed to survive complete immersion in seawater. Being rolled over or completely swamped in stormy weather seemed possible in such a small boat. There was also very little space for storage and organising supplies at sea. Perhaps it was working with Army day ration packs at the School that gave Julie the idea of multiple 24-hour food packs in sealable ½ gallon polythene tubs. Supplemented by sealable 1-gallon containers of stores for a few days and multiple bulk food items such as homemade fruit cakes, dozens of eggs (half of them sealed in waterglass), fruit, lime juice, and more.

Julie's idea of using sealable polythene tubs came from noticing that ice cream packaging had changed from cardboard cartons to resealable ½ and 1-gallon plastic reusable tubs. These seemed ideal for us. They could be filled, labelled and nested one on top of another to completely fill the space across the boat forward of the mast from floor to deck, extending forward to the buoyancy chamber bulkhead. Moreover, they could be 'free.' We put the word out to all our relatives and friends to eat lots of ice cream and save the containers for us. Julie started planning their contents, working out what we would need to maintain our health and good spirits sailing the boat for 24 hrs a day. When we eventually sailed, we carried 60 half-gallon and 20 one-gallon tubs.

An engine was hardly even considered. An inboard or even a small outboard motor would be heavy, take up lots of space, require fuel, spare parts, be smelly and expensive. And for what benefit? Would we use it to motor through calms in the mid-ocean? Why? We had no appointments to keep. For moving the boat around in windless harbours? No need. We could just use a paddle.

But what about a radio? A short-wave transmitter would need a lot of electric power, which would require an engine. But what if we needed help? Well, we would just have to be self-reliant. We decided we should not ask or expect anyone to ever come and look for us. If need be, we had to be able to rescue ourselves.

However, with a battery-powered short wave transistor receiver, we could receive marine weather forecasts from Britain as we sailed south from Scotland towards Madeira and receive time signals from WWV on the short wave. These would enable us to reset our watch or clock (in the absence of an expensive chronometer) to give us the accurate time of sun sights. And furthermore, some small marine receivers had a rotating aerial on top that could be tuned to the radio direction finding (RDF) beacons that lined the Atlantic coast of Europe in those days. With bearings from these beacons, we could draw position lines on a chart. Their intersection would give us some idea of where we were and supplement our astro-navigation. Long before GPS, this system was simple, and we hoped adequate, if not very accurate. Moreover a little radio would also be a source of news and entertainment. We settled on a relatively inexpensive Hitachi transistor radio with SW/MW and LW and a rotating RDF aerial.

Our list kept growing. A self-steering system, anchors, a sextant. One by one we researched them and bought them as our earnings allowed.

As the lists grew, we added the cost of each item. Could we afford to buy everything to leave in mid-1973, or would we have to wait another year? What could we economise on? This was long before PCs and spreadsheets, but we repeatedly recalculated income and expenditure by hand. It looked tight.

Christmas came, and Julie and I went to the old thatched farmhouse in Cottenham where my parents welcomed her. My father seemed an enthusiastic supporter of *The Aegre* project, but my mother was quietly nervous.

That January, the British newspapers were full of the story of the Robertsons, an English family cruising on a yacht in the eastern Pacific when a whale hit them, quickly sinking their yacht. They survived for 37 days in a life raft and a fibreglass dinghy. Their book, *Survive the Savage Sea*, led us to think deeply about how we would survive such an incident.

Julie and I often discussed what could go wrong aboard *The Aegre*, what we would do and how to prepare. The worst thing we could imagine at sea was the boat becoming full of water, perhaps following a capsize or being badly holed by hitting something. Putting sufficient buoyancy in either end to float the ballast was our answer to this. Dismasting seemed unlikely with our very short mast, but with the mainsail lug and boom aboard and woodworking tools, I felt confident I could build a temporary rig at sea if needed.

We wondered about carrying a self-inflating life raft in a canister. These were starting to become more common on yachts. The Robinson family certainly owed their lives to having one, but I wondered if the underlying premise behind such life rafts made them unsuitable for us. Self-inflating life rafts provide a relatively temporary safer place for survivors in the event of a boat sinking. They are designed to remain stationary in the ocean when deployed so that rescuers, alerted to the crisis presumably by an SOS radio message, come to the location of the sinking vessel, and can find the life rafts and their occupants.

But what if a yacht is far out to sea, is sinking, and no SOS is sent for whatever reason? Survivors may clamber into their inflated life raft, but what then? No one knows they are there. No one is coming to rescue them. The life raft isn't going anywhere. Sharks circle. Death awaits, slowly.

Of course, today, yachts carry an inexpensive portable Emergency Position Indicating Radio Beacon (EPIRB). These can be triggered near-instantly and send a signal and position via satellite to a world emergency system. Other vessels in the vicinity are alerted, and a rescue operation is initiated. But in 1973, only the military had forerunners of the system. They wouldn't be commercially available for another two decades.

We had to assume that no one would ever come looking for us. So sitting in a stationary life raft was not the answer.

We decided that a better way to increase our chances of survival was to be self-reliant. We would plan for the worst things we could imagine and how we would rescue ourselves. To us, *The Aegre* would be our life raft. She couldn't sink, thanks to buoyancy in either end, so provided she stayed in one piece, she would have everything we needed to survive. She might be full of water, and the mast might be broken, but if we could cope with that, we could sail on, eventually to reach a safe port.

So, no self-inflating life raft. That saved a bundle of money. But there were still so many other items we would need to buy. Yet again, we reviewed our list of predicted costs if we were to sail mid-year, and our savings. How much longer would we have to work in London? We hated it. We kept recalculating, making more and more cuts until finally we decided we could finish at the end of the month, but it was going to be hellish tight.

Then we would have to move all the boat stuff we had bought in London to the north of Scotland. Help came from another instructor from the school, Jamie Young, who loaned us his car, an elderly Morris 1000 'woody' estate. We loaded it up, filling every inch with equipment for *The Aegre*, waved goodbye to London, and headed north.

There's something deeply satisfying about heading out, be it driving away or casting off. On to a new adventure. No more late shifts on the building site. No more slow days on the Hairbrush and Cosmetics counter.

As the car hummed northward, I wasn't thinking far ahead. Perhaps in youth, we don't. Is it a sense of the unknown that attracts or frightens us? The fear of something ending, or the anticipation of something new? Perhaps it's a good thing we don't think of the further future. If we did, we might never venture out.

I wasn't thinking beyond sailing away. I couldn't have imagined it would be ten years before I would be back in London.

Chapter 6
Fitting out *The Aegre*

'The art of the sailor is to leave nothing to chance' — Annie Van De Wiele

D riving up, we just beat a storm, arriving at the Adventure School in NW Sutherland a few days before it hit. There was just time to unload the car, carrying everything by hand the mile to the empty school site and our little cabin. Soon the cabin was shuddering in the wind, snow building in drifts, hiding everything.

I loaded the 1100lb (500kg) of slate ballast from *The Aegre* into the windward side of the cabin to help hold it down against the wind. Inside, we huddled around a kerosene heater and wondered if the hut would blow flat in the middle of the night.

But apart from the wind, it was so peaceful after our hectic life in London. We had water from a nearby stream, a primus kerosene camping stove to cook on and a kerosene heater and pressure lamp to warm and light the cabin. Outside the snow settled deeply. It was so romantic. I felt like Dr Zhivago, holed up in the icy cottage with Lara on the Varykino estate in the Urals. But while the storm raged outside, rather than write poetry, we worked on our list of things to do for the voyage, things to buy, and our budget. We'd have no living expenses working at the school until we sailed, but with just pocket-money pay from John, no income either. Did we have enough savings to complete the fit-out of *The Aegre* and sail, with still some money left to replenish our stores in Madeira and pay harbour dues? We were relying on finding work in the West Indies on a charter yacht. We just had to get there.

The storm passed after a few days, and we ventured out into a new white snow-covered world. Our first priority was to visit Bob Macinnes, the boatbuilder in Scourie, nine miles to the south. How had he progressed with decking *The Aegre*?

We trudged through the deep snow back to the distant road and Jamie's car, now just a white mound. Luckily it started. We found Bob in his old Nissen hut boat shed working on a half-built clinker dinghy (known locally as a 'yawlie'). He was busy steaming thin wooden laths that would form the narrow frames between the boat's planks. A warm, cosy job on a cold day.

'Oh, so you're back,' he said, sitting down on his favourite stool and giving his pipe a puff. 'And how was London?'

'Never mind London Bob, how are you? And how is *The Aegre*?'

'Ach well, I've been giving her a bit of thought …'

We went next door to one of his sheds, and there she was, exactly as we had left her in September, five months before. Nothing had changed.

We were bitterly disappointed, but tried not to show it. I wondered how it would be possible to deck her in and still sail south in mid-summer.

'When can you start, Bob?' I said.

'Well, I'll need to finish the yawlie and order the timber, maybe in a week or two.'

'How about a cash advance?'

'Aye, that would be helpful.'

We were very subdued driving back to the Adventure School. My mind was in turmoil at the lack of any progress. It seemed like a significant setback. It was near dark when we set out on the 90-minute walk back through the snow to our cabin. We didn't speak much. We'd never imagined there would be no progress at all.

Things are never quite as bad or quite as good as they at first seem. That was another of Ridgway's sayings, and it helped us now as we rationalised the situation. In hindsight, we reflected that the lack of progress was perhaps unsurprising. Bob must have wondered if he should order and pay for the timber and put in his time without any certainty that we would return. He might have wondered if he would ever be paid. Maybe if we had given him a sizeable advance payment, things would have been different, but we'd had no money back in September. Meanwhile, he had firm orders from the local hotel to build new yawlies and repair old ones. Understandably, that was a safer use of his time.

And there was an upside to it. I could now work with Bob on the decking.

There would surely be many issues and questions we could now address together. In fact, it seemed better than him going ahead in our absence. As long as he started soon.

Maybe a project such as this demands some level of resilience. Ours was about to be tested further.

There was another essential visit needed, but we'd been putting it off. Living alone on the school site, just us in our little snow-bound cabin, was so peaceful. There was no one else for miles. Even the storm, with its shuddering winds and driving snow, was rather wonderful. And the white world it left us was breathtaking. We seemed self-contained, just the two of us, and maybe we didn't want it to end. But we knew John and Marie Christine must be back from Patagonia. They would be similarly isolated and self-contained, and probably enjoying it in their snug stone croft over at Ardmore.

But we knew we needed to meet them to discuss how the year's first half would play out. How would we work at the Adventure School and simultaneously prepare *The Aegre* and ourselves for a midsummer departure?

The Ridgway's croft was on the other side of the loch, a few miles away to the north-west of us. The only way to contact them was via a WWII field telephone between the School and their croft. The wire ran under the loch and was notoriously unreliable. After the storm passed, we tried calling them, but there was no answer for a week. Then suddenly the phone was picked up. It was Marie Christine. We arranged to visit them a few days later, on Sunday 18th February, the day of our first wedding anniversary.

Sunday came. It was bitterly cold, and the loch had a skin of freshwater ice, so we couldn't take a boat but had to make the two-hour walk around the loch. We found John in a dark, sombre mood. Eventually, he came out with what was bothering him. It went something like this:

'Your main interest and future lies in sailing and sailing boats. Sailing *The Aegre* to the West Indies is a logical development. You should try to do that if you want to make a future for yourselves in sailing. Don't waste your time playing around at Ardmore. Devote your energy to planning and organising the voyage. It would be wrong for you to start the season at Ardmore with your mind on something else.'

We were shocked. The foundation of our planning for the voyage was working at the school. In exchange, we would receive board and lodging, some pocket money, and much support until we left in midsummer. Now all that was gone. We would have to move out, but to where? We would need to find work, but where? *The Aegre* was in Bob's shed in Scourie, nine miles away, with weeks, if not months, of work required before we could leave. Our world was crashing down around us.

We trudged back through the snow in the gathering darkness, thinking our hope of a departure that summer was doomed. What could we do with *The Aegre?* Where could we possibly find work in north-west Scotland in February? And somewhere to live, preferably near Scourie and *The Aegre?* Should we just abandon the whole plan, put our boat up for sale and move to the south coast of England, where there was a thriving yachting industry, which meant lots of yachts and work? Start again?

It was dark when we left the footpath to climb up and over the hazardous snow-covered ridge to Skerrika and our tiny cabin back at the school. I hoped we didn't fall and injure ourselves or get lost. That would be an unfortunate end to a rotten day.

But again, things are never quite so bad or quite so good as they at first seem. Somewhere deep down, we knew John was right. We had wondered how we could focus adequately on working at the school while preparing for the voyage. Now John was following the advice he gave others, taking the bold decision, and confronting the issue before the season started. Perhaps he'd done us a favour.

Our shock turned into defiance. Back in our cabin, we scrawled a quote from Joshua Slocum's *The Voyage of the Liberdade* on the wall above our bed. It was the words of the poet Masaniello.

> *Away away, no cloud is lowering o'er us*
> *Freely now we stem the wave;*
> *Hoist, hoist all sail, before us*
> *Hope's beacon shines to cheer the brave.*

We were determined. I think Julie as much as I. We'd got this far and we weren't giving up now. We would just have to find new work and somewhere to live. We'd find a way. We would sail away on *The Aegre.*

John McLeod was the elderly owner of the nearest pub to the school, the ageing and rundown Rhiconich Hotel. In his crusty, parochial way, he was no supporter of the Ridgways and their fancy Adventure School. When he heard we had split from them, he immediately offered us work and lodging, Julie to work as a cook (the only cook) and myself as a handyman. I was to build an extension to the hotel using parts of old construction worker huts he had bought on the east coast.

But Julie's job, and with it the board and lodging, lasted just 24 hours. She'd cooked for seventy at the Adventure School but was adamant. No, she was not going back. No way. She didn't go into the details, but Mcleod wasn't an easy man to work for.

With nowhere to live once again, we drove over to Scourie through the snow in Jamie's car to see Bob Macinnes and tell him our sorry tale. He seemed to be our only remaining friend.

Scourie is a tiny village that lives on a bit of fishing; lobsters from the treacherous waters around Handa island, but more importantly, trout in the many small lakes dotting the marshy heath inland. Only the most intrepid fisherman come this far north to stay at the Scourie Hotel. From there, they'd be guided to little-known lochans where one of Macinnes's yawlies, and the trout, would be waiting.

'Oh ho ho ho!' Bob chuckled, his eyes twinkling behind his battered glasses. 'We'll have to work something out.'

Standing ankle-deep in wood shavings, leaning on a half-finished 12ft (3.66m) yawlie he was building, I realised he was as keen as us that the voyage went ahead.

'So what you need is somewhere to live. Let me see now.' Puffing his pipe, he turned and went to the small window at the back of the boatshed, facing out over Scourie below us.

'I think you should go and see Mrs McLeod,' he said, pointing to a distant house. 'She takes holidaymakers in during the summer. I think she'll have you for a bit. I'll give her a call. And Julie will need a job. Hmmm… well, over there in the hotel they will need a housemaid come the spring. Rhoda has been the housemaid for years, but she's struggling with the stairs now. I think she might need a young assistant. Go and see Mr Hay, the owner. Tell him I sent you.'

With Bob Macinnes as our supporter, it suddenly seemed like Scourie might take us in.

Mrs McLeod, who was no close relation of John McCleod of the Rhiconich Hotel, was like a homely, elderly favourite aunt and welcomed us into her cosily warm thick-walled stone cottage. She'd probably just made a fresh batch of scones. But we only stayed a few days before being offered a caravan her son Norman and wife Jean had behind their house nearby. They let it out in summer, but it was empty now and just fine for us at a low rent. We quickly moved in.

Next, it was off to the Scourie Hotel. The white-walled two-storey hotel started life in the 16th century as a fortified house, then became a coaching inn, and over the last 170 years it had become well known for its salmon and trout fishing. Mr Hay, the owner, was a small, quietly spoken gentle man wearing a brown suit and tie, the very antithesis of Rhiconich's John McLeod. Perhaps our story had preceded us because he said yes, he'd like to employ Julie as a housemaid to start in mid-March, about three weeks away, until we left in mid-July. We couldn't believe our luck. Open-mouthed, we looked at each other in amazement as we walked back to our caravan.

With three weeks to go before she started, Julie worked through our lists of all the things we still needed, writing to possible suppliers asking for catalogues and price lists. Sitting in the caravan in front of the kerosene heater, she wrote dozens of letters and then, each afternoon, she would meet the mail bus coming up from Lairg, bringing replies. Meanwhile, I worked on the extensions at the Rhiconich Hotel under the ever-present critical eye of McLeod, travelling backwards and forwards each day in Jamie's car.

It was bitterly cold both outside the caravan and in. We huddled around our heater, thinking about every possible aspect of the voyage. One weekend, our health and dealing with possible injury came sharply into focus. We had read of yachtsmen having their appendix removed before a long ocean passage but decided we'd not do that, but maybe get our teeth checked. Even as we thought about it, I had a numbing toothache. The Scourie doctor diagnosed an abscess in the root of a front tooth and gave me painkillers and antibiotics. To avoid any recurrence at sea, he arranged for it to be treated properly the next week in the Inverness hospital, 100 miles away. The pain killers weren't much good, and I spent a miserable few days in the icy caravan, cold and in pain, thinking how weak I was to be so disabled by a bit of toothache.

But sometimes, these things turn out well. I had an apicectomy (removal of the nerve) on two of my front upper teeth in the Inverness hospital, then went on to do some shopping in the town. Back at the railway station, the guard on the train to Lairg was an understanding fellow and said he would make room in his van for my 'personal luggage' at no cost. He raised his eyebrows a bit when I later arrived with 32 cubic feet (about 1 cubic metre) of expanded foam polystyrene sheets, 22 10-litre (2.64 US gal) clear polythene jerricans, 6 fathoms (36ft, 11m) of 5/8 galvanised anchor chain, and a tea chest of miscellaneous bits including a primus stove, two heavy-duty aluminium pots and a frying pan, a butane blowlamp plus spare butane cartridges, and more.

At Lairg, I had to move everything to the mail bus for the remaining 44 miles to Scourie. However Michael, the driver, knew us well by then, so there were no difficulties there.

My tooth abscess gave us a bit of a scare. We both got our teeth thoroughly checked but did worry about possible injury aboard. We ordered a medical home diagnosis book to take with us and talked with the Scourie doctor about where we might be going and the vaccinations we should get. He eventually supplied us with a comprehensive pack with everything from wound dressings to morphine ampules, creating an extensive medical kit.

Heavy weather sails were underlined in our to-do list. For sailing in light to moderate winds, we would keep the existing standing lug rig, but in strong to gale force winds and more, the second reef (to make the sail as small as possible) did not seem a good option. This was because the long wooden spar holding the top of the sail remained aloft, while most of the sail was bundled up and tied beneath it. It was cumbersome and ungainly. Acceptable for a few hours but not for the days and days we might have gale-force winds.

To me, a better arrangement for strong winds was a set of dedicated storm sails. While thinking about this in London, we found an ad in a yachting magazine for a traditional sailmaker in Orkney, Kip Gurrin, who was making traditional sails in natural materials. We wrote to him describing our boat and planned voyage and our need for heavy weather sails. He replied, offering to make a storm jib, a gaff-headed trysail and a sea anchor, all in flax. Somehow during the subsequent correspondence, the little gaff-headed storm mainsail evolved into a dual-purpose sail. Firstly, it would be a strong wind mainsail with a near parallelogram shape set conventionally behind the mast, but on looking at its proposed shape, I wondered if it could solve another problem, that of sailing with a strong wind directly behind us. Kip agreed to design the sail to be also set the other way up as a square sail, hanging across the boat in front of the mast, just like a Viking longboat's square sail.

Now he told us the sails were ready and invited us to visit him in Orkney, to pick up the sails and stay the weekend. We decided to take the ferry from the port of Scrabster on the north coast of Scotland over to Stromness in the Orkney Islands.

Kip met us off the ferry, transferring us to his little open gaff cutter *Blue Jacket* to sail across the harbour to the tiny island of Inner Holm and its one house, in which Kip, his wife and small daughter were living. It was late February, cold and very bleak, but their welcome was as warm as their potbellied stove. Kip soon had the flax sails spread out in the living room and was pointing out various features. They looked extremely strong, but rather heavy.

'I just need to finish sewing the bolt ropes around the head, tack and clew of each sail' he said, 'Here, I'll show you how you can help.'

Soon I was wielding a thick sail needle, sailmaker's palm and marlinspike to get the tension just right. Kip told us about working as a sailmaker on square-rigger sail training ships, his ambition being to establish a sail making business in Orkney while living on Inner Holm. When the rain briefly eased, he took us out to walk on the stone causeway linking the tiny island to the mainland at low water. Then the cloud lowered again, the rain set in once more, and we returned to finish the sail work.

The Gurrins were an adventurous couple and asked us insightful questions about every aspect of our proposed voyage.

'And what about food? How many days will you take? Fresh, canned and dried? Have you tried dehydrated soybean meat?' They certainly had. 'We've got a big sack of the stuff — it's called Protveg. It seemed like a wonder food when we bought it, but it's horrible. Would you like some? Please take as much as you can carry!'

It seemed like a good idea. We hoped it would taste better with lots of curry powder and gratefully took a large bag of it home with the sails.

Back in Scourie, we showed Bob the sails. In thick flax, they were quite a work of art. But were they too heavy? Too late now to change.

And then we were into another crisis. The instructors were starting to return to the Adventure School. Jamie Young, who had lent us his car to drive back to Scotland, hitchhiked up from southern England. He then borrowed his car from us for the weekend to drive the 93 miles to Inverness to meet his girlfriend off the train. He planned to drive one of John's newly serviced Land Rovers back from Inverness while his girlfriend would follow, driving his car.

Their return was delayed. Then somewhere in the dark, along the narrow twisty road above Loch Shin, Jamie's girlfriend fell asleep at the wheel. The Morris went off the road and down a steep hillside into the pines by the loch, then headlong into a tree. She was thrown out and somehow only suffered cuts and bruises. Jamie found her, got her back up to the road and appeared at our caravan door late that night with her in his arms. We patched her up. She was shaken, but her injuries were remarkably minor.

Jamie was philosophical about losing his car and just relieved that his girlfriend was uninjured, as we were. But for Julie and me, losing the car was another setback. Now I had no way to get from Scourie to Rhiconich to work on the hotel extension each day.

In truth, I was relieved, and so too probably was John Mcleod. I had no idea how to build his extensions, something which was becoming all too obvious to McLeod. So that was the end of that. But now, again, I was out of work.

Back in Bob Macinnes's boatshed, I leant on the half-built yawlie again, telling him our latest problem. He took all our difficulties calmly. Nothing seemed to upset him. As always, his eyes were sparkling, and he was chuckling quietly. Perhaps he was wondering how much more bad luck we could take. I was becoming fond of him.

Again he peered out of the small cobwebby window looking out over Scourie.

'Well now. A few years ago, Mr Hay at the hotel set up a steak bar in the summer for the holidaymakers. He always has to find someone to run the little kitchen. Do you think you could do that? It might not start for a month or two, though.'

Mr Hay, always elegantly dressed in a light brown suit, said he was sorry to hear our news. And yes, he would be opening the steak bar later in the spring. 'Let me think about it,' he said quietly, nodding slowly.

A few days later, we had a message to visit him again. He had good news. Would I run the steak bar kitchen from about May when it would open? His wife would teach me all I needed to know. Before that, would I like to work as a handyman around the hotel? No extension building this time. To start immediately. Julie would begin the following week. And best of all, he would provide full board and lodging as part of our pay.

We were thrilled. It was the best deal we could have imagined. Deep down, we thanked John Ridgway for forcing us to move on.

On that first morning as the handyman, Mr Hay suggested he would buy the caravan we had been living in previously, and we should stay in it, rather than in a small hotel room. My first job was to relocate it somewhere mutually agreeable close to the hotel. Things were getting better and better. Soon I had the caravan set up in a field below the hotel, looking directly out to sea over Scourie Bay.

Julie, able to turn her hand to anything, soon started as housemaid. Rhoda was very elderly and really couldn't manage the stairs at all but had worked at the hotel all her life. Mr Hay wasn't going to change that, but he did need someone to do the job. Hence Julie. Each morning, under the guidance of Rhoda, she took morning tea to all the guests in bed. She probably threw open the curtains as well, in her breezy way. She worked from 7 am until 2 pm, Then she was back at 7:30 pm until 9 pm, turning down beds and preparing for the following day.

For my part, Mr Hay really didn't need a handyman, but I filled my days cutting kindling for the hotels' open fires, carrying big laundry baskets in and out of the hotel and being on hand for any odd job that came up. It was a happy place to work.

With full board and lodging, we had no living expenses and could commit our entire income to *The Aegre* and voyage preparation. The budget would still be very tight but could now be balanced. We could surely leave if we could just finish *The Aegre* decking and sea trials by midsummer.

But there were so many things to think about—hygiene, for instance. There would be no flush toilet aboard, and this was long before compact portable chemical toilets. On the Atlantic rowing boat, John and Chay had used a simple bucket. We decided we could do the same. A large empty plastic paint pail at the hotel looked just right for a significant future role on *The Aegre*. The precise diameter to give support, relatively shallow and thus stable, and a sturdy metal handle. Another problem solved.

We modelled the cooker on the one in the rowboat too: another large paint pail, in steel this time, with a primus cooker mounted inside. We planned that the pail would hang from under the deck so it could swing as the boat heeled. To light it we'd use a butane cartridge blow lamp to heat the vaporiser. It looked stormproof.

But time was speeding by, already it was mid-April, and Bob still hadn't started on decking *The Aegre*. We had to be ready to leave in three months to make the most of the lighter summer winds or wait another year.

Bob was still waiting for the timber to arrive. I had removed all the original decking and spent countless evenings with him discussing the proposed changes. Anticipating the deck timber arriving, I set to and removed the existing decking and fitted the expanded polystyrene buoyancy sheets, layer by layer, into either end. I shaped each sheet with a hot knife I heated with our butane blowlamp. Unfortunately Mrs Macinnes's chickens, strutting around the shed, took a liking to eating the offcuts. I was a bit slow to notice but they seemed none the worse for it.

Larch for the deck framing arrived in late April, and Bob moved his most recently completed yawlie out of his boat shed and put The Aegre in.

We firmed up the plans for a flush convex deck covering the entire hull. The only openings would be for a two-foot (61-cm) square hatch and a similar-sized cockpit immediately behind it. Being curved, the deck would be stronger than if it were flat and give more headroom below. But how much curve? I wanted sitting headroom, sitting on the floor amidships that is, if nowhere else.

We scrambled about in the open hull, taking measurements and stretching pieces of twine from one end of the boat to the other. The best solution proved remarkably simple. With no deckhouse to interrupt the line, the deck amidships would form a straight line from the tip of the bow to the stern, curving off on either side to where it joined the hull. The highest rise amidships would be 9 inches (23 cm). The deck itself would consist of ⅜ in (9.53 mm) marine plywood to give strength with lightness. It would be supported every 2ft (61cm) by 2 in (5.1 cm) square larch frames, with hanging and lodging knees where they joined the top plank of the hull.

Once it was decided, Bob got on with it quickly. Each day after finishing at the hotel at 5pm, I would rush up to his workshop to see his latest progress. Bob seemed to spend all day thinking up questions for me. I looked forward to these evening discussions. He had spent much of his life as a fisherman and understood many of the problems we would face.

Often, I would arrive at his boatshed to find him sitting on his stool, puffing on his pipe and contemplating the hull of The Aegre before him. Looking up at me over his glasses, he would ask, 'And how are you going to cope with (this or that)?'

Which could lead to a discussion about anything to do with the voyage.

'And how are you going to manage the steering?' he asked one day. He had never heard of wind vane steering systems but quickly grasped the principle.

Navigation was a favourite topic of discussion. 'Well then, how are you going to measure how far you've travelled?' he asked another day.

We'd discussed the pros and cons of the various 'logs' on the market (instruments for measuring speed and distance travelled through the water at sea). I had concluded that none of them justified their expense for the sailing we would be doing, moving slowly and usually far from land.

'And anyway,' I said, 'By taking regular sun and star sights and plotting our position, we'll soon get to know what sort of speed the boat is doing.'

'But you could use a log if you had one, couldn't you?'

'Well, yes, but they're expensive, and I think we can manage without one.'

Bob, sitting on his small stool puffing his pipe, then pulled himself up and walked over to the workshop wall. There he unhooked an aged dull green brass cylinder, about 17in long, with fins at one end. It was one of many relics of the past that dotted his battered old boat shed. I'd noticed it before but had no idea what it was. Now, grasping it in his big hands, he rotated the centre section, which opened to reveal three dials. He said it was towed behind a boat, the fins making it spin around the fixed towing point. It would be hauled back aboard after a set time. When the centre section was opened, the dials would show the distance run since they were last put back to zero.

'My grandfather stopped using this 60 years ago,' he said, 'and it's been hanging there ever since. I think it needs a run. Take it along with you. I want it back, mind,' he added, smiling as he passed this ancient treasure into my young, innocent hands.

What do you say? 'Thank you — and what can I bring you back, Bob?'

It was an unexpected question and food for thought. Another chuckle.

'Ho ho... A bottle of rum from the West Indies. That would be just grand.' And so the deal was done.

Meanwhile, we were still looking for the lead ballast to replace most of the Caithness slate. We eventually ordered 7 cwt (356 kilos) from a firm in Glasgow. But how to transport it 300 miles north to Scourie?

Fortunately, the traditional Highland transport system could help—fish lorries. In the early 1970s, on nearly every night of the week in the season, lorries loaded up with fish at all the little harbours around the northern coasts of Scotland and then drove to the big markets in Glasgow and Newcastle. After unloading, they returned northwards empty. A phone call to Lackie Ross, who lived nearby and ran a fleet of these lorries, solved our problem, or nearly so.

'Well Nick, I'd be delighted to pick it up when I next have a lorry down there, but that may not be for quite a while,' said Lackie. 'Nobody's catching any fish just now.'

But we were well into spring, and the boats should start catching fish soon, or so Lackie thought. He promised that the first lorry down to Glasgow would bring our lead back.

As May went by, the decking and floors of *The Aegre* rapidly took shape. I spent as much of my spare time helping Bob as possible. He had arthritis in his right shoulder and hip and sometimes had off days when little or nothing got done. At other times he would map out on the plywood where he wanted it cut and then leave it until I came up in the late afternoon.

Then the lead arrived, and Bob could get on with the interior (before securing the deck panels). We decided to only build the floor and the bunk(s) inside. I would finish the rest later.

My initial idea for sleeping was to have two narrow bunks, one on either side up in the bow, which is the usual arrangement in small yachts. However, in *The Aegre*, the space in front of the mast would not be open. The polystyrene buoyancy would take the front half, and our food would take up the remainder of the area back to the mast, so the bunks would have to run along each side from the mast back to the hatch. There wasn't much room. But then, one evening, when Bob and I were installing the bilge pump, we stopped for a rest. We were inside the boat hull, under the open deck frames, lying across the boat on the hull planking, facing each other across the boat just behind the mast. We often lay there to chat between jobs. It was very comfortable, and I could fully stretch out. The shape of the hull fitting me perfectly. Bob too — sometimes he almost dozed off.

'Bob, how about building a little platform across the boat right here, just aft the mast, wide enough for a very cosy double berth in port?' I said. 'Then with the addition of a board across the back to hold you in, it would convert to a single berth at sea. We could then store water tanks underneath it. Being amidships, it would also have the least motion at sea. The sleeper could lie either way, depending on which side the wind is on and the boat heeling.'

'Aye aye, that seems like a fine idea.'

Moreover, we realised this arrangement would free up space on either side of the hatch/companionway. We could then mount our cooker and boxes of food in use on one side (they went to port) and the radio receiver, sextant and books opposite, under the starboard side deck.

The conversion of *The Aegre* to an ocean-going micro sailing boat was proceeding apace, but amongst the many problems nagging in my mind was navigation. Bob's loan of the antique log was a most generous gesture, but to navigate safely to Madeira and possibly the West Indies, we would need to know a lot more than merely our distance run through the water.

I had been studiously working through the coastal navigation correspondence course, being much more focused than I'd ever been on my A-levels at school or Optics at college. Many of the exercises were around the Thames Estuary and the English Channel. I was now expert in plotting a course at any stage of the tide from the North Foreland to Harwich going to the north of the Kentish Flats, across the Black Deep, west of the Gunfleet Sands and Pye Sand. True, magnetic and compass courses, dead reckoning positions, estimated positions and observed positions, dipping distances, allowing for leeway, I was on to it all.

But much of our planned voyage would be far offshore, well out of sight of land. For this, I needed to master astro-navigation, plotting one's position based on sightings of the sun and stars using a sextant and chronometer. I had bought the sextant, which was a start, but using it to determine our geographical position was still a mystery to me. Unfortunately, maths wasn't my strong point, I was almost as bad at it at secondary school as I had been at singing at prep school, but I knew John Ridgway had learnt enough to find his way across the Atlantic to Ireland. If he could, I could. Again, he advised me well from the rowing boat experience.

'It's easy to work out your latitude; you just need a noon sight of the sun,' he said. 'Then it's a simple calculation. You only need a sextant and the Nautical Almanac tables for the year. On the rowboat, I had a form, a template, that I covered in clear plastic and could then work through with a chinagraph pencil.'

I started to study it. John was right. I didn't need to know the accurate time for a noon sight, only our approximate longitude and approximate time. I would use the sextant to measure the angle the sun makes with the horizon, starting a few minutes before our expected 'noon', then recording the angle every few seconds as the sun goes up, until it seemed stationary, then started to drop. The highest reading is the noon altitude. Easy. Then some simple math to correct the sextant reading for known errors. Then some more easy math drawing on the tables on the day's page in the current year's Nautical Almanac, and out pops our latitude. It sounded easy in theory, and it was almost as easy in practice.

The Aegre
Registered at Lerwick LK92

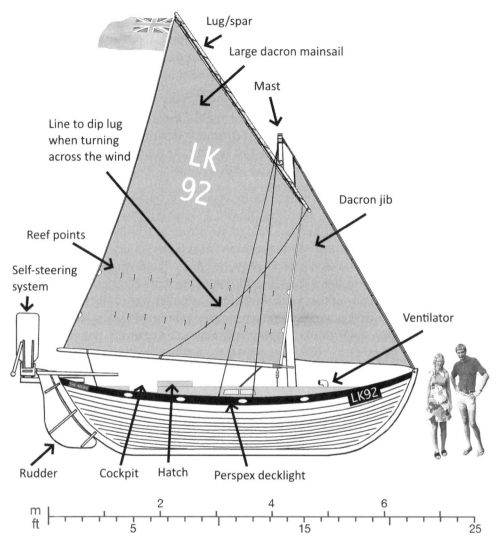

Lug/spar

Large dacron mainsail

Mast

Line to dip lug when turning across the wind

Dacron jib

Reef points

Self-steering system

LK 92

Ventilator

Rudder   Cockpit   Hatch   Perspex decklight

LK92

m
ft

2   4   6

5   15   25

The Aegre was a fairly typical Shetland style boat, 21′6″ overall length with a beam (width) of about 7 ft. For the voyage she was given an overall whaleback deck with a maximum rise of about 9″ amidships. She initially had 10 cwt (508 kg) of Caithness slate as ballast but this was replaced by lead ingots and fresh water tanks allowing the cabin floor to be lowered giving more headroom. A 2′x2′ cockpit and adjoining hatch were the only breaks in the deck.

Her main sailing rig was a standing lugsail and jib. Later a bowsprit and flying jib were added. In strong winds this was replaced with a much smaller gaff-headed storm mainsail and small jib, both made of flax.

The Aegre (Gene Carl Feldman)

However, I did need to see the sun around noon, and in the grey North Atlantic there can be days when it never appears. But this was where all my coastal navigation study would come in handy. By being disciplined and keeping a strict record of the course sailed, the distance run and likely leeway (due to wind, tide and currents), I could regularly plot on the chart an 'estimated position' in between noon sights of the sun.

From Scotland to Madeira, we would generally be sailing south, so our change in latitude would give us most of the information we needed. But latitude is really only half the story. To avoid running into Ireland unexpectedly, we needed to know how far we were east or west, i.e. our longitude. This, I discovered, is considerably more tricky to determine.

Luckily, I had found an easily understood little book called 'Celestial Navigation for Yachtsmen' by Mary Blewitt. I skimmed through it, noting that to work out a full latitude and longitude position, I'd need to take two sun sights, one at noon and one about three hours before or after local noon. I would need to know accurate Greenwich Mean Time when taking the morning or afternoon sight. Then, in addition to the year's Nautical Almanac Tables, I'd need a copy of the 'Air Sight Reduction Tables' Vol 2. Furthermore, I read, to work out star sights, I'd need another volume of tables, 'Air Sight Reduction Tables Vol 3.' But I thought that could wait for now.

The books of tables were easy; I could order them by mail, and they weren't overly expensive. But accurate time was more difficult. It has long been a problem at sea due to the vessel's motion and temperature changes, upsetting pendulum and spring tensions in mechanical clocks. In 1973 the only way yachtsmen could have accurate time on board was through using a marine chronometer. These highly consistent small mechanical clocks were wound precisely every day and protected from sharp shocks and temperature changes. But they were expensive, outside our budget.

Our alternative was a basic water-resistant mechanical watch that we would keep secure in the cabin and check every night against a time signal broadcast on the shortwave by WWV. This was a radio station in Colorado which we expected to be able to receive on our transistor radio. This station sends out a time signal every minute, and we planned to use it to determine the error on the watch (from Coordinated Universal Time, which is the same as Greenwich Mean Time). We could then calculate the correct GMT of any sun or star sight. It would not be as accurate as a chronometer, but we rationalised that we would be travelling slowly anyway. This did mean that our shortwave radio receiver now had an important role.

In summary, I made sure we had everything with us we needed to work out our position. I would practise with it once we got going. This sounds very casual, but in reality, the first passage to Madeira was almost due south, and the noon sights of the sun would enable us to check our progress.

Furthermore, radio beacons located along the coast of Ireland, France, Spain and Portugal would give a further check of our latitude with the simple Radio Direction Finding ability of our little shortwave receiver. As long as we had plenty of sea room and radio batteries and could keep seawater out of the radio receiver, longitude didn't seem critical. We just had to avoid hitting Ireland.

The question of avoiding Ireland brought on a debate about the best course for the passage south, from NW Scotland to Madeira. I was worried about the initial plan to sail down the west coast of Scotland between the Islands of the Hebrides and the mainland and then through the Irish Sea between Ireland and England, probably stopping in harbours along the way. We would have some shelter from the south-westerly Atlantic gales and could stop along the way if the weather turned bad. However, the relatively confined waters had lots of shipping, strong tides and currents, all creating difficulties. The prevailing south-westerly winds meant we'd have a headwind most of the way, and there would always be the danger of being blown onto a nearby lee shore.

I realised that the safety of a coastal passage like this was an illusion. There was an alternative. But taking it would indeed be a bold decision.

The alternative was to sail away from the dangers of the British coastline as quickly as possible after leaving Scourie in NW Scotland. We could do this by sailing slightly north of west for 40 miles, across the Minch to pass north of the tip of the most northerly of the Outer Hebrides, the Butt of Lewis. Then, anticipating the prevailing south-westerly wind, we would continue on this port tack straight out into the Atlantic for maybe another 100 miles until we were well to the west of the longitude of western Ireland. Then we would sail south on a starboard tack, leaving Ireland well to the east and clearing the SW tip of England. From there, if necessary, we could take a further tack out into the Atlantic to keep well away from the treacherous Bay of Biscay. But with any luck, the wind would swing around to the west, or even north-west, as we progressed south, allowing us to eventually set a direct course to Madeira, off the west coast of Africa. It would be about 1,500–1,600 miles (2,400–2,600 km), non-stop. We could surely average 50 miles a day (24hrs), so it would take approximately 32 days to get to Madeira.

We were suddenly planning a substantial voyage in our little Shetland boat. We had never even been offshore in her and here we were seriously contemplating a 30-plus day ocean passage. But with the enthusiasm and invincibility of youth, we just got on with it.

Back in Bob's boatshed, the extremely basic interior of *The Aegre* was complete, and Bob's work on the decking was going well. Now he was building the 2ft square hatch, which would slide forward to open, and immediately aft of it, the 2 ft square and 2 ft deep cockpit. Wooden washboards would slide in vertically to separate the cockpit and cabin in stormy weather.

We would have liked the cockpit to be self-draining so that any waves that slopped into it would drain back out to the sea through pipes in the floor, but this was not possible as the cockpit floor would be at or below the outside waterline, so any water that came into it would instead have to drain down into the bottom of the boat. We installed a high-capacity hand pump inside the hatch to pump it out again.

The days and weeks were quickly passing. It was May already, and I was now the cook in the steak bar café, serving lunch and dinner to a slowly growing number of tourists. It was easy work.

Now well into spring, the days were warmer, and we too seemed to have moved into a new life; one where the preparation for the impending voyage was everything, as if we were already sailors, just temporarily ashore. Every day there were problems to be solved, yet progress was made, be it with the boat, our stores, or more equipment arriving on the mail bus.

In between shifts, I worked with Bob on *The Aegre*, or spliced ropes that would control the sails, or collected and melted lead for the self-steering system counterweight. Julie was planning all our food and its packaging. My sister in England sent us empty polythene ice cream boxes for our food stores (her husband's waistline never recovered). Our lists were endless. But progress was excellent, and we set 31st May as the launch date. We would moor her in Scourie Bay, which was close by but not very sheltered.

I made a heavy concrete mooring and planted it in the agreed most sheltered spot in Scourie Bay, ready for *The Aegre*.

On 31st May, precisely a month after she had gone into Bob's workshop, *The Aegre* was ready for launching. Low water was in the late morning. Bob knocked out the end wall of his boat shed, and then, with the help of Bob's son-in-law Robert McLeod and Angus McKenzie, we eased *The Aegre* out and onto a rough wooden sledge that would pass as a temporary boat trailer, towed by Robert on his tractor.

Bob followed, bringing a trailer with all the bits and pieces needed to go aboard, mast, rigging, sails and water containers. On the beach, Julie and I loaded these all onto *The Aegre*. I went aboard and stowed them, lying on her bilge on the beach, the boat was heeled, and with the sound of the breakers in my ears, I could almost imagine I was at sea already. Now we just had to wait for the tide to come in. Sitting on the cockpit floor, I looked up and along the deck line and imagined myself crawling along the steeply inclined deck at sea and wondered how that would feel.

The tide slowly came in, and as it did so an onshore wind freshened blowing the boat sideways onto the beach. Soon Julie was wading up to her waist in the chilly sea trying to hold *The Aegre* straight while I, aboard, pushed off the beach with an oar. What dedication. Whatever had to be done I knew I could trust her.

And then we were afloat. and being towed out to our mooring while Julie went back to work. Meanwhile *The Aegre* rose smoothly to the swell, giving a gentle swoosh as she nosed through the chop. I looked down at our small, rugged boat. How would she stand up to a gale in mid-Atlantic? Would we really be able to live happily in such a small space as our little cabin? But even as these thoughts came into my head, they were dispelled. The clean lines of the flush deck, broken only by the tiny hatch and cockpit, gave a feeling of immense solidity. This, combined with all the built-in buoyancy and the short, sturdy mast, must surely make the boat almost invincible. That meant it was up to us to keep going. How often had I read that the crew usually gave up long before the limits of a boat were reached?

Soon she was lying sedately on our new mooring, looking very smart and business-like. The sun on the sea ripples were reflected on her varnished sides. The edges of the overlapping strake laps made a light 'glug glug' sound as she moved gently on the water, a familiar tune we came to know well. From the jetty, she showed the lines of the super-strong northern isles workboat she was. But she was going to be an extremely basic cruising boat: no engine, no electrics, no transmitter, no proper nautical chronometer, no toilet, no self-furling sails, no refrigerator or freezer, no running water, and of course, no GPS or computer. Such luxuries were still years away.

The boat was on the water, but there was still much to do, like setting up the mast and sails and loading all our stores and equipment. We'd need to take her out sailing too. How would she handle with so much more weight in her than before? And we'd need some strong wind to try her storm sails. How would the cooker perform, and where were we going to stow everything with no storage areas built in the cabin? There was so much to do.

It was already the end of May. The north-west coast of Scotland has a narrow window of calmer summer weather. Our target was to depart by mid-July, just six weeks away. Could we make it?

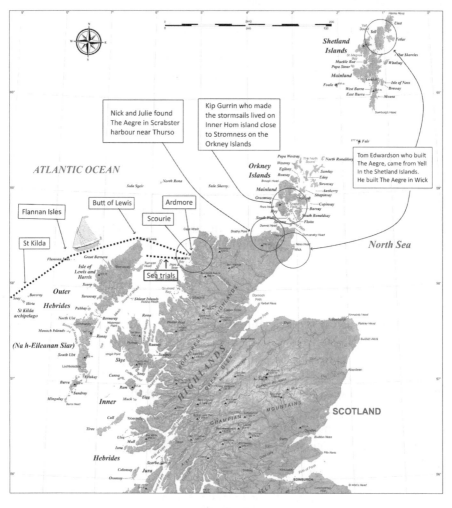

Scotland

Chapter 7
Sea trials

'Of course, for a seaman, next to being actually at sea, the greatest enjoyment comes from preparing the boat for a voyage.' — Sir Robin Knox-Johnston

O ur little world in Scourie changed that day with the launching of *The Aegre*, as if suddenly we were sea folk, temporarily on land, but at home on the sea. The beginning of our new life.

We were no longer trudging up the hill to Bob's boatshed but rather just down to the short stone wharf by the beach and rowing out to our boat rocking gently on the swell, her varnish work glinting in the sun. *Come, sail me,* she seemed to say, *let's go, let's go.* So soon this would be where we lived, our lives ruled by the weather and the tide. I could hardly wait. We just needed to rig her, do sea trials, and load food and water. Surely we could sail off south within a month or so?

If only it could all have been that simple.

An immediate problem was the cheap inflatable dinghy we'd bought from a mail-order catalogue to get to and from the shore and to take with us. Now we found it barely supported two people and was awkward to row. Air continually leaked, so it was always soft. It was like a dangerous children's toy. I cursed it, but somehow it got us from the beach to *The Aegre* and back every day. Once aboard, there was much to do; the mast and supporting rigging to be put in place and the two sets of sails set up and trialled. And much more. My list was several pages long.

After the launch, the mast was first. Even with all the rigging attached, I could easily stand the short piece of varnished solid Oregon pine upright and lower it through the hole in the deck. Below in the cabin, Julie guided the mast foot onto a gold half-sovereign, for luck, sitting in a notch in the keel. Then I attached the rigging to hold the mast secure.

The cooker was next, hung on two steel arms attached to the underside of the deck to the left (port) of the hatchway. Preheated with our butane blowlamp, the primus was alight and roaring almost instantly. Soon we were standing in the tight little hatchway, drinking our first cup of tea aboard our compact cruising boat. With her flush deck, she looked rather good. Almost ready to go anywhere.

I pulled up the sails on the first calm afternoon with the boat secure on the mooring. In theory, I could do this while standing in the hatchway, with no need to go on deck, but in reality, some deck work was needed. I crawled around on the curved decking. We had no guardrails, just a low gunwale about 2 ins (5 cm) high around the edge of the deck.

Then I tried reefing the mainsail, and found I could do this easily from the hatchway.

Next were Kip Gurrin's storm sails. I lowered the large mainsail and lashed it down on the deck in chocks Bob had built for it on the starboard decking, then hauled the thick, heavy, and stiff flax sails up on deck and rather laboriously set them up using the boom from the large mainsail. Then back in the hatchway, heaving alternately on the throat and peak halyards, raised the new storm mainsail. Once set, it looked small and strong. The changeover had been slow and awkward, but at least I now knew I could set all the sails.

Meanwhile, Julie tried to bring order to a chaotic scene in the cabin below. From the cockpit, the narrow bunk across the boat just aft of the mast was like the far side of a swamp of all our kit. There was no quick solution to the chaos below, but we thought we'd gradually find a place for everything. A higher priority was to take *The Aegre* out under sail, but we were working six days a week at the Scourie Hotel, now full of anglers chasing trout and salmon

We planned a trial sail on our first day off after the launching, but it was foggy, and there was no wind. A heavy swell from some distant gale was rolling into the bay, rocking us gently. We busied ourselves aboard, enjoying the sense of being on the water as we started to stow stuff into the farthest crevices of the boat.

Early in the afternoon, a light breeze flickered across the water blowing away the fog. Being impatient to get going, we soon had the sails set and let go of the mooring. We slowly wafted out of the bay, a heavy swell breaking on either shore close by. It was rather frightening. Just outside the bay, the wind fell away, and we were totally becalmed, the sails slatting from side to side as we rolled heavily in a short steep sea. Julie was soon seasick. I felt so sorry for her. With almost no wind we soon headed back, ghosting our way into the bay's calm and onto our mooring. So much for our first sail. But it did show how well *The Aegre* sailed in extremely light airs, and Julie wasn't upset about briefly being seasick. A good first effort, we agreed.

The weather on our next day off was just the opposite, being windy, cool and grey with low cloud. Whitecaps to the waves in Scourie Bay foretold rough seas at the mouth and off Handa Island. Common sense might have kept us ashore, but we wanted to test the storm sails, so in full wet weather clothing, we headed out to *The Aegre*, set Kip's flax storm sails and tacked out of the bay. Big swells were rolling in, but the boat easily lifted over them as we surged out of the bay. Silver spray flew the boat's length as we burst through the tops of waves.

Leaving the shelter of the bay, conditions quickly became worse. Just off Handa Island, the tide was running hard against the wind, creating steep, short and violent waves. *The Aegre* was thrown about wildly. Now even our storm mainsail was too big. I lowered it, tied in a reef, and reset the much smaller mainsail while the rocks on Handa to leeward steadily drew closer. Immediately we were sailing strongly again, but now under full control, the boat just on a slight heel. We squashed together on the windward edge of the small cockpit, Julie not feeling seasick this time as *The Aegre* surged along, making light of the big seas as we headed back into Scourie Bay and onto our mooring. I felt like laughing. This boat was so good!

There was a reasonable weather forecast for our next day off, and we planned a more ambitious trip to Lewis, the largest island of the Outer Hebrides, about 40 miles (64km) west of us, and back. We left mid-evening, heading out into the long grey dusk of a summer's night at 59 degrees north. There was no other shipping and few lights on the coast astern as we headed west, beating into a light sea and steady south-westerly wind. Julie turned in to get some sleep for 4 hours on our little bunk below. I'd wake her at 2 am.

Now on deck alone, it was chilly. I wore a few layers of wool and my new Helly Hansen oilskins. The wind was steady, the sea light and *The Aegre* was just heeling gently, the full rig easing her along at four to five knots, needing little effort from me to hold her on course. Below in the cabin I could see Julie tucked up, fast asleep beneath our duvet. Was I dreaming, or was this real?

One by one, the lighthouses astern dipped below the horizon until we were all alone in the twilight of the far north summer night. With the boat sailing so smoothly, I tried setting the wind-vane-controlled self-steering system. Soon I had its steering lines attached to the tiller and the wind vane adjusted.

I sat back and watched in delight as it held the boat on course. It was so simple, but so liberating. No longer did I have to steer all the time. Now I could sit on the cockpit floor, out of the wind, my eyes at deck level to keep a lookout.

As if in a dream, I watched *The Aegre* relentlessly marching to windward in the twilight, making good speed across a light chop. The sails set firm, not a wrinkle or a flap to be seen. The boat was leaning at a steady angle. Only the swish of the bow wave disturbed the silence. It was as if we could go on sailing like this for ever.

Freed from steering, I looked at the chart, clipped to a piece of plywood. Sitting on the cockpit floor, I held it on my knees and plotted our estimated position by the light of a small oil lamp. No longer was this a homework exercise.

Soon it was nearly 2 am, and already there was light in the eastern sky. Sunrise would be at about 2:20. The wind had strengthened and we were now shipping spray over the windward bow, water running across the foredeck. With the tiller still in the hands of the self-steering and keeping one eye on the compass, I lit the cooker and made a cup of tea to wake Julie with. She looked so peaceful I hated to disturb her, but this was the life we'd chosen. 'Wakey wakey, 2 am, time to wake up, here's a cup of tea, and a quarter of a Mars bar.' It would become our typical night watch handover routine.

Julie woke uncomplainingly, then sat snuggled under the duvet in the early morning twilight, drank her tea and savoured the bite of chocolate and her last few moments in bed in the sheltered cubby that was our cabin. Then she was up, pulling on her thermal underwear, then rolling out of the bunk and standing up in the hatch to pull on her wet weather gear and gumboots. A little blearily she looked out at the grey horizon all around. In the south-east was the beginning of the dawn. She didn't look impressed.

'The wind's up a bit. Where are we?'

Excitedly I replied, 'About 20 miles off Loch Laxford, Lewis is about 20 miles ahead. We should see it in about two hours. The wind is up a bit, the barometer steady, and the self-steering is holding a good course. No ships sighted, but I think I'll tie in a reef. No need to press the boat more than necessary.'

Twenty miles? It could have been two hundred. For the first time, we were far offshore in the middle of the night, totally independent, on our own little cruising boat, and all was well.

I dropped the mainsail to the deck, tied in a reef and reset it. *The Aegre* was quickly back up to the same speed as before but hardly heeled now. Soon the self-steering was back in control.

With Julie now sitting in the cockpit I showed her the course we were steering on the compass, my latest estimated position plot on the chart and how to trim the self-steering if the wind shifted a little. 'If anything changes, wake me up,' I said.

I pulled off my oilskins in the narrow hatchway and then ducked into the cabin. For the first time at sea on *The Aegre*, I crawled onto the bunk and snuggled under the still warm duvet. Ahhh, it was so comfortable. But what's this? With a torch I could see water running down the mast onto the side of our bunk. It must be the spray on the foredeck. I thought I'd sealed it. Obviously not well enough. But there was nothing that could be done about it that night.

I settled back, breathing deeply, feeling the boat heel a little, then back, the boat easily rising and falling over the light sea, the water rushing by half an inch from my ear. My first night's sleep aboard *The Aegre*. Aft in the twilight, I could see Julie's dark shape in the cockpit framed against the night sky. A rounded figure, like a travelling bag woman, in multiple layers of clothes to keep out the chill of the night. I wondered if this was how she'd imagined it would be …

Then Julie was calling me, waking me with a warm cup of tea. 'Six am, Lewis is ahead, wakey wakey.' We exchanged places and slowly closed with the grey north-east coast of Lewis a bit north of Tolsta Head. With the self-steering still in control of the helm, I made a big breakfast of bacon and eggs. There was no sign of Julie's seasickness that morning but instead there was something magical about eating fresh egg and bacon sandwiches forty miles out at sea on our own little sailing boat. There was nowhere else I'd rather have been.

I knew the day was coming when we'd just keep going, but not this time. With the washing up done, we turned around to head back to the west coast of the mainland, forty miles beyond the grey horizon.

A rusty freighter heading north rolled across our bow with no sign of seeing us. Then the wind eased to give us an easy sail back. The Old Man of Stoer, a prominent offshore rock stack west of Ullapool, was the first to appear over the horizon to the south-east as we headed back to the prominent cliffs of Handa Island and finally into Scourie Bay.

We were back on our mooring by mid-afternoon, almost disappointingly early. *The Aegre* had shown herself to be relatively fast and very well balanced, despite floating about 9 inches lower than when sailing empty. We'd learnt a lot about sailing and living aboard her.

That same day, my parents, Eleanor and Vere, arrived to visit for a week, having driven the length of England and Scotland. They brought more polythene food boxes, two sizeable home-baked fruit cakes, and the gift of a pair of powerful binoculars, which we came to treasure. Implicit in this was their support for our adventure, but I imagined they were worried. Did we really know what we were doing?

They were keen to see *The Aegre*, and we ferried them out to her in our feeble little dinghy. I hoped it wouldn't collapse as they sat on its squishy sides.

Once aboard *The Aegre*, Eleanor and Vere were an enthusiastic audience as we proudly talked them through how everything worked. We showed them all our stores, navigation instruments, freshwater tanks, self-steering system, foolproof cooker, big bilge pump, two sets of sails, and short-wave radio receiver. They tried our bunk and agreed it was very comfy. Given the opportunity, I began to think they'd like to come with us.

On their last night with us, my father gave me a small envelope and, smiling, said,

'Here's a little something from us. Open it when you reach the West Indies.'

Imagining maybe a celebratory meal, we tucked it away safely somewhere. That day seemed a long way off.

But then my parents were gone. I was too busy to feel sentimental. It was already early July. We wanted to sail before the end of the month, so we'd be sailing south in the peak of the summer.

Every night we'd review our to-do lists. I realised we'd never actually be ready to sail. We'd just have to set a target few days, carefully watch the weather, and then just go. If we had everything on board, we could work things out as we went along.

One important job was a fresh coating of antifouling paint to the underwater section of the hull. There was no nearby slipway, but back at the Adventure School there was a sheltered beach where *The Aegre* could dry out between tides. We sailed around Handa Island to the school on our next day off and propped the boat up on the little beach as the tide fell. Then, working fast, we scrubbed the bottom and slapped on two coats of anti-fouling paint.

It was dry when the tide rose again to float us off. But then John and Marie Christine invited us to stay for a farewell dinner. Our friendship with the Ridgways had been restored, and now, with too much good cheer, we left much later than planned. There was no wind at all out on the loch. Lance Bell, the school's handyman gave us a long tow out to the mouth of Loch Laxford in the late evening twilight eventually casting us off from his workboat *Ada Bell*, with a cheery 'Good luck', but even there, hardly a breath of wind ruffled the water. We spent the rest of the night barely breasting the tide past Handa and wafted back onto our mooring off Scourie at about 4.30 am in the early light of the dawn.

A couple of hours later, Julie was back at work in the hotel, taking early morning tea to the guests. She wasn't quite so breezy that morning.

We were soon to leave but deliberately hadn't sought any publicity. We wanted to be free from ties and obligations, be able to leave whenever we wanted, go wherever we liked, and change all our plans at a moment's notice. We were children of the sixties. But somehow, the press heard about our plans a week before we hoped to leave, and suddenly there were phone calls at the hotel for us.

'Are you going to sail across the Atlantic?'

'How long is your boat?'

'How many of you are there?'

Do you have a motor/radio/cat/dog/parrot?'

Naively we answered. We'd never spoken to reporters before. Our answers became fact. Soon we read in the paper that we were leaving at the end of the week, sailing to the West Indies via Madeira.

Walking along the stone wharf, a little boy stopped me and said, 'Are you the man that's sailing to America?'

I smiled to myself as I realised I was.

Then we were as ready as we could be and just waiting for our updated sea charts to arrive in the mail. The weather seemed settled, with an uncommon light wind from the north-east. Ideal for sailing across to the northern tip of Lewis and it would become a tailwind if we turned south-west, a perfect course for us. It seemed auspicious.

Then on July 24, the charts arrived on the mid-afternoon mail bus. Excitedly we rang Bob and others to say we'd leave that afternoon. We met him and many friends on the stone wharf a short time later. I shook Bob's hand for a long time, trying to express my thanks for everything. He, together with John Ridgway, had got us this far. Not only had Bob done the work on the boat, but he had given the exploit his approval. This opened many doors in Scourie for us. He would have come with us in another time, another age, another life, and we would have loved to have had him along.

Neither of us could really believe we were off, but there was no time to be sentimental. With the goodbyes said, Julie and I clambered into our little dinghy and rowed to *The Aegre*.

We were soon alongside the varnished hull. She was low in the water with all the stores and our belongings, and we had little difficulty in scrambling aboard, watched by everyone on the wharf nearby. Feeling nervous with their eyes on us, I deflated and stowed the dinghy while Julie put away the last few odds and ends below. Then I raised the big lugsail. *The Aegre* swung around into the wind with the tan Dacron mainsail billowing above us. I took a last look around the deck. Were we really ready?

'Here we go then,' I called back to Julie on the helm, and cast off our mooring, then gave the traditional three long farewell blasts on our foghorn. Some car horns answered from the shore. I'd been looking forward to doing that for so long. We really were off.

Julie steered her off before the light north-easterly wind to sail out of the bay. Our little boat was as keen to go as we were. The small group on the wharf quickly became just small blobs of colour, then were gone behind the hill as we turned north-west towards Handa Island. How could such good friends and supporters disappear so quickly? One moment we were with them, the next alone.

The tiny white cottages of Scourie gradually merged into the hills astern, the coastline opening on each side as we drew away from the coast. Ahead of us, the open sea.

Chapter 8
First passage: Scourie to Madeira

'There is but a plank between a sailor and eternity' — Thomas Gibbons

Was this really happening? Were we really off, heading for Madeira 1,800 miles to the south? It was a little after 5 pm on Tuesday 24th July, 1973. I was 23, Julie 19.

Excitedly I joined her in the cockpit. She was steering, and perhaps more nervous than I, she looked down at the compass. 'What course shall I steer?' she asked.

What course? What course? No need to look that up. I'd worked it out months ago. I reeled off the figures to take us north-west across the Minch to the Butt of Lewis, the northern tip of the Outer Hebrides, our turning point into the North Atlantic proper. As Julie brought the boat onto the course, I trimmed the sails and we started to reach across the wind, soon making good speed. I put Bob's log over the stern, and the long line paid out before tightening on its deck cleat. In the clear water astern, I saw it start to spin the miles away.

As we pulled away from the coast, the yellow streak of Sandwood Bay appeared far off to the north-east. Astern, the ridge of Foinaven grew to dominate the skyline, while the Old Man of Stoer stood out from the cliffs to the south. I took sights on all three with our hand-bearing compass and then plotted our position on our chart. Excitedly I called to Julie, 'Since leaving Handa, we've averaged five knots. If we keep this up, we'll make the Butt of Lewis in eight hours.'

Julie, on the helm and beginning to feel seasick, was unimpressed.

With the excitement of leaving over, we both needed a cup of tea. I 'went below' to put the kettle on. Except I was on *The Aegre*, so I just sat down on the cockpit floor, legs in the cabin, cooker by my left elbow. Our cooker hung in the swinging pail was proving ideal. The hot drink gave us renewed energy, and while Julie continued to steer, I prepared the boat for the open sea, lashing our big Danforth anchor down just aft of the mast and bringing the anchor lines below. Our tiny cabin seemed very disorganised. We had never got around to building anything inside except the bunk and a bookshelf. I could never decide on the best way to arrange it and eventually decided that practical experience on the first passage would show the best arrangement. We just had to live with the chaos below till Madeira. We'd never have left if we had waited until we were completely ready.

But the cabin really was a mess — it looked like a maritime junkyard. Some order was needed. I decided to use the coils of anchor lines, spare sail sheets and many other pieces of rope to insulate everything else from the damp exterior planking which was exposed almost everywhere. On top of the lines went all our clothes and possessions, mostly in polythene bags. Fortunately, Julie had thought more about the food, which was all stowed up forward in polythene boxes as planned, except for a crate of oranges which we'd managed to squeeze under the cockpit decking to port, accessed very awkwardly from behind the cooker.

As we drew away from the coast, the sea settled down and our motion eased. Julie started to feel a bit brighter and offered to make dinner, so I took over the helm and set up the wind vane self-steering system to the smell of frying onions. Soon *The Aegre* was steering herself as if by magic, with no loss in speed.

Julie had planned a celebratory dinner for the first night out, but times were hard, and food supplies in the local shop were limited. Sausages and bacon, canned peas with instant mashed potato. It wasn't quite up to the standard of the Scourie Hotel. Sharing a single bowl, we smiled at each other in the dusk. Here we were, heading out to sea at last. Together we'd done it, well, we'd got this far. With a little salt spray and a sea view, it was a feast.

Dinner was soon over, and with the cockpit deck only nine inches above the sea, washing up was just a matter of dipping the bowl over the side. Then we moved into the system of four-hour watches we'd planned. Julie was the sleepiest, so she turned in, leaving me to the evening gloom. The Cape Wrath lighthouse twinkled to the far north-east and the Stoer Point lighthouse to the far south-east, both soon to disappear below the horizon. Then just darkness. Now we were really alone.

'The other fellow' (the self-steering system) held us on a steady course, *The*

Aegre continuing to cream along to the north-west towards the Butt of Lewis, still far away. With no need to steer, I could sit on the floor of the cockpit out of the wind, my head just above deck level, one eye on the horizon for ships, the other on the compass, my legs in the cabin under the hatch. As the twilight deepened, the little cabin in front of me was dimly lit by the flame of our small kerosene anchor light hung below to double as our cabin light. I could see the shape of Julie on the bunk, snug, dry and asleep. We were finally off, I couldn't help smiling at the wonder of it all.

Although it was July and midsummer, it wasn't warm. Starting from a latitude of 59 degrees north meant that the nights were chilly even in summer, while daylight hours were long. Sitting on the cockpit floor, I was out of the wind but still wearing warm woollen socks, woollen long johns and jeans over the top, a Helly Hansen Polar jersey, two home-knitted woollen jerseys, and a woollen balaclava over my head. On top of all that, I was wearing Helly Hansen oilskins and gumboots. I was warm and dry, but it was awkward to move around.

We changed watches and places at midnight. A shared Mars bar gave us renewed energy. The Cape Wrath and Stoer Point lights had dipped below the horizon a good hour before, but far in the distance ahead we could now just see the white pinprick like flash of the lighthouse on the Butt of Lewis. I showed Julie where we were on the chart and explained what compass bearing the Butt light should be on to be sure of clearing the island before we altered course to the west to head out into the Atlantic.

Then I was standing in the hatchway to undress. 'If there's any problem, wake me up,' I said as I stripped off my oilskins, carefully timing it between bursts of spray from the bow. Then, pulling the hatch closed behind me, I crawled forward to the lovely warm bunk running across the boat. I knew she would, but my mind was racing as if I'd drunk too much coffee. I lay with my eyes open, listening to the water rushing past a few inches from my ears, the boat heeling a bit more then a bit less, searching for her way across the sea. In the dim twilight I could see Julie aft in the cockpit silhouetted against the starlit sky. We were really off at last.

I took some deep breaths and tried to relax. Could I ever sleep? I closed my eyes. The boat felt strong and steady, and Julie would wake me if anything changed on deck. I made myself doze. Sleep must have come.

Julie takes up the story:

It was a beautifully clear starlit night, and I sat rather nervously admiring it.

I had another look at the chart and went over what Nick had said. It all seemed logical, and I thought I could cope. I certainly didn't want to wake Nick up for anything as it had been a hectic day, and he needed a few hours of sleep. I felt much refreshed and not seasick now that I was taking full responsibility for the boat.

I kept checking the course, but it seemed all right. I wondered if I could alter the self-steering lines by myself if the wind changed or we had to alter course. I hoped we wouldn't pass the Butt until Nick's next watch.

It was amazing to be going along so well, with no apparent effort. The sea was smooth, like going through a sea of mercury.

I took the bearing of the light every half hour or so as I didn't want to miss the point at which we should alter course. I began to feel cold despite my layers of clothing and huddled down more in the cockpit to get more shelter from the wind. How cosy it was down below! Like a completely different world.

To pass the time, I started to sing quietly to myself all the hymns I had learnt at school and was amazed at how many and how fully I remembered them. Then a feeling of isolation crept over me, and I wanted to wake Nick up for reassurance, but he looked so peacefully asleep that I didn't like to. Sudden unfounded fears of sea monsters made me grip the sides of the cockpit and check my life harness. I imagined long, slimy tentacles pulling me into the sea and being too horror-stricken to scream.

After three hours, the Butt light was on our port quarter, on the bearing at which Nick said we should turn. I undid the self-steering lines and turned the boat more off the wind onto the westerly course Nick had said. I thought I should adjust the sails somehow and let the sheets out a bit, but I wasn't confident that I had done the right thing. I wished that Nick would stir and should out, 'Everything OK?' so I could confide my worries, but even the slightly different motion of the boat hadn't woken him. There was only about an hour of my watch left, so I steered myself, partly for something to do but mainly because I was unsure about altering the wind vane. Nick had explained it to me several times, and I understood the principle of the thing. I just found it difficult to put into practice.

On the dot, I called below to Nick, 'Time to wake up, wake up sleepyhead,' until he stirred.

'How's it going? Have you altered course yet?' he said. I brought him up to date as he got dressed. He soon got the self-steering working, and I left him to watch the dawn.

We didn't feel like much breakfast when we changed watches again at 4 am, so we just had a cup of tea and some crispbread. Julie retired to the bunk while it turned into a grey day on deck, the first of many, but most importantly, the north-easterly wind was holding.

In our original plan we had anticipated that the prevailing south-westerly wind would predominate, hence our plan to sail west until we could clear Ireland on a tack south. But here we were with the opposite. While it might not last long, this wind allowed us to take a more direct (south-westerly) course to sail out to the west of Ireland. When the wind reverted to the south-west, we could, if necessary, go onto the port tack to head further west away from Ireland. With no engine and a not overly powerful lug rig, we had to avoid any possibility of being blown onto the west coast of Ireland. With this unexpected wind direction, I plotted a new course that would take us south-west but keep us well clear of the north-west tip of Ireland. It would take us past the Flannan Isles and then on past the islands of St Kilda, the outlying islands to the west of Lewis.

Coursework finished, I secured our chart board up underneath the deck and out of the way, then reset the self-steering, bringing *The Aegre* onto the new course for the Flannan Isles. These are just a small collection of rocks surmounted by a lighthouse, about 20 miles west of Lewis and the same distance ahead of us. With *The Aegre* on the new course, I looked dead ahead and there in the far distance, I could just see them on the distant horizon.

Aboard the wind was holding, and in the light sea, we were making good speed, the self-steering vane keeping *The Aegre* on a steady course. By lunchtime the isles were abeam, and we were heading for the island of St Kilda, about 40 miles away and amazingly, just visible on the horizon.

St Kilda is even more remote than the Flannan Isles. According to our Pilot Book, there were actually four small islands. They're the most westerly in the British Isles, about 40 miles out into the Atlantic, west of the Outer Hebrides. Despite being so small and remote, St Kilda was inhabited for at least 2,000 years, the last crofters only being relocated to the mainland in the 1930s. As *The Aegre* continued slicing through a light sea towards them, I gazed at the lonely islets on the horizon and wondered about the life of the people crofting here far out in the Atlantic, rarely visited and subjected to the worst of the North Atlantic weather.

Not that things were easy on *The Aegre*. The wind had been steadily increasing all afternoon, the sea building, and it had started to rain. I had been off watch and 'asleep' all afternoon, but had got little rest as the heel angle, motion and noise had worsened with the rising wind. In the cockpit poor Julie looked exhausted. Now coming on deck, I could see the sky ahead was ominously black. Fearing the worst, I decided to reduce sail before it became completely dark.

This would be my first go at changing at sea from the big Dacron mainsail to the flax stormsail Kip Gurrin had made for us. In theory, it was easy— lower the mainsail, swap the halyard and boom to the gaff storm sail, raise the storm sail while all the time Julie held the boat on an appropriate course to the wind. The reality of crawling around in the twilight on the tiny heaving deck of *The Aegre*, wearing all those layers of clothes and a life-harness that continually became entangled in everything, was not easy. The shackles were tight, my hands cold, and the violent motion made everything difficult. I expected it to take ten minutes; it took an hour. Exhausting for both of us.

But it was worth the effort. The sail set beautifully. *The Aegre* was quickly back up to speed, now sailing comfortably on just a slight heel and not feeling stressed. Ahead the sky was near black, but with the storm sails set, we were as prepared as we could be.

Astern, the dark, lonely shape of St Kilda, the last piece of Scotland, slowly faded. It would be our last sight of land for more than four weeks.

With a course now set to take us well to the west of Ireland, we sailed into the darkness.

Unexpectedly, the wind held steady until the early morning. The bad weather promise of the dark clouds came to nothing, but rather, in the early morning during Julie's watch, the wind started to die away, and by midday, we were almost becalmed.

The stormsail hung limply, until I reversed the evening sail change procedure and set the big lugsail to make the most of any light breeze. I spent the rest of my morning watch lying on the deck beside the cockpit under the weak sun, listening to BBC Radio 2 on our little transistor radio and waiting for the weather forecast.

Already it was as if the news came from another world. France had resumed nuclear bomb tests on Mururoa Atoll in the Pacific; the just-released Bond film, *Live and Let Die* with Roger Moore, was doing well at the box office; and Fleetwood Mac's single *Albatross* had reached 14 in the pop charts. *Albatross* floated out over the airwaves and seemed just right as *The Aegre* gently rolled on the light glassy swell fifty miles off the west coast of southern Scotland. The occasional gull-like petrel, wings fully extended, glided silently past inches above the long swells. And finally came the weather forecast, which was for moderate south-westerlies later in the afternoon.

Off watch for the afternoon, I left Julie to the glassy sea and was soon asleep on our comfortable bunk.

Julie woke me at the end of her afternoon watch four hours later. She looked more relaxed and confident. Immediately I noticed a change in our motion. No longer were we idly rolling about. Instead, we were on a steady angle of heel, the bows alternately rising and falling as we chomped along into a light sea, eating up the miles. The marine forecast had been right and as planned, Julie had put us on a port tack and set the sails. So we were now heading close-hauled out westward, away from the coast, out into the Atlantic.

For 24 hours, the wind held, slowly strengthening. More spray started to come aboard. *The Aegre's* bows were fairly fine, so there was little shuddering or jarring as we beat across and into the building chop. The self-steering held the boat on a steady course out to the west, as if proud of itself, *saying look at me, I can do this forever*.

But down below for Julie and I, conditions were not very good. Every deck seam had its own drip despite liberal coatings of mastic, and water still ran down the mast onto our bunk despite a new attempt at a seal.

It was our fourth day out, and as the wind strengthened, I reefed the big mainsail and then with Force 7 forecast replaced it with the gaff stormsail. It was another struggle on *The Aegre's* pitching deck, but once set, the boat was much less stressed and going almost the same speed. At 5 pm, we pulled in Bob's log to find we'd made 72 miles to the west in the previous 24 hours. Optimistically I calculated that if we could keep this going for another two days we could turn south, confident of safely clearing the west coast of Ireland.

But it wasn't to be. The wind was blowing even more strongly by the middle of the evening, and *The Aegre* was frequently burying her lee rail. Spray from the bows was going higher than the mast. We suddenly both felt exhausted, the culmination of the unusual routine of non-stop 4 hours on, 4 hours off watches for 4 days solid. We decided to heave to for the night. This would give us a rest, and the weather might improve by morning.

Heaving to meant stopping the boat in the water, and we could do this by setting the small sails to work against each other so the boat sat almost motionless in the water. *The Aegre* needed no assistance to remain in this position, but we continued our four-hour watch routine. We hadn't seen a ship since leaving and had a sizeable radar reflector near the masthead, but still being run down seemed a possibility, so we kept a lookout. Besides, where else would the second person go other than the cockpit floor? The bunk was strictly a one-person position with the necessary leeboard in place. But with the conditions outside increasingly bad, we wanted the hatch closed and the drop boards between the companionway and cockpit in place. And we both wanted to be inside. A watch could be kept by the person sitting or lying beneath the hatch, pushing the hatch cover forward periodically and standing up for a quick look around.

Julie took the bunk while I rearranged the bags of now wet spare clothes on the floor and the mooring lines, other spare lines and fenders, to make an almost comfortable position under the hatch. It was better than being outside in the wind, rain and spray, but I had to keep my oilskins on because of all the drips.

We settled in for the fourth night, wryly reminding ourselves that we had wanted to do this. The night slowly passed. Hove to, the rig was holding the boat almost stationary, although we seemed surrounded by white crashing waves every time I looked out. I felt we were quite safe. At midnight we shared a cup of coffee from a Thermos flask made up after dinner and half a Mars bar, but decided it wasn't worth changing positions.

We saw no ships, but slept surprisingly well in the almost gentle rocking motion of the boat. A slow grey dawn showed the sea and the wind to have gone down a little, so we resumed sailing westward under the stormsail and jib. One day was beginning to merge into another as we became more tired and distant from our previous lives of structured days and sleeping all night.

This was now our fifth day at sea and nagging at my mind was growing uncertainty about our position relative to Scotland and Ireland. Since leaving Scourie, we'd kept a detailed log, The courses sailed, distance, wind direction and speed, sea condition, estimated leeway, and barometric pressure were all there. I'd then plotted our dead reckoning position every four hours and adjusted it for estimated tide flows and leeway to give an estimated position. I hoped this would be accurate to within a few miles.

I wished I could check this with an observed position. My most recent was the sighting of St Kilda, but that was two days before. We were now far from land. The only way now to get an observed position was by using the sextant to take a sighting of the sun or stars, but we had rarely seen the sun, and I hadn't tried taking any sights. I estimated we were a hundred miles offshore and heading further out, so I decided an accurate position wasn't critical at this time.

However, in the absence of the sun, we weren't wholly relying on dead reckoning, and then allowing for leeway, ocean currents and tides to create an estimated position, because we could use Radio Direction Finding (RDF) signals from shore stations received on our Hitachi transistor radio to give us an approximate position. Since leaving Scourie, we'd been using RDF beacons for a bit of reassurance. I would sit on the cockpit floor, my chart table on my knees, holding the Hitachi radio with its rotating aerial on top. Using a list of RDF stations, their call signs (in morse code) and frequencies, I could tune into those nearest to us and measure the compass bearing of the strongest signals. I'd then draw these as pencil lines on the chart from the beacons, our position being roughly where they crossed. Combining these positions with our dead reckoning and estimated position, we tracked our progress south-west with some confidence, if not a lot of accuracy.

But right now, for us, the weather was rapidly deteriorating, the sea steadily building as the wind increased. Close hauled as we were, taking the building waves on the starboard bow, it wasn't long before the decks were streaming with water and the drips down below were all going again.

I switched to the gaff stormsail before nightfall, and then had to tie a reef in it about 2 am.

With the noise of the wind and waves in my ear, I worried about the prospect of a full gale. I thought about the Viking ships and how they must have coped with this weather. Still, as I went below off-watch, I was full of confidence in *The Aegre*. We had the added benefit of a full deck and buoyancy in either end. While Julie huddled outside in the cockpit, I stripped off my oilskins and crashed onto the wet bunk, trying to avoid the water streaming down the mast on its way to the bilge. Ignoring it, I was soon asleep.

Julie woke me four hours later at 6 am, bringing me sharply back to the whining of the wind in the rigging. She looked tired, cold and frightened.

'They're still broadcasting that gale warning,' she said despondently, crouching on the cockpit floor, head beneath the hatch. 'It's not looking too good out there.'

Understatement was becoming like a code between us. What she meant was that it was pretty awful.

Luckily the self steering was holding the boat on course, allowing her to make a cup of tea while I stayed on the bunk. I tried to consider all aspects of our situation. We were well over a hundred miles from the west coast of Scotland, the nearest land to leeward. We'd have to drift for quite a long time before covering that distance. With the boat so small and low in the water, we had found her to drift very slowly. But even if we drifted at 2 knots to leeward, it would take 50 hours, and in reality, we were probably making less than 1 knot, and these summer gales were usually short-lived. No real danger there then. Would the boat be able to stand up to the seas themselves? Well, I thought so. But we had to give her the best chance.

After pulling on a few more layers of wet clothes on the bunk, I stood up in the hatch, pulling up my oilskins and clipping on my life harness, and surveyed the scene. It was now really very windy and rough. *The Aegre* was doing her best, but we were barely making any progress despite all the effort and stress. It was time to stop sailing, but how to minimise the drift downwind to the shores of Ireland?

Traditionally lifeboats (and *The Aegre* was not dissimilar) have used a sea anchor, a drogue attached by a long warp to the bow, to hold the front of the boat into the wind and waves and to minimise movement through the water. Kip Gurrin had made such a drogue for us from flax with a metal ring sewn into its mouth to hold it open. Now was the time to put it out on a long warp.

I lowered the sails, then laid the drogue out over the bow on a long line. It immediately gave a steadying effect to the boat, though sometimes there was a sharp tug when the movement of the boat coincided with a large wave. I'd hoped *The Aegre* would swing around to lie bow into the wind and sea, but this didn't happen, probably because of the bare mast catching the wind. Instead, she lay somewhat across the oncoming seas, taking the waves fairly easily on the starboard bow, with little water coming aboard. I found that if I lashed the tiller down a little (away from the wind), she was pretty stable in this position apart from the occasional violent jerks as the drogue was swept by a wave. I tried hanging a length of heavy chain from the warp to act as a spring, which reduced the shock of the warp suddenly tightening. There was little left to do.

The big seas and driving spray reduced visibility at sea level (where we were) to such an extent that there was little point in keeping a lookout. I checked the lashings on the metal radar reflector high on the mast, and everything on deck, then slid back the hatch to join Julie below. Officially she was off watch, so she took off her oilskins and lay on the bunk while I arranged myself on the bags of clothes, warps and lifejackets. We tried to ignore what was happening outside by turning up the radio and reading.

Our little transistor radio was proving its worth. RDF, weather forecasts, time signals and news and current affairs turned up loud to block out the noise of the gale outside. Well, almost all the noise. Occasionally we'd hear a huge wave breaking with a great roar and come sweeping towards us, finally hitting us with a BUFFFF and throwing us over onto our side, the top of the wave sweeping across our Perspex deck lights.

Despite the conditions outside, the day passed quickly. Neither of us felt hungry, so we didn't bother with lunch. Soon it was evening and getting dark, and if anything, the weather was getting worse, or maybe it just always seemed like that with the dusk. But the weather forecast predicted it, and for it to ease within 24 hours, so I wasn't over-worried.

Still, it seemed a long night, and there was little point in running formal watches. We just tried to catch up on sleep despite the cramped, wet conditions and violent motion. We seemed to get used to it. There was just nothing romantic about this at all.

By daybreak conditions were easing, and breaking waves were hitting us less often. The tops of waves were falling over themselves rather than being blown off by the wind. I soon had the reefed storm sails set and the self-steering looking after the helm. Once more we were heading south, powering along, up and over the big swells, and when the sun came out as well, it was sailing at its best.

We were just a week out from Scourie and seemed to have adjusted to the rhythm of life aboard *The Aegre*, the four-hour watches and frequent sail changes. To the reader four hours may not seem very long, particularly if the wind and sea are constant and the self-steering is in control of the helm. It seems like all the watchkeeper has to do is keep a lookout for ships and watch the compass and the weather. But four hours on, four hours off over the whole 24 hours, day after day, can be trying. We likened it to living under a table with no lights whilst someone randomly throws buckets of cold water at you. Try it for a week non-stop. And we knew we were only a quarter of the way to Madeira.

In all, five depressions swept over us, bringing gale force winds for a day or two, then easing for another day or two until the next depression moved in. We experimented with setting the sea anchor, and then with setting just the tiny storm jib and lashing the helm down. Effectively hove to, *The Aegre* was steadier with the little jib, and it became our preferred set-up in very heavy weather.

We'd emerge after each gale, cheerful after catching up on sleep. I loved sitting squashed together on the side deck of the cockpit watching the gradually declining seas and admiring the occasional shearwater as it glided by, clearing the waves with its wingtips. The sky would clear and the sunshine dazzlingly on the white breaking wave-tops. We'd make great speed, surfing down one wave and driving up the next. There was nowhere else I wanted to be.

Then the barometer would start dropping again as another depression came in from the south-west. We weren't surprised. This was the kind of weather we expected in this area.

Twenty-four hours later, the wind would start to ease, and we would resume our way south.

By late in the twelfth day, we were in the clutches of our fifth gale. The weather forecaster said it was worse than those before, but it seemed much the same to us. The wind and sea steadily rose until we abandoned sailing, resorting yet again to the storm job and lashed helm. We lay below, now squashed together on the bunk for both warmth and comfort. As was now customary, every so often an extra big wave would break over us, water spurting in around the sides of the hatch and foam covering the Perspex deck lights. We'd gained confidence in *The Aegre* but still couldn't help feeling nervous. We had become acutely aware that there were no guarantees out in the middle of the ocean. Our survival depended entirely on our preparations of the boat and ourselves. We thought we had anticipated almost every eventuality, but was that enough?

As it became light, all we could see to the horizon were long swells and breaking tops, while the wind whined through the rigging. On deck everything was secure, just the little flax jib holding us steady, as we slowly drifted eastward towards Ireland.

On our little radio a Galway station was the loudest, but even they interrupted the racing results to warn of the terrible gale blowing off the west coast. We returned to the BBC only to hear of an oil tanker being blown ashore at Milford Haven 300 nautical miles (556 km) to leeward of us on the coast of Wales and heavy rain and floods inland. I thought of my mother sitting dozing in her favourite chair by the big open fireplace in our Cottenham cottage late in the evening. With her head resting in one hand, she'd be staring into the embers, while big gusts of wind roared in the chimney. Maybe she'd be thinking of us, somewhere out there, and praying we were safe. I felt cruel giving her such worry. But we were safe — well, sort of. A bit wet, yes, but the boat was fine. We knew approximately where we were and still had plenty of food and water.

Unfortunately, Julie was still sporadically seasick and was now becoming depressed by the continual bad weather and our poor progress south. I felt much better but was struggling to keep Julie's spirits up. I made scrambled eggs for lunch to try and get some food into her. She was all for giving up and selling the boat in Madeira. Admittedly the two weeks at sea seemed to have consisted of one long round of howling gales, but I reminded her that we knew this first part would be the worst, and soon the weather should change to warm light northerlies, to push us south. I don't think this gave her much comfort but fortunately, the next morning, our fourteenth since leaving Scourie, the whining of the wind in the rigging did start to lessen and the wind slowly swung around to the north, and the barometer started to rise. We guessed the depression was moving off to the north-east.

As it became light, I set the gaff stormsail and as the sun rose, we sat together again in the cockpit hand steering, just so pleased to be making good speed south again. *The Aegre* tore along, bursting over the tops of the lumpy sea. But it wasn't long before we remembered just how much work the self-steering did for us and thankfully reconnected it. It was time for breakfast.

It was our last gale on this passage. The wind gradually moved to the north-east and became very light, and it seemed a fraction warmer. The sea went down, and our spirits went up.

The light northerly seemed to be holding, and soon I set our big mainsail, and then the sun came out and with it our spirits lifted.

On watch, but with the self-steering on the helm, I updated our position on our chart. Bringing together all the courses, distances, estimated currents and leeway, I put our estimated position as about 50 nautical miles (93 km) off the south-west coast of Ireland. It didn't seem that far. What we needed was an observed position. I got out the sextant and the Nautical Almanac and, around local noon, attempted to take a noon sight of the sun. I played with the sextant for 30 minutes, eventually deciding I had a reading of the sun's maximum altitude. My skill with the sextant was going to have to improve. But I was confident it would.

I then did the simple math, drawing on the Nautical Almanac for the sun's declination that day. My calculated latitude was (surprisingly) close to that of my dead reckoning and put us just south of Ireland. We felt very relieved to have finally cleared Ireland. For so long, we had almost been able to feel its lurking presence just over the horizon to the east of us. With it gone, we suddenly had 300 more miles (556-km) of sea room to leeward, but it also meant a new danger too, that of more shipping. The paths of any ships sailing from the English Channel to North America would cross our route within the next couple of days, a frightening prospect. I imagined a big freighter heading west, clearing the Channel and Ireland, and turning on the autopilot. They wouldn't expect to see a tiny sailing boat 300 miles out, coming down from the north.

I checked the radar reflector shackles on the halyard, and we resolved to keep an extra good lookout.

The light northerly held and we gently sailed south. Life on board became easier. On watch, the self-steering held us on a meandering course southward. I set up a line from the end of the boom forward to the bow, locking it in place so that everything moved less, reducing chafe. Off watch, we could easily sleep in the gentle rocking motion and the quiet snore of the bow wave. This was the weather we'd been hoping for.

Sixteen days after we'd left Scourie, Julie was on watch, and now feeling much happier, woke me excitedly. 'A ship, a ship, come quickly!'

I hurriedly rolled out of the bunk and put my head out of the hatch. Sure enough, there was a ship, a real ship. It was a rusty old freighter, rolling along on a course that would take her across our bows, not missing us by much. Julie let the sails out a bit to slow us down. There was no point in contesting right-of-way here, especially as they had given no indication of having seen us. It came boring on and swept across our bows about 100 yards ahead. There was no one to be seen, and it had almost disappeared over our horizon within fifteen minutes.

With the calmer weather, Julie was feeling much better and decided to make Protoveg curry for dinner. This was the soybean 'meat' given to us by Kip Gurrin in Orkney. After experimentation, we'd found it to be just about eatable with lots of curry sauce. It was high in protein and free, and we resigned ourselves to getting used to it.

After dinner, we sat talking in the cockpit, enjoying the sunset for perhaps the first time, The Aegre ghosting along in front of the light north-easterly breeze, the only sound the occasional sound like a snore from the bow as we accelerated a little down a wave. We felt we were emerging from a long winter. The sea and the sky were changing from the greyness of the North Atlantic to a beautiful blue. Now we were two hundred miles out to sea off the west coast of France and a thousand miles north of Madeira, a tiny dot in the ocean far ahead. While all alone, we felt close. All seemed well.

But as always, our lives were dominated by the weather. Yes, we had northerlies now, but they were often light, and the temperature was rapidly rising. A pattern settled in of two or three days of light northerlies, then a day or so becalmed, followed by a few more days of light northerlies. Even with our big lugsail set, our pace became sedate, and we eased along over a calm sea heeled at a very gentle angle. The self-steering was holding us on a slightly wandering course over a vast blue meadow. This was a great change from the previous two weeks but brought its own problems, as we were quite unaccustomed to the developing heat.

We were into the so-called Horse Latitudes, an area of light and variable winds between the south-westerlies to the north of us and the north-easterlies to the south. Fortunately, we had plenty of drinking water, but on deck, we had no shade, and down below our cabin, formerly a snug, warm haven from the cold gales of the North Atlantic, was becoming hot and stuffy. The passage of air from the hatch to the single ventilator up forward was largely blocked by all our stores stowed forward of the mast. It seemed we were better equipped for the cold, rough weather of the north of Scotland than the hot sun and light winds off Portugal and the west coast of Africa. Julie and I were children of the north, both fair-skinned and blonde. Like many British people, we had no idea how to cope with the sun and heat. We initially welcomed it, but our skin didn't tan well. We had little in the way of sunscreen creams, and soon we were pink, burnt, hot and sore.

But with the self-steering system working well, there was no need to steer on watch, and we both evolved our own activities. I would start my watch by checking the course we were steering and every aspect of the rig to ensure no lines or sails were chafing on anything and no unwired shackles were coming undone. I would write up the log with course and weather details every hour, take a noon sight with the sextant and plot our position, checking it with RDF bearings on the coast of France, Spain and Portugal. I'd re-fill the Primus cooker and small cabin oil light with paraffin and check the bilges were dry, all the while keeping a lookout for other vessels. But this still left time for just watching the waves and the way of *The Aegre* as she dipped and curtseyed her way along. There was time too to study the cabin and visualise how the layout and stowage could be improved.

Between watches alone, we talked endlessly, favourite memories and old friends being the most popular topics. We speculated about the future. What would it be like in Madeira? And the West Indies? What would we do when we got there? Eventually, one of us would go off to bed and the other would be left alone again.

Alone, but not lonely. Before we left, I had often been asked if we wouldn't be lonely, just the two of us out on the ocean for weeks with no one else to talk to. I'd reply that I didn't think so but secretly wondered if we would. Now, three weeks out from Scourie, we spent big chunks of every day and night alone on watch, but I didn't feel lonely. On watch, I would be alone but solely responsible for keeping the boat safe and going as well as possible. Down below in the cabin, just a few metres forward, was Julie, asleep. When I finished all my maintenance jobs, I would often relax, lying in the shade if possible, on the cabin floor, feet up in the cockpit, my left ear pressed to the radio, quietly listening to the world news from Deutsche Welle radio (in English) or the BBC World Service. It was like eavesdropping on a world far over the horizon, a world we used to live in but now seemed distant from. I heard that Britain had just joined the Common Market, Pink Floyd had released *The Dark Side of the Moon*, and NASA had put Skylab 3 into orbit 270 miles above Earth. Every night I looked for it high above us, thinking they might be our closest neighbours. Julie listened to the radio on her watch too, and over meals, we'd discuss events in that other faraway world.

Another week passed, and then another. Being far west of the Bay of Biscay, we were spared the dreadful weather it's famous for. The more westerly route we were following is advised for all ships voyaging under sail from Britain to the south.

With the improved sailing, our morale greatly improved. Our daily mileages were unspectacular, usually between 50 and 70 miles a day, but the warmer weather and easy motion made up for everything.

Four hours on, four hours off, four hours on, pull in the log! We still measured our distance travelled through the water on the antique log lent to us by Bob MaciInnes, his words 'I want it back, mind' ringing in my ears. I'd put it on the end of a 60 ft 5mm line attached to a big cleat on our stern. As it dragged through the water, its fins caused it to spin. We pulled it in every 12 hours to open the cylindrical casing and read off the distance run. Spinning behind us, I was always worried that a shark might take it, so we never polished it or attempted to clean it. However, although many sharks studied it, I guess it wasn't to their taste, for they always left it alone.

Each day we'd guess our 12-hour mileage before it was revealed.

'Thirty-one miles.'

'No, I reckon thirty-six.'

'It's … thirty-three.'

It was our twice-daily game. We became pretty accurate.

Although we now had many days of light winds, there were few when we were totally becalmed. Each day we would be 50 or 60 miles further south, a fact confirmed by the temperature, which daily got higher, the sea, which rapidly got bluer, the constantly changing bearings of the numerous RDF stations along the west coasts of France, Spain and Portugal, and finally, reassuringly, by my noon sun-sights of the sun with the sextant, my new toy. I wasn't yet fully confident with it but was becoming more so every day

Sailing was now most enjoyable. The self-steering system easily controlled the boat, our only problem being a leisurely gybe. This left us free to read, listen to the radio, or even just lie and look at the stars as we gently rolled along. Our favourite position on watch was still sitting on the cockpit floor, wedged into the corner, head at deck level, legs and feet stretched out in the companionway. One eye on the compass, another on the horizon. Every few moments, the snore of the bow wave breaking gently to leeward. Rolling gently south, this was surely the life.

We were still 300 miles north of Madeira (I thought) when, idly tuning around on the RDF frequencies, I picked up the Morse signal for MAD (– – • – – • •) beeping at us out of the ether. The irony wasn't lost on me, but I knew this was actually the RDF signal being transmitted from Madeira. Madeira is only a small island, though the largest in a group of three, lying 250 miles off the West African coast. They were tiny specks on our North Atlantic chart. It had seemed so easy to miss them and sail right on past, but with the help of the RDF signal, dead ahead according to the bearing on our little Hitachi radio, it now seemed impossible to miss the island.

Initially faint, the signal grew steadily louder over the next few days as we drew closer. I was gaining confidence in handling the sextant too, and on the evening of 24th August, I brought our position on the chart up to date and then said to Julie, 'Keep a good lookout tonight! We should see the lights on the island in the early morning.'

It was 31 days since we had sailed out of Scourie.

I should have said 'might' or 'maybe, perhaps if we are anywhere near where I think we are.'

I had the middle night watch and saw nothing despite keeping an extra good lookout. But the wind had eased a bit, and our speed had slowed. I wasn't too worried. At 3 am, I woke Julie, and we changed watches.

I lay down on the bunk, water swishing past my ears as we gently rolled along, my mind buzzing. What should we do if we saw nothing tomorrow, or the next day, or the next? But the radio signals must be coming from somewhere. And we still had plenty of food and water. We could always sail east to Africa. But I couldn't have been too worried, because I was soon asleep.

'Wakey wakey, time to wake up!'

I opened my eyes, it must be the end of Julie's watch, but it was still dark. I looked aft; out through the hatch, I could dimly see her sitting up on the side of the cockpit, looking ahead.

'What's the trouble?' I called out. It obviously wasn't the end of her watch.

'There are some red lights out here which don't seem to be moving, still quite a long way off. Come and have a look.'

I crawled out of the bunk to look out of the hatch. It was warm, and we were still ghosting along under the self-steering in front of the light northerly, across a smooth sea. Sure enough, in the distance ahead were two red lights, one above the other. She said they hadn't moved during the 30 minutes since she had first seen them. I got out the chart and the North Africa Pilot book, studying them carefully for the nth time. And then the List of Lights. I soon realised what we were seeing.

'They're the aerobeacons on the island of Port Santo, a small island to the north-east of Madeira. There's no doubt about it.'

So we were almost there. It seemed incredible. My navigation must be right. We sat staring ahead, unable to stop smiling and saying 'wow!', *The Aegre* gently sailing beneath us. Soon we'd be there. But at this speed, it would be a while yet. I went back to bed. I still had two hours of sleep to go.

When Julie next woke me, it was light.

'What can you see?' I called to her from the bunk.

'An island, dead ahead, but still a long way off, come and look,' she replied.

A few hours before we had been all on our own on the ocean, and now, suddenly, here we were with land ahead. For a year, I had wondered if we would ever sight Madeira like this.

In the daylight, we could no longer see the red aero beacons we'd identified in the dark. However, the island in front of us was easily recogniseable as Porto Santo from drawings in the Pilot Book, being dominated by a single conical mountain that fell away to a coastal plain on the western side. But mysteriously, there was no sign of Madeira, the much larger and higher island adjacent to Porto Santo. Visibility seemed good. So where was it? Why couldn't we see it?

All day we crept along, inching closer in the light wind. There was still no sign of Madeira. Then in the late afternoon, when Porto Santo was almost abeam, the much larger island of Madeira slowly emerged, exactly where we had expected it to be. It had been completely hidden by a thick wall of mist.

Hand compass bearings taken on Port Santo and Madeira positively identified where we were. From this, I calculated that at our present speed, we would reach Funchal, the main port on Madeira, at about lunchtime the next day, Sunday 26th August. Arriving at midday on a Sunday didn't seem a good idea. From yacht cruising books, we learned that port authorities often charged high overtime rates at weekends. Were we in such a hurry, we asked ourselves? Time was one thing we had plenty of. So instead of rushing on, we decided to sail around into the shelter of Porto Santo, heave to there for Saturday night and Sunday, and then sail on into Funchal on Monday morning. This would avoid any chance of having to pay overtime and give us time to prepare the boat and ourselves for going into port.

As evening came on, we slowly closed on the western end of Porto Santo, then sailed slowly eastward into the lee of the small island to spend the night south of the main town of Cidade Vila Baleira. We used cross bearings on four lighthouses to plot and maintain our position.

With the jib pushing us one way and the mainsail another in the light breeze, *The Aegre* came to a standstill. It was suddenly still and quiet, the boat all but stationary in the calm waters seven miles off the beach.

Ashore, the island seemed to be alive in the dark. There were pinpricks of house lights, and a row of orange streetlights all along the coast. Tiny headlights crawled along the shoreline. People getting on with their lives. Civilisation. So strange after 32 days and nights alone on the ocean.

The next day, Sunday 26th August 1973, was Julie's 20th birthday, and exactly a year since we had taken delivery of *The Aegre* back in north-west Scotland. For Julie it started early, as I woke her at 2 am to take over the watch. We were still stationary in the calm waters seven miles south of Porto Santo. *The Aegre* rolled gently on the long north-westerly swell that curved around the island into the bay. Madeira, now clearly visible, was rising majestically in the south-west, 40 miles away.

We spent the day preparing to go into the main port of Funchal, giving the boat a tidy up, bringing the anchors and chain up on deck, airing our shore-going clothes and having a rest. I worked out the tide flows and then plotted a course and departure time from our present position to Funchal, to arrive mid-morning on Monday.

It was just dark when we set sail that evening on our run in, the last lap of the passage. We were glad to be sailing again. The day spent hove to had become boring, and we were impatient to get going.

Our course took us between the Islas Desertas, another island, this one to the south-east of Madeira, and the easternmost cape of Madeira, a gap 10 miles wide and well-lit by lights on the outermost points. There was a steady breeze from the north-east, and we could make a comfortable 4 knots (7.5 kph). There was a swell coming up from astern, and I was worried that this might develop into a rough patch of sea as we passed over a big shoal between the two islands.

Luckily the wind held steady, and the sea remained relatively calm. We passed quickly between the islands under the gaff mainsail and our bigger jib.

It all hardly seemed real. Here we were, fast approaching Funchal, Madeira, having sailed non-stop from NW Scotland. But there had been nothing to it, we blithely agreed; all we had to do is get out there and do it. It wasn't money or years of experience, just single-mindedness and determination.

As it became light, we sailed along the dark southern coast. Preparing to enter Funchal, I hoisted our specially prepared little Portuguese courtesy flag, and beneath it, the yellow Q (Quarantine) flag, as is required of visiting foreign vessels, and our own little Red Ensign flag. Just like real ocean voyagers, we were coming from afar.

Now Madeira was no longer a faint black outline. More detail was emerging every minute. After the barrenness of rocky NW Sutherland around Scourie and Ardmore, Madeira's vegetation was strikingly luxuriant. Amidst it, hundreds of small, red-roofed houses were clustered along the coast, mixed in with high-rise blocks of flats or hotels. The western sides of the valleys soon started to be lit with the soft pink light of the sunrise.

Ghosting along a mile offshore, we stood in the open hatch and cockpit, entranced. But even as we stood staring, the wind was dying on us as we sailed into the shelter of the 8,000-ft (2,438-m) high island.

Soon the wind completely died. Now we were steadily drifting towards a line of breakers dashing against the rocks immediately beneath a towering hotel block. It would be an uninspiring end.

'Don't worry, I can always paddle us off,' I called to Julie, hoping I sounded more confident than I felt. We were rather close, even for my liking. In my head I heard the comments of the pre-voyage sceptics: 'They didn't make it then.' 'No, got wrecked on Madeira, I heard.' 'Yes, just along by the Travelodge.'

But then a slight breeze came across the water, flecking the surface as if a thousand tiny birds were running on it. The mainsail gently filled, and silently we started to move. The bow lifted a little, then fell with its reassuring ssshhhh. We were on our way again, out into deeper water. I've always been lucky.

The breeze held, and we slowly eased along the island's south coast, the green terraced hillsides populated with small white cottages with orange terracotta tile roofs. With Julie on the helm, I stood in the hatchway with the Funchal harbour chart in front of me, plotting our way along the coast. Soon the bay that is the outer Funchal harbour opened up. But where was the entrance to the inner harbour? Where should we go? I studied our chart of Madeira yet again and re-read the Pilot Book directions.

The reader will know that Julie and I had never sailed into a proper harbour before, one with a city attached, cruise ships, oil tankers, fishing boats, pleasure boats, dredgers, commercial docks, lighthouses, quarantine anchorages, multiple random buoys, and so on. Sure, we'd sailed into Scourie Bay a few times, but it only had two moorings, Robert Mcleod's and ours. This wasn't anything like that.

But the sun was shining, and the light breeze holding. Fortune favours the brave, we said to ourselves as we slowly sailed in towards the town, the anchor, chain and warp ready to go. Aloft the Portuguese ensign fluttered on our starboard shroud and below it our plain yellow Q flag indicating we were in quarantine, i.e., we were entering the port from foreign waters and needed Customs, Health and Immigration clearance. We had our own red ensign showing our nationality as British on the port shroud.

We hoped someone from the harbourmaster's lookout would see us coming in, recognise us as a foreign boat from our flags, and send a pilot boat out to tell us where to anchor. But nobody took any notice of us as we slowly threaded our way in through the outlying fleet of anchored small craft.

As we got closer to the shore, we could make out more detail until, almost at the last minute, we identified the inner harbour entrance and sailed in on the light breeze. We could now see a few yachts anchored at the far end, close to a big stone jetty, so we headed in that direction.

Before we'd gone much further, we noticed an official-looking chap wearing a crumpled navy blue cap standing in the stern of a heavy grey battered-looking rowboat in the inner harbour, apparently waving at us. Still holding the light breeze, we sailed in then spun *The Aegre* around to head up into the wind and stop alongside him.

'You not fishing boat, no? I thought you local fishing boat,' he said in Portuguese English. Apparently he was the pilot. He went on, 'You follow me,' and urged his rower onward, guiding us into the shelter of the inner harbour where in sign language he indicated that we were to anchor close in the lee of the large stone jetty adjacent to the centre of town. It was lined with people out for a stroll. We were today's entertainment.

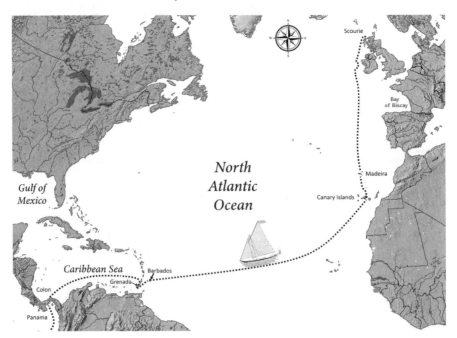

The North Atlantic

Then after giving us rough directions to the Customs, Health and Immigration offices ashore he was rowed away, still standing with his hands on his hips, rather imperiously, in the stern of the heavy old rowboat.

Under the hot sun, the atmosphere was almost surreal. *The Aegre* drifted slowly astern on her anchor in the still water, pointing seaward in the light breeze to a background of the noise of cars and people.

While Julie lashed the tiller and tidied up the cockpit, I dropped the sails, flaked and secured them under their simple cover on deck, checked the anchor warp was secure and prepared our second anchor, chain and warp, just in case.

But the harbour was near windless, the sun beating down on us, its heat reflecting off the nearby stone jetty and concrete harbour walls. The light was intense. We'd never needed sunglasses in Scotland but wished we had them now. For some protection we draped our flax stormsail over the boom, to form a rudimentary tent. Under its shade I slowly felt myself calming down from the drama of the weeks at sea and the final hours sailing in.

It was comfortable in the shade and I started to settle into a post-arrival paralysis, musing on the wonder of a life on the sea and sailing… So it had taken us 34 days for this 1,800 mile passage from Scourie, we'd arrived still sane, with plenty of food and water. Nothing on the boat broken. Why, the voyage being more than 1000 miles, now qualified us to join the illustrious (to us) Ocean Cruising Club. Around us were half a dozen other international yachts, but no one seemed aboard. I studied them, their lines, their rigs, they looked so strong and well set up.

Then Julie interrupted my daydream, calling to me from the cabin where she was sorting out her shore going clothes, 'Come on, don't just sit there, we have to go ashore and clear Customs'.

And so began the next chapter of the voyage.

Chapter 9
Madeira sunshine

'Cruising is fixing your boat in exotic locations' — Unknown

T*he Aegre* was unnaturally still. But around us were other boats, people, and the roar of traffic from the nearby main street, all so strange after being alone at sea for weeks.

With everything stowed and shipshape, and *The Aegre* settled on her anchor, I prepared for going ashore, exchanging my ubiquitous swimming trunks for my crumpled best (only) trousers. Trying to brush out the salt stains, I wondered why Julie's sun dress had survived so much better. No matter, I pumped up our pathetic little inflatable dinghy so we could go ashore to visit the Customs, Health and Immigration office. We'd also visit the post office and buy fresh bread and fruit. Suddenly it was exciting. Now hardly able to stop smiling, we pulled the hatch shut and stepped off *The Aegre* into the floppy, flimsy dinghy. Drawing away from *The Aegre,* we saw her from the outside for the first time in nearly five weeks. She looked so small and low in the water. We started to joke about ocean voyaging with nine inches of freeboard.

It was only a short distance to the slippery stone steps, where a bit of a swell, or maybe the wash of harbour traffic, made landing tricky. We tied the dinghy to a nearby rusty ring, wondering if it might be stolen, but felt it unlikely because it was quite the worst dinghy tied there. Then up the rough stone steps, suddenly seeming unusually firm and solid under our feet after 34 days at sea. It was hard to balance, as if the ground was constantly coming up to meet our feet. Feeling disoriented, a bit dizzy and almost land-sick, we walked the short distance to the main street, where the press of people, the cars, scooters, and motorcycles, were almost overwhelming, everything moving so quickly. We felt like travellers from space suddenly landed, our blonde hair and fair complexions in stark contrast to the shorter, dark-haired

Portuguese people around us. It would take us about a week to become used to walking in the town.

We easily found the harbour offices and quickly finished the official business. Yes, there were just two of us on board. UK passports. No dogs, cats, or parrots. No firearms. No liquor. No problems.

Then to a bank to change some of our few pound notes to Portuguese escudos. Our budget was tight. We had left Scotland with a bit over £100 in the bank, and some cash, hoping this would last us till the West Indies in mid-December, four and a half months later. Impossible to live on so little, you might think, but remember we had a boat full of food, enough we planned for 100 days, say three months. And it was 1973, when a pound bought quite a bit. So now we changed a little to escudos. We would just have to see how frugally we could live.

We soon found the market. The fresh fruit and bread seemed cheap. So far, so good. Then to the post office, and yes, there were some letters for us from our parents. We bought postcards to send back to England and Scotland, then took a short walk around the town, our legs slowly adjusting to walking.

Back at the jetty, we saw *The Aegre* lying calmly to her anchor. Even closer to the jetty was another very compact cruising boat we had admired when we had anchored close by. Beside her, *The Aegre* looked old-fashioned, but hey, we consoled ourselves, we were here; she was ours, and we knew her to be a solid, seaworthy boat.

Unsurprisingly our dinghy had not been stolen, and we were soon back on board, stowing the shopping. Then there was a knocking on the hull,

'Hello, anybody aboard?' It was a scraggly-haired blonde-bearded, chubby youngish man in a dinghy who introduced himself as Sven Lundin, the owner and sole sailor aboard *Bris*, our neighbour. Soon aboard and ensconced in the cockpit of *The Aegre*, Sven told us he had built *Bris* in Sweden in 1971 and sailed from Gothenburg via the north of Scotland. A similar course to our own, taking 45 days. He said he was headed to Brazil.

Sven was the first visitor of many. Initially there were only six other foreign yachts, all moored adjacent to us. Julie wanted to meet the people, me too, but I also wanted to study their yachts. I had so much to learn. I was fascinated to see these highly organised, beautifully fitted-out cruising boats. Before Madeira, I'd never been on one apart from John Ridgway's spartan 30-foot entry in the 1968 Golden Globe race.

The crews of other cruising yachts were interested in *The Aegre* too, perhaps because she was so much smaller than every other cruising yacht (apart from *Bris*) and by far the most 'traditional' in both boat and rig. We would be invited aboard their yachts for coffee, lunch or dinner and to exchange stories. All were headed to the Canary Islands and then across the Atlantic to the West Indies, some further. We'd marvel at the spaciousness, the joinery, the gadgets, the fridge and freezers, the toilets and hot showers and the comfort of their boats, and of course, we'd invite them back to *The Aegre*. We would be a bit embarrassed to show them around. It didn't take long. She was so basic. No engine, no electrics, one burner primus cooker, no shower, no toilet, no chronometer, no freezer, no fridge. Just 9 inches above the water. Small camper vans were better equipped than us. But our visitors were all polite and respectful. Coming non-stop from so far north we'd sailed further than many of them. Clearly the seaworthiness of *The Aegre* was indisputable.

After they'd gone, we would console ourselves. We'd say they were all old, well, at least mid-thirties. We felt like the new kids on the block playing truant, as if we'd borrowed Dad's little fishing boat for the weekend and just kept going.

We had another group of visitors that brought practical help, local fishermen. They were fascinated by *The Aegre*, which was about the same size as their own open boats (and *The Aegre* was still prominently registered as a fishing boat, LK92, in Lerwick, Shetland). We gave them the full tour. We learnt they fished for the metre-long pitch black and incredibly fierce-looking espada (known as black scabbard fish in English) commonly found around Madeira and the Canary Islands. They usually live between 800–1300 metres (2,600–4,300 ft) down, but they come up to 200–300 metres (660–1000 ft) to feed at night. The fishermen would arrive back in the harbour at dawn with their catch all ready for the market, where they fetched top prices. Laughing and with lots of smiles, they'd slip a few big fillets over to us with much 'Expressao de aplauso' (Bravo!)

Espada was welcome on our diet, which otherwise comprised bananas and vegetable stew. Bananas were particularly cheap, but Julie said that according to our food book we needed to eat about 8 kg daily (18 lbs) to get enough protein. We were so often given huge bunches that sometimes that seemed an option. But generally, we settled for a vegetable stew in the evenings comprising potatoes, sweet potatoes, green peppers, green beans, carrots, aubergines, ladies' fingers, sweetcorn and grated cheese. We had brought two enormous slabs of cheddar from Scotland, which looked like enough for 200 days, never mind 100. Julie called it 'Ragout des legumes au gratin', and it suited our one-pot Primus perfectly. We ate it every night for weeks and seemed healthy enough.

With all this food talk, the inquisitive reader is probably wondering how we coped without a toilet on board in the harbour. Well … We tried to make the most of every trip ashore, but realistically in the early morning or late evening, or when we just felt lazy, we needed a less troublesome way. At sea, we had the white Snowcem bucket we kept on deck when not in use. We would squat on it in the cockpit, where we had a great view of the ocean and were well supported by the cockpit sides as we rolled along. Diplomatically we'd use it for the serious stuff when the other was off watch and asleep, then a quick flush over the side. But how was that going to work in a harbour? Well, just the same for the small stuff. Remember this was 1973. There were fewer than ten yachts in the harbour. Onboard sewerage holding tanks were almost unheard of. The reality was that everyone's sewerage was going straight into the sea. And still, the water looked startlingly clear and clean. But it could be a bit disconcerting if someone came rowing by and saw Julie or me sitting low in the cockpit, head and shoulders at deck level, and slowed for a chat. And stayed and stayed, clearly wanting to be invited onboard to have a look around. Tricky.

It was also one of the downsides of being so close to the quay. Being near the town centre, the quay was a popular strolling point, a great place to catch a bit of the evening sea breeze, pause and look at all the yachts, particularly those closest. Sometimes it felt like our every move was watched.

But we loved the life we were living. The memory of Julie's seasickness misery, the endless cold grey Atlantic gales off Ireland, the incredibly cramped conditions below, everything being sodden with seawater and the relentless four hours on, four hours off seemed to have faded, replaced by fresher memories of the balmy weather, light northerlies and following seas of the final few weeks. And then our delightful life in Madeira.

It came to seem like a foregone conclusion that we would sail on. I guess Julie and I discussed it, but I can't recall us giving serious consideration to calling it a day, turning around and sailing back.

We did some stock-taking, though, reflecting on the passage from Scotland. The boat had certainly proved herself. Not comfortable at all, but we had never felt endangered, or at least I hadn't. The curved whaleback deck had made her incredibly strong. Massive waves sometimes seemed to crash into us, and she'd just roll a bit and shake them off like a boxer in a training bout. She sailed surprisingly well to windward or off the wind, steering herself in all conditions. Our rig had proved up to the task, although awkward to handle. That could be improved, as could the chaos down below due to lack of organised storage. Our food and water had worked out perfectly, to Julie's credit. We'd planned to have food and water for 100 days and estimated we had at least another 70 days' worth left. The cooker had proved a great success, able to give us hot food and drinks in the worst of weather. In fact the envy of many of our visitors.

And somehow, Julie and I had found we made a good team at sea. We looked after each other well. We would joke that running a four hours on and four hours off watch system, we didn't see that much of each other, less than a couple working 9–5 jobs. We always had lots to talk about, be it the radio news we'd been listening to on the BBC World Service or Deutsche Welle's English broadcasts, some memory we'd been reflecting on, a book we'd been reading and sometimes the future. By that I mean the next passage, the next port, or seemingly much further on, the West Indies. Beyond that seemed too far ahead to think about. Of course we would go on. A few weeks in Madeira for boat maintenance and improvement, then next stop Santa Cruz in the Canary Islands.

But it was going to be more than a few weeks in Madeira, governed as we were by the seasons. Good weather could never be expected sailing from the north of Scotland to Madeira, but the least bad weather was in mid-summer, July and August, hence the timing of our passage to Madeira. But for the next long passage, across the Atlantic to the West Indies, we'd be in a quite different weather system, that of the north-east trade winds. These blow from North Africa across the Atlantic to the northern part of South America and the Caribbean. They extended further north and were more reliable in the northern hemisphere winter. Our destination, the islands of the West Indies, had their own hurricane season from June to the end of November, which was definitely to be avoided, so we didn't want to arrive there before mid-December. Allowing two months to sail there, with a short stop in the Canary Islands, a bit south of Madeira on the way, meant staying in Madeira until early October. And it was only late August right now.

A two-month holiday in Madeira? Well, not exactly. There seemed no chance of any paid work, but we'd planned to use this time to improve *The Aegre* inside and out, making the most of the fine weather and the experience of the boat gained on the passage south. And maybe a little holiday. It was to prove unexpectedly beneficial in another important way too.

What about seeing something of the island and the people? With ubiquitous jet travel today, the point of travelling is the destination, the journey there a mere period of inconvenience. But for us on *The Aegre* in those days, the journey was almost everything. Our occasional companions were voyagers on other sailing boats, our destination a port, a safe harbour, and the people there who were connected to the sea, be they ashore or on other vessels. Our talk was of the sea and sailing. We didn't see ourselves as tourists but as sailors, sea-going folk. We came to know some of the fishermen, the boatmen working around the harbour and some of the market stall-holders, but our community, our people, were those on other sailing boats. Indeed we made friendships there that have lasted fifty years.

As for every sailor, the needs of the boat came first, and for us aboard *The Aegre*, there was much to do. Our highest priority was to protect the outside of the wooden hull from the dreaded boring teredo worm, the terror of every wooden boat owner in the tropics.

We'd coated the underwater section of the hull with antifouling paint in Scotland, but only up to her original waterline. Now, with all the stores loaded for the voyage, she was sitting much lower in the water. We knew we needed to raise the waterline, i.e., remove the topside varnish rapidly disappearing underwater and replace it with antifouling paint. To do that the boat needed to be out of the water for some days in fine, clear weather. Neither was possible on the cold and wet north-west coast of Scotland, whereas conditions in Madeira were ideal.

Now we had both the time and dry, hot sunshine. Perfect conditions.

There was a small slipway at the Clube Naval do Funchal (yacht club) nearby. The manager was friendly and agreed to pull *The Aegre* up onto the shingle beach on a rudimentary frame and park her alongside other local boats. They'd do it tomorrow. Well, he actually said *mañana*.

Eventually they did pull her out on a makeshift cradle, and quite carefully too. Five hectic days followed as we scraped off all the varnish that was now below the real waterline. Then we marked in a new waterline and applied two coats of epoxy undercoat and two coats of antifouling. Then we sanded and applied another coat of varnish above the waterline and black paint for the top plank.

We came to know the yacht club boatmen well as they tried to teach us Portuguese. They all came to help with the re-launch, which turned into an exceptionally well rum-lubricated celebration that miraculously, we and our boat managed to survive without further damage. The next day when I went to pay for the use of the slip and the boatmen, I was waved away with a shrug,

'*Nao e nada*' (Is nothing).

'*Gratis*' (Free).

'*Expressao de aplauso*' (Bravo).

We liked this place!

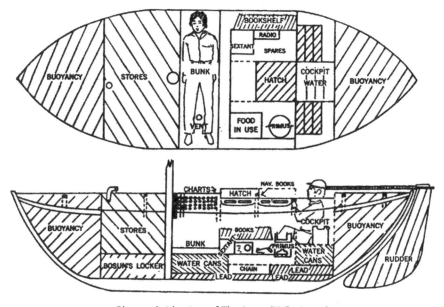

Plan and side view of *The Aegre* (N Grainger)

Back on our mooring, with our varnish work gleaming, I set about building in more interior joinery. During the voyage down we had had plenty of time to plan it, and I now set to and built in storage racks and shelves on either side of the narrow passage down to our bunk which ran across the boat just aft the mast. To be honest, I'm the Sweeney Todd of boat building; I aspire to a level of craftsmanship far beyond my capability. But with the woodworking tools I'd brought with me and pieces of scrap timber picked up in the yacht club yard, I knocked together a stowage framework inside the boat that served us well from then on.

A third area that required improvement was more intellectual, that of astronavigation, and here, as in other areas, our luck continued to hold.

Sailing down from Scotland, we'd relied heavily on keeping a careful log and then confirming our estimated position with RDF beacons ashore. We'd rarely seen the sun until the last part of the voyage, when I started to take regular noon sights for latitude. We were sailing south, and then the RDF signal from Madeira told us the island was dead ahead. Easy. But to sail westward to the Caribbean, I would need to determine our longitude, which was more difficult. I knew the theory but was embarrassed to admit the paucity of my experience in the seasoned field of ocean yachtsmen slowly assembling in Funchal harbour.

Then Pat Chilton and his wife, from Brixham, England, sailed in aboard their 38′ (11.6m) Nicholson ketch, *Mary Kate of Arun*. In the tradition of cruising yachtsmen of those days, Pat was a larger-than-life character. In his early 50s, he had recently retired from the Navy, where he had served in the Fleet Air Arm for 32 years. He'd been a fighter pilot during the war and later a test pilot. Now here he was sitting next to me, jovially explaining how to use sun sights taken mid-morning and mid-afternoon, and the Nautical Almanac and the Air Sight Reduction Tables to calculate both latitude and longitude. Of course, he was used to doing it flying at 700 mph (1,127 kph) whilst at the controls of a subsonic jet and knew all the shortcuts. With lots of jokes, he explained it all to me. He made it so simple, and I've been grateful ever since.

Soon one or two yachts were arriving every day from Europe for a brief stop on their way to the West Indies. They were all much larger than us. At the opposite end of the scale, we laughingly said that in terms of crew density (people per foot of overall length), the leader was solo yachtsman Tom Blackwell aboard his 55ft ketch *Islander*, timber-built in the 1930s.

Tom was well into his 60s. He had inherited some of the Blackwell part of Crosse and Blackwell of Branston pickle fame. He had been in the Navy when his father died, but then, he said, 'I was orfff!' He'd bought *Islander* and had been sailing around the world singlehanded ever since. He had a piano down below and, even more impressive to us, a proper chronometer. This was an electronic Bulova Accutron wristwatch that used a tuning fork oscillating at 360 Hz instead of a balance wheel as the timekeeping element, and it didn't tick but hummed. It was guaranteed to be accurate to one minute a month, two seconds a day. It was a forerunner to modern quartz watches, which use a vibrating resonator. Tom kept it well protected in a special hardwood box. We drooled over it.

Then we discovered another solution to the chronometer problem. Heino and Brigitte Sass, from Germany, were in their mid-thirties and heading out from Europe to sail around the world in their 32 ft GRP sloop *Brisa*. Anchored nearby, we'd smell fresh coffee wafting over from their yacht each morning, and it was hard to resist their invitations to come aboard and share a cup.

Heino and Brigitte had something we'd never seen before, a domestic quartz clock. It looked better suited to a kitchen wall than their homely saloon, but then they told us of its extraordinary accuracy. They used it as their chronometer. We'd never seen anything like it. Within ten years everyone had one, but in 1973, in Madeira, it was as high-tech as you could go.

Just before we left, our friends from Scotland, John and Marie Christine Ridgway, together with their daughter Rebecca (5), flew down from the North of Scotland to stay in an apartment in Madeira. With great excitement, they came down to the harbour to meet us. We all went for a sail on *The Aegre*. Then they took us on a sightseeing tour around the island.

We had now been in Madeira for seven weeks, and to keep up with the seasonal winds, we needed to head south to the Canary Islands. We were as near ready to go as we could be. We filled our water tanks with Madeira water, reputed amongst mariners to be among the world's purest and most long-lasting, and the Ridgways came to see us off, bringing masses of fresh fruit, bread and other goodies.

Finally, with the Ridgways back ashore and the big lugsail swinging from the mast, I lifted the anchor. On a light breeze, we slowly made way, waving goodbye to the Ridgways on the stone quay, and with three long blasts on our foghorn, farewelled the remaining yachts and the waving boatmen at the Clube Naval. The wind strengthened a little as we emerged from the inner harbour, *The Aegre* heeling to it and picking up speed as we set a course for the open sea.

Back ashore, the Ridgways drove to their apartment high on the hillside above the town. From there, they looked out over the ocean to the south and watched our small tan sails become smaller and smaller until, finally, we disappeared into the vastness of the ocean.

I was not to see John, Marie Christine and Rebecca again for 29 years.

Chapter 10
On to the Canary Islands

*'But where, after all, would be the poetry of the sea
were there no wild waves?'* — Joshua Slocum

Cruising on a small sailing boat, the contrasts are startling. In Funchal harbour, we'd grown used to the still hot air of the sheltered anchorage, the nearby noise, hustle and bustle of the city, the market and its cheap fresh food, the company of friends, assumed safety, and the lassitude that comes from sleeping undisturbed for eight hours every night, then waking to sunbeams moving slowly across the cabin as the boat gently rocks, welcoming another easy day. Maybe not in paradise, but close and very different from being at sea.

At least we were spared the shock of sailing out into bad weather. With the prevailing wind from the north, the high mountain mass of Madeira sheltered us as we wafted out south under our big tan lugsail over a calm blue sea. Gradually we drew away, the heat and noise of Funchal fading as the vast sea horizon grew ever wider ahead.

I proudly looked around the boat. Everywhere I could see improvements. The varnish gleamed. The chaos below had been turned into order, with everything neatly stowed in its place. On deck, snap shackles were everywhere they were needed to make sail changes slick and easy.

There was fresh food for dinner, sitting together in the cockpit in the dusk, the light quickly fading as it does in the tropics, *The Aegre* steering herself in the balmy following breeze. Already life at anchor in Funchal seemed far away. Resignedly we prepared for our first night back at sea, and Julie turned in for a four-hour sleep. We'd swap places at midnight.

Now I was alone in the cockpit for the first time in nearly two months.

Already Madeira was invisible astern in the darkness. We were really on our own again.

With a torch, I reviewed the chart. We were going to the Canaries for two reasons. Firstly, because it was on our way. To pick up the NE trade winds, we needed to head well south on the eastern side of the Atlantic, well past the Canary Islands. And secondly, legend had it that prices were lower in these Spanish islands (Madeira being Portuguese). So, a good place to replenish our food. But a strange name for a group of islands. Was it full of canaries? No, I discovered, the name came from dogs, or possibly seals on the islands, the Latin for dog being canaria, and given by the first Europeans to visit.

It would be a short passage, we hoped, to Santa Cruz on Tenerife, just 300 miles to the south of Madeira. The only hazard was the Selvagen Islands, a small cluster of dry, uninhabited islands just to the east of the direct course, known for their (reputed) buried pirate treasure. Expeditions in 1813, 1851, 1856 and 1948 had failed to find it. We weren't planning on a 1973 dig and aimed to keep well to the west of them. We expected light winds from the north, which would make the sailing easy, but were warned that sudden strong winds could come from the east, off the Sahara.

I settled down into the shelter of the cockpit, turned on the radio, and tuned around to find the BBC World Service. What had happened in the world since we'd arrived in Madeira and become pre-occupied with harbour life? I quickly caught up; A military coup in Chile led by General Pinochet, an OPEC oil embargo which was triggering a worldwide energy crisis, and Art Garfunkel had released his first solo album, *Angel Clare*. All far, far away from us as I looked out to the ocean and darkness all around.

Soon it was midnight, and we were back into our middle-of-the-night watch change routine. Already life in Funchal was as if in the distant past.

The light northerly breeze held overnight, the next day and the next night. It was a gentle introduction back into the way of the sea. With clear skies, I got out the sextant and put Pat Chilton's instructions into practice to plot our position.

My noon sights were becoming very consistent. Although the boat was constantly moving, I became used to taking sun sights and correcting them for various errors, such as being very close to the sea surface. However, the mid-morning and afternoon sights were of much less use because we needed accurate Greenwich Mean Time for them. Our time was still coming from a regular clockwork wristwatch (no Bulova Accutron or quartz clock for us), which we checked and corrected every night using the time signal broadcast every minute by the radio station WWV on the shortwave, but the watch ran inconsistently from one day to the next. This was frustrating, and added an unknown error to each position line I calculated.

However we were sailing almost due south, so we really just needed our latitude, calculated from the noon sight without the need for accurate time. Our log spinning off the stern, giving us the distance run through the water, provided a check. Finally, Radio Direction Finding beacons on the Canaries made them impossible to miss as long as our little transistor radio kept working. We just had to keep to the west to avoid the Selvagen Islands midway between Madeira and the Canaries.

The balmy weather continued for a third day, but at about 2am on the fourth day, everything changed. Julie was on watch and woke me shouting, 'Nick! Nick! Quickly, On deck, now!'

Waking, and instantly feeling the boat stressed and surging across the water, I scrambled up and stuck my head out of the hatch to face a howling wall of wind. It was dark and cool, but the sky was clear, and the stars twinkled brightly above us.

The wind seemed to have come from nowhere. At the helm Julie was braced, holding the tiller with both hands. We were roaring along downwind, surrounded by two huge waves of phosphorescence. With me ready in the hatchway, Julie rounded *The Aegre* up into the wind, our speed throwing spray the boat's length, and I dropped the big lugsail, flogging wildly, to the deck.

What a relief. Turning back off the wind, we slowly rolled along under the jib. The wind held and soon I set the gaff stormsail. Twenty-four hours later, we were off the port of Santa Cruz, Tenerife. There the wind fell away to a mixture of nothing and then violent gusts sweeping down from steep brown barren cliffs rising behind the long harbour wall over which we could see some yacht masts.

With no engine, we made the most of occasional gusts that came sweeping across the flat water, and in between times, using a paddle over the side, we entered the long narrow harbour. We passed a line of Korean fishing boats noisily unloading big black tuna and continued to the end, where we could see some of our companion yachts from Funchal already anchored. They'd spotted us coming and were waving, pointing to where we should anchor. With the anchor down, sails stowed and the dinghy inflated, we sculled across black oily water to join them for a cold beer and take in our new ugly surroundings.

In 1973 the anchorage for cruising yachts visiting Santa Cruz on Tenerife was not in a pleasant harbour close to the centre of town, as in Funchal, but in a distant corner of a foul, oily dock for foreign fishing boats, five kilometres out of town. The constant coming and going of tuna boats, the 24-hour unloading, the noise, the smell and the dismal surroundings put us off staying long.

Just getting ashore from *The Aegre* was hazardous due to the black, sticky oil from the ever-present fishing fleet, which lay on the water and coated all the rocks around us. It got on our feet, then our clothes, then the boat. It had already formed a dark line around the hull of *The Aegre* and our little inflatable. It ate into the dinghy fabric, which now hardly held air and needed to be pumped up whenever we used it.

Santa Cruz, the capital, was supposedly a duty-free port, but nothing was free except the cockroaches. It was like a nightmare to suddenly find one calm afternoon in the harbour that it was raining cockroaches. They landed all over our deck and scuttled down every vent and crack. We had always been careful not to bring cardboard containers on board to avoid them. It would take us months to finally get rid of them.

We took the occasional ramshackle bus to go shopping in the city. Many things were cheaper than in Funchal, especially tinned sardines, so we bought a lot and replenished our 24-hr food boxes.

As in Madeira, our thoughts were not on sightseeing but on the coming main event, the Atlantic crossing, all 2,400 nautical miles of it (4,450 km).

Preparing for this, the mainly windless conditions in the harbour were perfect for working out how we would set the gaff stormsail upside down as a square sail for the transatlantic passage in the expected strong following NE trade winds. This had seemed like a crazy idea when we had discussed it with Kip Gurrin back in the Orkneys early in the year, but theoretically, we thought it would work. Now in these calm windless waters, I tried setting the sail in this way. It took me some time to set it up on our small deck, but once up it seemed like an ideal rig for the fresh NE trade wind we hoped to take us across the Atlantic

On Sunday 28 October 1973, Julie and I were almost ready to leave but decided to first celebrate our first meeting on this day five years before in Cambridge. It had been at a meeting of youth-hostellers, she was with two girlfriends, she was only fifteen. Never could we have imagined it leading to this. Now, 2,000 nm out from Scotland, in our best shore clothes, showing salt stains, rust marks, and now traces of black oil, we walked from the fishing dock around the coast a little, along a deserted pristine sandy beach to nearby San Andres, a little village just north of the harbour, where a tiny bar advertised 'Bifsteak' for 50 pesetas, which, at 139 pesetas to the pound, we thought a pretty good price. In the near empty bar we ordered the Bifsteak then sat drinking vino tinto de la casa looking out to the blue sea and far horizon, and thought back to that auspicious day in Cambridge all those years ago, and wondered where those friends were now.

After ten days, we had started to almost like Santa Cruz, but then for three consecutive days, we woke to find an even thicker than usual coating of black sludgy oil over the whole surface of the harbour. We longed for the clean open sea. It was time to go.

Chapter 11
Transatlantic passage

'Out of sight of land, the sailor feels safe' — Charles C. Davis

On Thursday 1st of November 1973, Leon Jaworski was appointed Watergate Special Prosecutor. The end was coming for Richard Nixon. We didn't know it then, but we would follow the saga, blow by blow, on our little transistor radio as we sailed all the way across the Atlantic.

We sailed out of Santa Cruz that same day, finally off across the Atlantic, loaded with food for one hundred days and 227 litres (60 US gallons) of water. We had sailed more than 2,200 nautical miles (4,000 kilometres) to get to the start line. Not a bad shakedown cruise. Now for the 2,700 nautical miles nonstop Atlantic crossing to Barbados, the most outlying West Indian Island.

Perhaps the most asked question in the years since has been, 'Weren't you frightened setting out to sail across the Atlantic in such a small boat?' Indeed, this would be our first real ocean voyage. There would be no coast nearby that we could run to if needed. But I don't recall being frightened, although undoubtedly we were a little nervous. We reduced our fear by thinking of everything that could go wrong well ahead and how we would handle it and ensuring that we had the necessary resources. At Ardmore, John Ridgway had drummed into us Adventure School instructors the importance of self-reliance. Aboard *The Aegre*, we took this seriously. We determined that whatever disaster we could think of happening, we had to be able to rescue ourselves. For instance, if we lost our mast in bad weather, we'd just have to build a jury rig so that we could sail on. But what if we hit something and the boat was badly holed? Thinking of this possibility, we'd built buoyancy into both ends of *The Aegre*, enough, we calculated, to float her even if she was completely full of water. We believed her to be unsinkable.

Furthermore, having lead ballast (firmly secured), we believed her to be self-righting in the event of a capsize. Sure, we didn't have an inflatable life raft, but for us, *The Aegre* herself was our life raft, and rather than just providing some rather dubious shelter in the event of some disaster until some outside persons rescued us, *The Aegre* could be sailed on so we could rescue ourselves. We had enough food and water for 100 days, more than double the maximum expected length of the voyage. Moreover, it was subdivided into multiple watertight containers to withstand spoilage, even if the boat was filled entirely with water.

But some risks were more challenging to manage, for instance, if one of us was severely injured or became sick. We thought the chances of injury were relatively low because all the sails, spars, and anchors were relatively light. Even in the worst conditions, the forces generated were not high, so the chance of fingers or limbs being caught in ropes and severed was low. Yachtsmen have also been injured in bad weather by being thrown across the cabin, breaking ribs, arms and legs. There was no chance of that in *The Aegre's* tiny cabin. We did carry morphine ampules for short-term pain relief, just in case. Appendicitis was a potential risk, and whilst some yachtsmen had their appendix removed before an ocean crossing, we didn't. Other forms of sickness seemed more likely in port rather than at sea. Hygiene was clearly paramount, as was the safe handling of knives, fishhooks and woodworking tools. We took a thick Ship Captain's Medical Manual and tried to keep safety at the top of our minds.

Admittedly other more nebulous fears showed their colours on watch alone between 1 and 3 am on moonless nights, like being dragged down in the clutches of a giant squid; being unwittingly run down and broken in half by a supertanker; being attacked by pirates with machine guns; one or both of us dying from salmonella poisoning; falling overboard when on watch alone; the boat catching fire, and other awful things. But these are like the fears you can have wherever you live. If you took them seriously, you might not get out of bed in the morning. Some are just fantasy; the risk of others can be reduced with simple preventative measures. The remainder must be put aside. Or stay home in bed with the sheets pulled well up.

Once we explore the dimension of fear, it seems to diminish. So no, we were not frightened, but a little nervous. Had we really thought of everything?

So equipped in mind and on board, we headed off. Atlas maps of the North Atlantic and landmasses bordering it show the distance from North Africa to the Caribbean as relatively short, no further than from Scotland to the Canaries. However, this is not so in reality. It's actually about twice the distance, the projection of the map giving a false impression, but we were hoping to average better speed than on the voyage south from Scotland because, rather than battling headwinds, we expected to have the prevailing north-east trade winds behind us most of the way and a favourable current carrying us along.

From our research, we knew that the northern edge of the NE trades was some distance south of the Canaries, almost at the latitude of the Cape Verde Islands. For the best winds and fastest passage, we should sail before the light northerlies that prevail off the Moroccan coast, almost as far as the Cape Verde Islands, 800 miles to the south, before turning west as the wind shifted toward the north-east. Then the wind would be behind us, as would be a 0.5-knot westerly current worth 12 miles a day. No, it wasn't the shortest way, but the fastest. This was a slightly more scientific approach than the advice given to a friend making the same passage on another small yacht. He was told to 'sail south till the butter melts, then turn west.' He got there too.

But as the wind filled in, it came from near ahead, the opposite of that predicted, and we spent the next five days close-hauled, bucking into a light sea. *The Aegre* sailed well close-hauled in light conditions. We would trim her so the lee gunwale was just on the waterline. The self-steering vane would easily hold her on a steady course, and she'd march along hour after hour, day after day. We could focus on stowing everything away properly, lashing things down, making sure nothing was chafing on anything else, organising our food and water for the coming weeks, and the kerosene for the primus and our night light below.

The Aegre became shipshape, and the peak of Mount Teide (3,718 m, 12,198 ft), the volcano that soars above Tenerife, dropped far below the horizon astern. We found our sea legs again and adjusted back to our life at sea and its succession of 4-hour sailing and sleeping windows mixed with midnight cups of tea. Breakfast was with the dawn, crackers and cheese for lunch and a one-pot dinner we ate standing in the hatchway, sharing a spoon and the pot with the sunset, wondering what the night would bring.

But days of beating into a head wind are wearing. The boat heeled and constantly bucking over a steep short sea, and we were relieved when eventually the wind crept round to the north, behind us and strengthened, the sun came out, the sea became blue, and the swell increased. Was this the north-east trade wind we'd heard so much about? Would it blow us all the way to Barbados?

Rather than reef the mainsail as the wind freshened, I dropped it altogether, and the jib too, and set the square sail as I'd practised in Santa Cruz. Then we were off on a helter-skelter ride before the NE trade wind.

Under the square rig for the first time, *The Aegre* surged forward smoothly down each wave with a roar from the bow. A little duck and a curtsey by the stern whilst another wave top broke out to leeward with a gentle roar. Then a slight easing when you could hear the hiss of the foam, so close you could put your hand out to touch it. Then you could feel the boat building into another surge forward, then another surge, then another, all guided, hour after hour, day after day after day by the wind vane's invisible hand on the tiller.

Blowing from astern, we had more than 20 knots of trade wind and an endless succession of big rolling swells with their tops gently breaking. Ahead, flying fish took off in huge swarms, trying to escape the silvery blue and green dorado now streaking beside us as we bowled along night and day. We'd bought a small illustrated book in London on ocean fish of the world and would thumb its pages identifying fish like the dorado that we'd never seen or heard of before.

With the mast braced aft by the mainsheet hauled to the top of the mast and the sheets all cleated firm, the line to Bob Macinnes's old log out astern was taut, the log spinning the miles away, getting the run of its life as we headed for Barbados, 2,700 miles away. This was sailing. This was living. *The Aegre* was in her element. The self-steering windvane would blow near flat one way, then the other, hauling the tiller back and forth, somehow keeping the boat on a near steady course.

The harder it blew, the faster we went. We tore along effortlessly. Our best day's run (24hrs) was 103 miles, but most days were almost as good. It was a good speed for our little overloaded boat, so deep in the water and with less than a 6m (20 ft) waterline length. All we had to do was keep everything working and hang on.

Big seas would come sliding up from astern or on the quarter, towering above us. Sometimes as they approached, we would see a line of skipjack tuna or dorado swimming in the front of the wave as if surfing, then *The Aegre* would be off, accelerating down the face of the wave, and so it would go on and on, for hours, for days.

Always an optimist, I was busy with my slide rule (this was before electronic calculators were invented), working out that if the wind held, we would complete the 2,700-mile passage in 31 days. But of course, it's dangerous to do that, and sure enough, the wind didn't hold. It gradually died on us, and we were becalmed for 48 hours. The sea assumed a glassy look, and we were fried by the sun, our latitude now being just 20°N of the equator.

With so little room below, finding a shady spot on watch was difficult. For the first time, the deck was too hot to walk on in bare feet. To cool off one day, I decided to go in for a swim. I did wonder what it would feel like to swim mid-ocean and if I could get a photo of the boat.

I carefully looked around to ensure there were no sharks nearby as we did have a shark following us quite often, but no, not today. Then, after securing a line around myself and tied to the boat (so there was no chance of a slight breeze coming up and *The Aegre* sailing off without me), I jumped over the side.

Just as I did so, it occurred to me that the shark of a few days before might be sheltering in the shadow beneath the boat. I did a quick check as I hit the water, but no, nothing there. Then, holding the camera in one hand above me, I slowly swam away from our little world. The water was warm. *The Aegre* rolled slowly on a long slow swell, the square sail hanging lifeless. Hundreds of miles from land, it was both exciting and scary. It wasn't long before I pulled myself back to the boat and rolled back over the gunwale into the cockpit. Julie was relieved to have me back.

When the wind returned, it came from the south. We sadly watched the barometer fall and, by the middle of the next day, were hove to in the middle of a full gale from the WSW. We were used to bad weather from the last passage, and at least it was warm now. We wouldn't have minded it for a day or so as it gave us a chance to catch up on some sleep, there being no point in keeping watches, but it went on and on.

Eventually, it gradually abated as the depression to the north of us slowly moved eastward, and the wind swung around more to the west (dead ahead). Finally, 17 days out from Tenerife, that weather system passed, and we were becalmed again for a further three days. So much for our 31-day passage.

Reviewing those first 20 days, we had made 1,000 miles (1,852 km) in the first 12 and then only a further 150 miles (278-km) over the next eight. But we carried on eating and drinking the same amount regardless of how many miles we sailed. We were now just starting our 7th 10-litre jerrican of water. We had 22. We decided to reduce our water allowance from 5 pints a day (2.8 litres) to 4 (2.3 litres), between us.

The 21st day (three weeks out from Tenerife) was notable because we caught our first fish. A small shoal had been swimming alongside us for a week or more which we'd identified as triggerfish or leatherjackets. I had tried every piece of our complicated Scottish fishing tackle in my efforts to catch them, but there was no fooling them. They were grey and about the size of my hand and thin but almost round with rough sand-paper-like skin and small mouths. We noticed that they were feeding on the baby goose-necked barnacles already starting to grow around the waterline. I snagged the biggest with a speargun (not at the first or even the second attempt, I admit). Those first two fillets, straight into the sizzling pan in the middle of the Atlantic, set a standard that has been hard to beat these last 50 years.

The calm gave way to another short period of NE winds but quickly faded into days of light squally variable winds. Often we only made 10 miles in 24 hours. We were mid-Atlantic and still had about 1,300 nm (2,400 km) to go. Unfortunately, we were now in the New York–Cape Town shipping lane. We couldn't really manoeuvre with no wind or engine (a paddle doesn't count for much mid-Atlantic) and felt vulnerable as a succession of supertankers appeared over the horizon and rapidly bore down on us. Was anyone on them keeping watch? Even if they were, would they see us? Would this one, or that one, pass behind or in front of us? In the quietness of the still ocean, we would hear the dull thumping of their engines deep in the hull of *The Aegre* long before we could see them. As they came closer, their huge bow waves were hypnotising. But they all seemed to see us and altered course in time, some still passing quite close. *Bettina* of Oslo slowed down to close with us, asking if we were all right, even writing our position in huge figures on the back of a large chart which they hung off the side of the bridge. We didn't like to ask for a cold beer or a replacement cheese grater for the one we'd lost overboard. As they went on their way, we thought of the officers sitting down to a proper lunch, maybe with a glass of wine.

Eventually that day, around nightfall, a gentle breeze came rustling quietly over the sea, and a ripple became discernible from *The Aegre*'s bow. We leaned her over, so the sails hung in the best position to give a little drive, and the silence started to be broken by an occasional gentle snore from the bow. We tiptoed around in silence lest we frighten the wind away, preparing for the night and being underway again. Behind us, the line of oil tankers, now just a twinkling of navigation lights, slowly slipped away beneath the horizon. Alone again, we headed WSW, on and out into the dark night. Somewhere out there, 1,200 miles over the horizon, was Barbados. Watch on watch, the days and nights blended into each other as we slowly made our way into the western Atlantic a little north of the equator.

For us back in 1973, there was no email, instant messaging, video conferencing, or contact with the outside world, apart from distant short-wave radio news services we could pick up at night if the sun-spots weren't giving too much interference. We were quite alone. So with just a pen and a damp foolscap pad, we each wrote of our days in long letters to our parents.

Towards the end of November, the north-east trade winds seemed to settle down and blow as expected. Living in our own world aboard *The Aegre*, we continued our steady routine of four-hour watches, the miles slowly going by. We'd pull in Bob's trusty old log morning and evening, guessing what the reading would be with increasing accuracy. The self-steering system and rig generally continued to work well, requiring daily maintenance in the way of greasing the lines where they passed through blocks, but otherwise, there was little we had to do other than keep a lookout and an eye on the compass. We read voraciously during the day and at night, lay in the companionway, feet up in the cockpit, listening to the radio and the Nixon saga, or just watched the sea and the stars.

But as November turned to December, the north-east trade wind failed us again and the sea flattened out, becoming glassy and silent. With no engine, half a day of no wind is delightfully restful. Once we had abandoned sailing, the sails could be dropped and stowed, the boat tidied, food and water stores updated and reorganised, sleep caught up on.

But then, after 24 hours, it becomes a little worrisome. Why was there no wind at all? Had we sailed into the centre of some giant ocean gyre where there was no wind and never would be? After 48 hours, the sea became flat in every direction to the horizon. This was our most prolonged single period of being becalmed, three and half days and nights. Eighty-four hours. Looking back at our log, we counted that we'd spent 8.25 days totally becalmed since leaving Santa Cruz. We began to think we might not get to Barbados before Christmas, and hoped our parents wouldn't become too worried.

But then, about the 11th December, the north-east trade wind filled in again, and *The Aegre* settled back into a steady rhythm, giving us 80 miles every day.

It was now about six weeks since we'd left Santa Cruz. Six weeks without a shower, a bath or any sort of proper wash in fresh water. Didn't we rather smell? Wasn't it uncomfortable with all the salt everywhere? How did we cope with that, I'm sometimes asked?

To answer, I should explain that growing up in England in the 1950s and

60s, there was no shower in our Cottenham house, but there was a bath, and I was expected to have a bath every Sunday evening (whether I thought I needed it or not). Daily showering wasn't so common, but changing underwear, yes.

So, sailing off on *The Aegre,* we didn't miss a daily shower. During the first three weeks of the first passage to Madeira, when the weather was unrelentingly wet and cold, I don't think we ever emerged from our Helly Hansen fibre pile 'polar' jerseys and long johns. Keeping warm was a much higher priority than smelling pleasant. But I don't recall smelling badly anyway. We wouldn't have been sweating much, and well, maybe we just slowly got used to it and didn't notice.

But once it started to warm up, and now sailing across the Atlantic in the tropics, we were comfortable during the day in shorts, swimming suits, T-shirts and a hat. We experimented with going naked, but neither of us felt comfortable and generally preferred wearing some clothes. Possibly it was cultural, but for myself, quite often working on deck with the sails and rigging hardware, I felt vulnerably uncomfortable naked. Fishing naked could be tricky too. I learnt the hard way when pulling in a fishing line mid-Atlantic and discovering in an excruciatingly painful way that it had been caught up in the tentacles of a Portuguese man-o-war stinging jellyfish. From personal experience, I can tell you that tentacles and testicles should never be mixed.

But how did we keep clean? And wasn't the salt on our clothes and skin a problem?

With a limited amount of freshwater aboard, our intention was to only consume it, not use it for washing. But in reality, we now both used a small amount, maybe half a cup, for a freshwater wash/wipe, most days. But salt was everywhere, on our skin, clothes, and bedding, which made them feel damp and cold on a chilly night. We accepted it, just as we didn't notice each other's smell.

But the passage was nearly over. Many days out from Barbados, we picked up an RDF signal from the island, dead ahead, confirming our course. Better still, we soon received local commercial radio from the capital, Bridgetown.

'Here is the weather forecast for today for Bridgetown, Barbados. Todaaay is going to be sunny aaaaand fine,' we heard from the announcer every day. Our kind of weather, we agreed.

The low east coast of Barbados gently appeared over the horizon on the 13th of December, pretty much in agreement with our navigation. We'd been out 43 days and sailed approximately 2,700 miles since Tenerife. We could soon see and smell the cultivated lushness of the rich sweet land. We altered course to clear South Point, the most southerly cape, and by noon of the 44th day, we were sailing across Carlisle Bay and into the Careenage at Bridgetown, our little yellow Q flag flying. Yes, we were coming from across the ocean and wanted to clear Customs and Quarantine.

The Careenage is a small dock at the site of a British settlement in 1628, in the open mouth of a small river. Sailing ships were careened here (pulled over onto their sides so their bottoms could be scrubbed of barnacles). It developed into the main port area with docking for the sailing schooners that provided transportation between the islands of the West Indies. In 1973 it was still being used for this and was a mass of classical-looking working schooners, international yachts clearing customs, and larger sailing fishing boats.

We tied up alongside an English yacht we'd met in Santa Cruz, *Peter Rabbit*. A photo of that arrival moment in Barbados survives, showing Julie on the deck of *The Aegre*, in her best (only) bikini, in faded lavender, barefoot, her blonde hair in two plaits, looking trim, suntanned and healthy. Was this moment as good as it could get?

Tied up to *Peter Rabbit*, we filled in the Customs forms about all the livestock and firearms we had on board. Once cleared, we eased out to anchor nearby close to the gently shelving yellow sandy beach of Carlisle Bay, just along from the Royal Barbados Yacht Club. Soon the anchor was down and burying itself in the sand beneath the clear water as we swung to the strong offshore breeze. I dived into the sparkling blue water to go down and ensure the anchor was correctly set and found myself surrounded by small multi-coloured fish.

We were in Barbados. Wow! We'd made it. But what now?

Chapter 12
Barbados

*'What are you prepared to give for your dream? If it is not
everything … stop pipe dreaming.'* — T.F. Hodge

B e careful what you wish for. Achieving a grand ambition is a mixed
blessing. Its achievement can be an anticlimax, even a disappointment,
and lead to deep questions, such as, what was the point of it all? Was it
all worth the effort? Our ambition had been to sail the Atlantic on our own
boat, and here we were, anchored just off the Royal Barbados Yacht Club.
Other yachts were sailing in every day from Europe. Everybody around us
had sailed across the Atlantic, which somewhat diminished the achievement.
But we were proud to have done it ourselves on our little engineless Shetland
sailing boat. And I came to realise that achieving a grand ambition can inspire
confidence. What other challenges might we take on in quite different fields
if we could do this?

At the time, I don't recall feeling disappointed that we'd arrived, that our
ambition had been achieved, or that Carlisle Bay seemed as if it could be
anywhere. Nor were we wondering about our next grand challenge other
than the need to find work. We were far too busy coping with the reality of
the moment, this being that we had no choice but to anchor out in the Bay,
but with our inflatable dinghy at the end of its life, we wondered if we could
make it into shore or back without it deflating around us.

But of course, we did and then walked into Bridgetown to the post office
to see if there were any letters for us in the Poste Restante, and to send a
telegram to our parents and letters to them, the Ridgways, Bob Macinnes,
and other friends.

Then back to the Royal Barbados Yacht Club, just above the Carlisle Bay
beach, to proudly sign the visitors' book, shower, and drink the traditional

rum and coke, sitting on the balcony looking out over the bay. In front of us was an international gathering of recently arrived yachts, with *The Aegre* near the front, not far off the beach. Many were possibly escaping the first OPEC-induced oil shock, whose effects were starting to bite in Europe. We heard England was now on a three-day week, with two and a half hour queues at petrol stations. I felt a bit embarrassed as if I'd escaped just in time.

Then we went shopping for essentials, fresh bread and fruit, and, not to be forgotten, a bottle of Mount Gay rum, Barbados's best, for boatbuilder Bob Macinnes.

Our spirits were high, but the urgent need to replace our dinghy dominated our thinking. We needed money, and somehow, we'd have to find work. We temporarily resorted to hitch-hiking rides ashore and back in other yachts' dinghies, but I felt ashamed to do so and sometimes we just swam ashore and back, clothes held high in one hand. Perhaps the low point was swimming the shopping out to the boat one evening. Clearly, the holiday was over.

We expected to spend the 'winter' working in the West Indies aboard a charter yacht. Then, well before the start of the hurricane season, we would take *The Aegre* north, up the east coast of the US via the intra-coastal waterway, for the early northern summer. Then possibly head back to the UK across the North Atlantic mid-summer via the Azores, to the UK. But in December, freshly arrived in Barbados, that all seemed far away.

We quickly heard of work for a skipper and cook on a 50ft sloop for the charter season. I wondered if we could do this and how *The Aegre* would fare abandoned by us for weeks.

Then we remembered the envelope my father had given us before we left, with the words, 'If you get to Barbados, open this.' Back in Scotland, we'd stowed it carefully for that mythical day. Now we searched the boat as if looking for the last can of corned beef.

Finding it, we savoured the opening moment, speculating what it might contain. Five pounds? Ten pounds? Enough for a celebratory meal or fresh food for a few more days? But no, beyond our wildest imagination, it contained a cheque for five hundred pounds — real wealth on a small cruising boat in the West Indies in 1973. At that moment, our lives changed forever.

We quickly calculated this was enough to buy a proper inflatable dinghy and re-provision the boat for at least another hundred days of sailing, maybe a hundred and fifty. Suddenly there was no need to stay and work in the West

Continued on page 135

① My parents married in 1941.

② Julie and my motorbike, it wasn't quite her style.

③ John and Marie Christine Ridgway.

④ Julie, top of her class.

⑤ On my arrival at Ardmore, pre-haircut.

⑥–⑩. Tom Edwardson building *The Aegre* in 1966 using 11 x ½ inch mahogany planks per side, the 12th, the top plank, was larch, all with copper fastenings. (Photos: Andrew Bryce)

⑪ Bob Macinnes gave her a stout curved deck of ⅜ marine plywood that covered the whole boat supported by 2" x 2" larch beams.

⑫ Aboard *The Aegre* we visited Ardmore and the Ridgways during sea trials (Photo: Jim Archer-Burton)

⑬ Cycling in Lapland (Photo: Tim Ewer)

⑭ John Ridgway and *English Rose III*, the 1966 Atlantic rowboat

⑯ Our snug cabin midwinter at the Adventure School in NW Scotland.

⑮ Married in London, February 1972

⑰ Launching *The Aegre* near Ardmore before the overall decking was added.

⑱ Bob Macinnes examines the storm mainsail made of thick flax.

⑲ The antique log Bob Macinnes loaned us, last used 60 years before by his grandfather. "It needs a run" he said.

⑳ The decked in *Aegre* emerges from Bob's boatshed above Scourie.

㉑ Loaded onto a makeshift sledge, *The Aegre* is towed half a mile to the water.

㉓ Looking aft on a grey day off Ireland.

㉒ Julie gives the near indestructible cooker a try.

㉔ Just after arriving in Funchal, Madeira.

㉕ Raising the waterline in the Madeira sunshine.

㉖ Relaunching.

㉗ Marie Christine and Rebecca Ridgway aboard *The Aegre* sailing off Funchal.

㉘ A trial setting of the storm-sail upside down as a square sail in Santa Cruz harbour, Tenerife, Canary Islands.

㉙ Becalmed mid-Atlantic I went swimming to take this snapshot of *The Aegre*.

㉚ Taking a noon sight under the square sail.

㉛ Servicing the self-steering system at speed mid-Atlantic.

㉜ Fish swam close beside us at their peril.

㉝ Self-steering in a following sea.

㉞ Shower time mid-Atlantic.

㉟ Arrival in Barbados after 44 days at sea.

㊱ No room aboard for late arrivals to *The Aegre*'s Barbados Xmas party (Photo: Brigitte Sass)

㊲ Anchored in Carlisle Bay, Barbados

③⑧ Our wonderful new inflatable dinghy

③⑨ Off to Grenada.

④⓪ Hauled out in Grenada.

④① Transiting the Panama Canal, *The Aegre* lashed alongside Tom Blackwell's 55ft ketch *Islander*, here passing through the Galliard Cut.

④② About to depart from Atuona, Hiva Oa (Photo: David Samuelson)

④③ *The Aegre* hauled up on the beach for a refit at Puna'auia, Tahiti. Moorea in the background.

④④ July 14th, Bastille Day on Tahiti — one year out from Scotland.

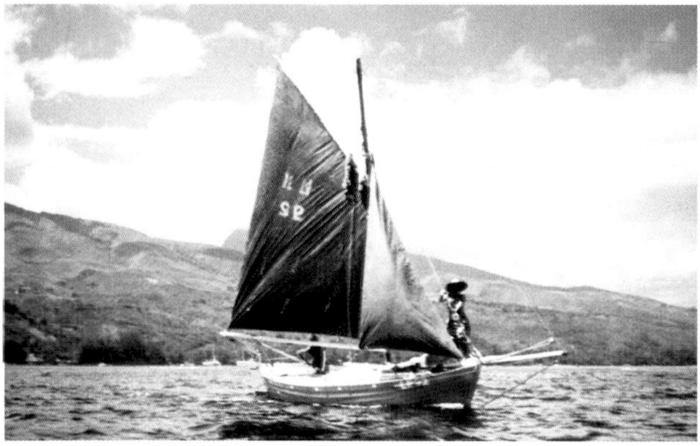

(45) Departing Tahiti for Rarotonga. (Photo: Bob & Sharon, yacht Marluva)

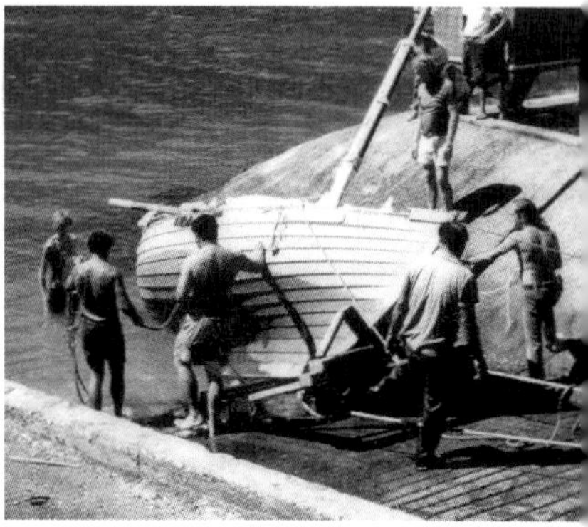

(46) Heartbreakingly, *The Aegre* crashes onto her side. Ken Bailey (in white shorts) and his boatbuilder friends look on.

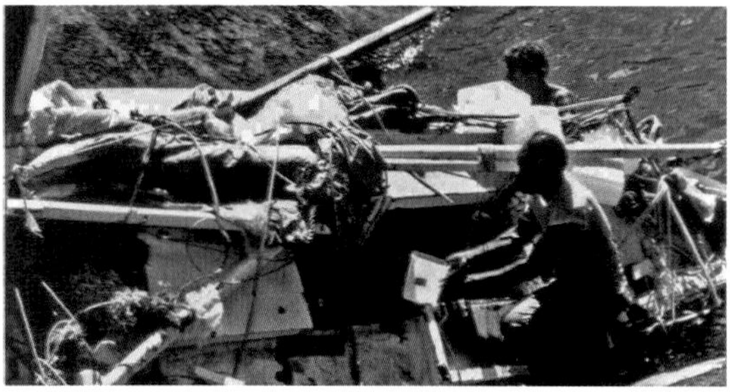

(47) The deck view. It was no time to be house-proud.

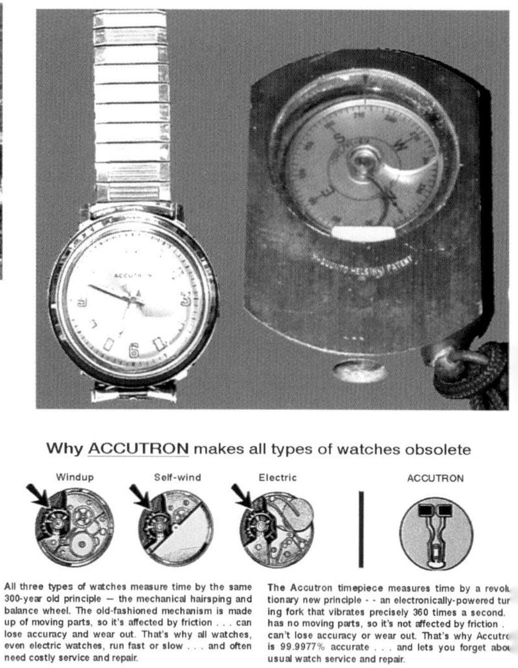
ACCUTRON
Why ACCUTRON makes all types of watches obsolete
Windup
Self-wind
Electric
ACCUTRON
All three types of watches measure time by the same 300-year old principle — the mechanical hairsping and balance wheel. The old-fashioned mechanism is made up of moving parts, so it's affected by friction . . . can lose accuracy and wear out. That's why all watches, even electric watches, run fast or slow . . . and often need costly service and repair.
The Accutron timepiece measures time by a revol
tionary new principle - - an electronically-powered tur
ing fork that vibrates precisely 360 times a second.
has no moving parts, so it's not affected by friction .
can't lose accuracy or wear out. That's why Accutr
is 99.9977% accurate . . . and lets you forget abo
usual watch service and repair.

(48) Survivors of the capsize, our Bulova Accutron chronometer and Suunto hand-bearing compass.

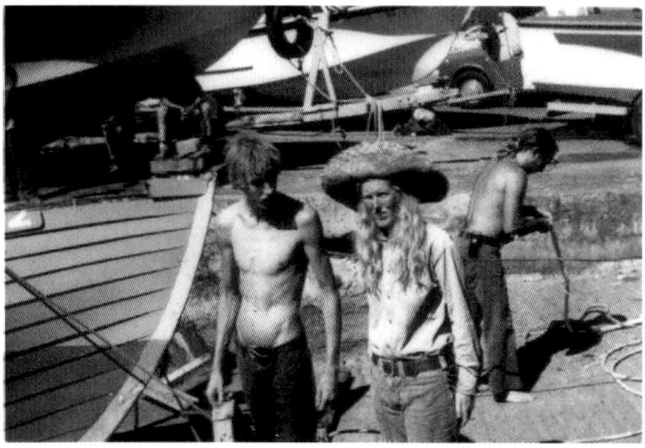

(49) "You all right Julie?"

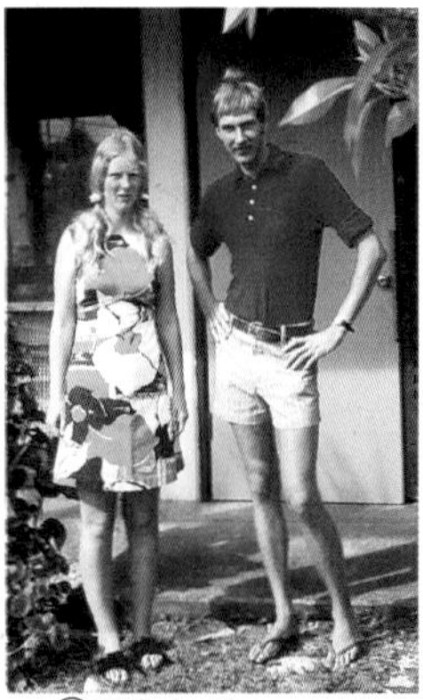

(50) Life in Pago was good for a while.

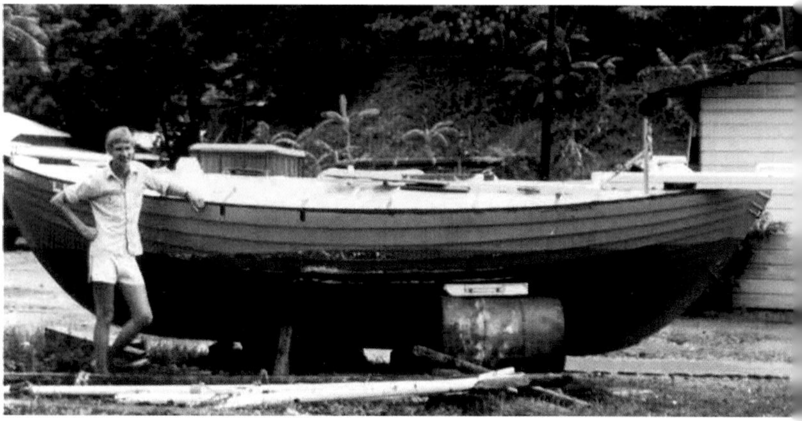

(51) Sadly leaving *The Aegre*, my lovely boat.

Continued from page 126

Indies. Suddenly returning to the trouble-stricken UK via the North Atlantic looked decidedly unattractive. Suddenly, we could sail to the Pacific.

It was almost too big an idea to comprehend.

We could stay just a short while in the West Indies, perhaps explore a little of the Grenadines, then while the winds and the season were with us, head west, onwards, with the trade winds across the Caribbean to Panama. Then through the Panama Canal and out into the vastness of the Pacific. A hundred days from Barbados could take us to the middle of the South Pacific, to Tahiti... five thousand miles beyond our imagination.

I stared at Julie, nodding and saying repeatedly, 'We could do it — we could do it'. I don't know that she was quite as enamoured with the idea as I was, but nor do I recall her objecting. Perhaps she was trying to grasp the implications of sailing into the Pacific, while I was just completely caught up in the very idea of it.

I was dazed by the opportunity, but reality intruded. There is always maintenance and improvement work to be done on a cruising sailing boat. Right now, there were two things at the top of my list: a new inflatable dinghy and a much-improved sunshade to go over the boat in harbour.

It was going to take days, possibly weeks, to convert the cheque to cash, so in the meantime, we made a sunshade with our final few pounds. The flax stormsail draped over the boom had been a failure as a tent, as there was little space or light beneath it, and rain came straight through it. We replaced it with a big square of cream canvas stretched over the boom set high above the deck and held out wider than the boat by light wooden spreaders running across the boat and secured down to the gunwale. Beneath it, the deck became a shady saloon. It was a huge success.

Some of the money eventually arrived at a local bank, and we bought the new dinghy, an Avon Redstart inflatable with plywood floorboards. Robust and proven, it was a favoured model among sailing voyagers but expensive (£120), and took a fair chunk of our £500. But we knew it was vital to cruising life in every harbour and even as a potential (sailable) life raft. I loved it. No parent was ever so protective. It was always carried, not dragged up a beach, and at night in harbour secured safely on the deck of *The Aegre*.

Meanwhile, the cruising fleet in Barbados's Carlisle Bay was growing. Now in the final weeks before Christmas every day's afternoon sea breeze brought in a new wave of transatlantic voyagers escaping the European winter and the OPEC oil crisis. We'd met some of them before in Madeira, including

Heino and Brigitte Sass, aboard their 32ft GRP sloop *Brisa,* and single-hander
Tom Blackwell, in his sixties, alone aboard his forty-year-old 57-foot ketch
Islander.

But not every arrival was so big. Shane Acton sailed in alone aboard *Super
Shrimp,* a bilge keeled 18ft ply Caprice. He anchored close by, and we were
amazed to discover that he'd grown up in a village near Cambridge, about
three miles from Cottenham where I grew up. *Super Shrimp* had much more
space below than *The Aegre,* although I didn't like the way I could feel the
waves lapping against her sides through the thin plywood. But he went on
to complete a circumnavigation, returning to Cambridge with *Super Shrimp*
eight years later.

Another arrival in a small vessel was Geoff Stewart, alone aboard an open
21ft 9in GRP engineless Drascombe Longboat. Up till then, *The Aegre* had
seemed cramped. Geoff had just fibreglassed a piece of plywood across the
open hull between the buoyancy tank/side seats and slept under it. His
passage non-stop from Las Palmas in the Canaries had taken him 59 days,
making us feel much better about our 44 days.

Although there were now many international yachts anchored around us,
there was initially little interaction between the crews. We seemed alone in
rowing around, welcoming in new yachts and getting to know everyone. To
try and change that and celebrate being alive and in Barbados, we organised
a party aboard *The Aegre.* Everyone laughed when we rowed around inviting
them. How could the smallest boat in the bay host such an event? We hoped
they'd stay in their dinghies alongside *The Aegre,* but no, everyone had to
come on board. That night we discovered the deck would hold more than
thirty-five large people. Just. Only one fell off. Sitting in the companionway, I
was the barman, not a difficult job; there are only so many things you can do
with Mount Gay rum, coke, lime and ice. Life was more hazardous for Julie,
playing cocktail waitress in a bikini and circulating amongst our guests. How
she managed that as the drinks flowed and the evening wore on is anyone's
guess. But it was a great party and was much talked about. Subsequently there
was always a party somewhere for the next week through Christmas and New
Year. And we were invited to every one of them.

Christmas Day came. We were more than a little homesick and, in a way,
glad when it was over. Both of us came from families that made much of
Christmas.

Now, together but alone, aboard *The Aegre* anchored in Carlisle Bay, it was
never going to be like Christmas with our families, and we missed it. Lying

on our little bunk, we gave each other presents, with the boat gently rocking on the mooring. For Julie, a big straw sunhat (which had been quite tricky to smuggle aboard and hide), a belt, two books, a young women's magazine, and a new notebook to keep her diary in. Julie gave me a new pair of swimming trunks (badly needed), some chocolate and a bookmark. We had a big salad for lunch. It was our first Christmas away from home.

Out in the Carlisle Bay anchorage, the Christmas week culminated in a grand New Year's Eve party aboard a wooden English gaff cutter sailed from the UK by a retired doctor and dentist. That night, I rather overdid the Mount Gay rum, or maybe it was the gin. The difficult part was then sculling back to *The Aegre*, well, not the sculling, but finding *The Aegre*.

Fortunately, we were in the habit of hanging a little kerosene anchor lamp off the forestay every night in harbour. Thankfully now we could just make out our little light in the distance. Rolling back onboard from the dinghy was a messy business because I forgot about several half-full paint cans. Julie's account of it all in a letter to her Mum was not flattering. The next morning, we didn't feel much better, even the gentle roll of *The Aegre* on her anchor was too much and half asleep I rowed us to the beach. Groaning we rolled ourselves out over the dinghy side and onto the warm sand, to lie, eyes shut, in the stillness breathing slowly. But now the sand seemed to be gently rocking. Waking, I found we were surrounded by similarly beached partygoers from the other yachts, looking like small pink stranded whales, survivors like us, not just of the night, but of the year.

What would the New Year bring? For us it would be sailing the Pacific. We'd been putting together a plan throughout this time, Julie having come around to the idea. We estimated that our remaining money would last another six months or more, living frugally. And if we left soon, we could spend these six months catching the best wind, first across the Caribbean to Panama and then out westward from Panama to the central Pacific.

Before leaving, we needed to recoat the bottom of *The Aegre* with antifouling paint, and we wanted to see a little of the West Indies. With insufficient tide to dry the boat out to repaint the bottom, we needed a small slipway, but every slipway known to yachties in the region was expected to be fully booked.

Except, we learned, in the nearby island of Grenada, 140 miles to the south-west. Grenada is a small country that comprises the main island of Grenada itself with the capital St George's, and six smaller islands in a chain to the north, known as the Grenadines, leading to St Vincent. South of Grenada are Trinidad and Tobago.

Trouble was brewing in Grenada, which had been under British rule since 1763 until 1958, when it became part of the Federation of the West Indies, but was to be granted independence in February 1974. The existing Premier, Eric Gairy, was to be appointed Prime Minister. But all was not well, we learned. The New Jewel Movement, a Marxist-Leninist group led by the popular Maurice Bishop, wanted to overthrow the government, and there were rumours of violent conflict in the streets of St George's and an armed response by the military supporting Gairy. As a result, many yachts were giving St George's a miss this year. From further research around the yachts in Carlisle Bay we learnt that the St George's yacht club had a small slipway that would be big enough for *The Aegre*, and that we might just be lucky and find it unused.

Furthermore, everyone told us Grenada was beautiful and an ideal starting point for a cruise north through the Grenadines (small islands to its north) before heading off west for Panama. So we decided to sail to Grenada, hoping to pull the boat out on the yacht club's slipway and paint the bottom. Then we could sail north through the Grenadines to (relatively large) St Vincent to restock with food. Finally, we might then retire to the little island of Bequia just south of St Vincent, regarded as one of the most beautiful in the whole of the West Indies, for final preparations before heading off west on the 1,200 nm passage across the Caribbean to Panama. It seemed like a good plan.

An older, wiser head might have thought it foolish to deliberately go to a small island which was about to be gripped by a Marxist-Leninist uprising, intending to pull a yacht (comprising our home and total assets) out of the water. But an older, wiser head probably wouldn't have been aboard *The Aegre* in the first place. Sometimes I think we did have a rather naively benign view of the world.

Untroubled by such dark thoughts and keen to be on our way, we had one last evening with our many friends in Carlisle Bay, and then we were off to Grenada.

Chapter 13
Grenada and the Grenadines

'Until you have the courage to lose sight of the shore, you will not know the terror of being forever lost at sea.' — Charles Cook

The island of Grenada is only 140nm (260km) south-west of Barbados. After the Atlantic passage, it hardly seemed worth getting out the sextant. Just a bit of dead reckoning navigation, I decided, as we headed off on Sunday 13th January 1974. Being mountainous, I thought we'd see it at thirty miles or more.

Three days later, I knew we'd missed Grenada. Hello Trinidad, here we come. Reluctantly I got out the sextant and fixed our position. Oh dear.

Which is why it took us five days to sail to Grenada, not two and a half. The last two days were spent beating hard to windward. The gods were kind to us that time, and I was never so complacent again.

We found the small Grenada Yacht Club slipway, and sure enough, the next yacht booked on it had cancelled. We could have it for three days. Soon *The Aegre* was up out of the water, and we were busy scrubbing.

As Julie wrote in her diary: *Got boat out of the water yesterday — money in advance — went to bank, queued to get in — windows broken — reports of looting. We scrubbed stbd side, hard work, did port side this morning — Primer first- tomorrow another coat of primer. On Sat two coats. Then launch on Sunday! It's one day extra — we'll have to pay for it. I hope it's good this time. A lot of flies inside the boat. We've both been bitten a lot.*

There certainly was tension in the air. With reportedly 68% unemployment, there were many unhappy people and a revolution to oust the unpopular Eric Gairy was under way. The action seemed to be in the main town located around the bay over in the neighbouring flooded volcanic cone.

Julie wrote about it: *Yesterday went to bakery with Skipper [a dog that had hung around us on the slipway]. Skipper has no road sense. Read newspaper over shoulder, horrible reports, man killed, his stomach cut open with a cutlass. Gairy said police could help themselves from the shops as he could not pay them. We'll be glad to leave.*

Every day, there was growing tension and demonstrations. Whilst working on the outside of the hull, I made sure I could let go the chocks holding the boat trolley with a single swipe from a sledgehammer, to launch us back into the bay like the Yarmouth lifeboat. On deck, I arranged the sails so I could hoist them for a quick getaway. At night I slept with the sledgehammer and a large machete by my hands.

But at no time did I feel we were actually in danger, but still we were relieved to soon be back in the water and preparing for a cruise north through the Grenadines. The marina near us was almost full of yachts, and no one seemed too concerned by the impending revolution. The general view was that both sides knew the yachts brought a lot of money to the island, and no one wanted to upset this industry.

Seeking advice about our onward passage, we worked the other cruising boats in the marina. It's easy when you are young and have a distinctive small wooden boat with a traditional rig. Also, there's no problem with the pecking order. We were at the bottom, and we knew it. But that's not entirely true. Departing from Scotland, from a latitude of 59 degrees north, we had sailed further than most others, and that carried its own small prestige.

One fair-sized and somewhat worn but very seaworthy-looking ketch, Alsanol Too, impressed us, and with no shame, we called out, introducing ourselves, hoping to be invited aboard. The owner, Dr Alex Bell, was a dentist from Ecuador who had just completed a two-year circumnavigation with his crew. He was very welcoming, and full of knowledge and encouragement. He got out his charts to show us his course. Pencil crosses, showing his daily position fixes and the connecting lines, snaked out right across the Pacific. We were in awe of how far we had to go in a much less speedy boat than his.

Suddenly Alex stood up and gathered all the charts into his arms. 'Here, you're going to need these,' he said, 'I won't need them again. They're yours.'

We were stunned by his generosity and couldn't thank him enough. He gave us more than 100 charts of the Pacific and a Pilot book (invaluable for sailing directions),

Alex, if you ever read this, thank you again, and I've still got a few of the charts kept safely for you. They've got a second set of pencilled fixes on them now, out across the Pacific.

But where to stow so many charts? A cat's cradle of thin shock cord and small brass eye screws between the deck beams immediately under the deck solved the problem. We rolled all the charts up and squeezed them in. They were dry and out of the way, but accessible. And they gave a bit of padding for our heads too.

According to rumour, a large demonstration was expected in St George's a few days later. We sailed that morning, to a backdrop of shouting and chanting from a big crowd in the town's streets, then gunfire. It was a tragedy in the making that sadly had many more years to run.

Thus we sailed out of beautiful St George's. It seemed almost obscene to be heading out for what we expected to be a leisurely series of day cruises north to St Vincent while people were being shot at. Somehow we reconciled it with our powerlessness to make any difference.

Now with a clean bottom, the agile and speedy sailing ways of *The Aegre* were fully restored. After thousands of miles we were as used to sailing her as any commuter driving their car to work, but all our sailing so far had been on the open ocean. We weren't used to sailing close to rocky shores, coral reefs and other yachts. Between Grenada and St Vincent there were hundreds of rocks, little islands and coral reefs, and almost no lights. Sailing at night would be really dangerous for us. So we planned to find a sheltered anchorage every night and have a good sleep.

A cruise north through the Grenadines would sound idyllic to most sailors, but we initially found the reality less so, a strong headwind and westerly current making our progress slower than expected.

On the first night we anchored in the shelter of a headland near the village of Gouyave, still on the north-west coast of Grenada. The next day the headwind persisted, and we slowly tacked our way north to eventually anchor for the night in a bay on the western side of the uninhabited Ronde island. It was a different sort of sailing. The small islands were spectacular, the breeze steady and warm, the sea and the sky blue, the anchorages safe, and there were a few other yachts around. It was growing on us.

Our destination for the next night was Hillsborough Bay, on the little island of Carriacou. It promised a sheltered anchorage. But importantly, I wanted to send a postcard from here to my Uncle Jack, he who had gone to sea in a boat with a calico skin. Canon John Barry, my mother's sometimes wayward brother back in Northern Ireland, a key mover in the St Columba curragh voyage to Iona back in 1963 and now an avid follower of our voyage. For years Jack had been the Rector of the Hillsborough parish church in County Down, Northern Ireland. I thought receiving a postcard from us in this other Hillsborough would entertain him. In the mid-afternoon, we sailed into the bay, anchored, and quickly rowed ashore, only to find it was an early closing day—no postcards for sale. We settled for a postmark on a short letter to him.

Later that afternoon, at anchor, we were visited by some teenage boys in an outrigger pirogue (a dugout canoe with an outrigger on one side). They brought fresh limes to trade. We pleaded poverty. They asked if we were working (no). They looked at our sailing boat and asked where we had come from. We told them. They smiled and said, 'You're rich.'

We were humbled, and bought their limes.

Onwards, the next day, to anchor for the night on the western side of Cannounan Island in Charlestown Bay and then finally we sailed into Kingstown, St Vincent. We were going to St Vincent for its bank. The last of our money was being sent there so we could replenish our stores for the passage to Panama and have cash to do the same in Panama before heading out across the Pacific. But the money hadn't arrived yet.

'Maybe after the weekend,' they told us. But by Monday, we hardly needed it. Emerging from the bank, we wondered what to do for the weekend, but first, we followed our ears. It was late on a quiet Friday afternoon in this small town, but pulsing from somewhere, in the wind or through the ground, was a steel band rhythm and more. It was in the distance, coming and going with the breeze. Was it coming from this direction or that? Could we find it? We set out to walk. At every intersection, we used our ears to get one turn closer. It was definitely getting louder. And louder. Suddenly we were upon it, a crossroads entirely taken up by perhaps 100 people, everyone playing something, from traditional steel drums to steel lamp-posts to pieces from wrecked cars. The rhythm was flowing this way, then that, then somewhere else, then back again. Endlessly. We were entranced.

It was long past dark when we got back to *The Aegre*. On the nearby wharf, we noticed a big newcomer, a Canadian naval destroyer, apparently on a goodwill visit. A notice on the wharf advertised that the ship would be open for visitors the next afternoon. We thought we'd go. Our real motive was to meet up with the Navigation Officer and take a look at, and possibly get a tracing of, a chart of the approaches to Colon, the Caribbean end of the Panama Canal, a chart missing from Alex Bell's extensive donation.

The next day, in our best shore-going kit, we queued up and went aboard, asking to speak to a Navigation Officer. We were quickly introduced to a friendly, smartly uniformed Lieutenant. He was welcoming and took us up to the bridge, where he peered at *The Aegre* with binoculars while we studied the chart. After lots of chatter and jokes, he invited us to have pre-dinner showers (ok, ok, we must have smelt pretty ripe) and then to a cocktail party on board arranged that evening for local dignitaries.

In her diary Julie wrote of it: *I wore my yellow T shirt and tartan long skirt. N wore grey/white stripey trousers and blue/white flowery shirt. Jolly smart. Met Jim Merriam again [the navigation officer], Tex, the second in command and Barry Baker, the Supply Officer 'Tell me what you need!' Coffee and dancing in the wardroom. A good time had by all.*

The following day we reciprocated in our own way, conducting tours of *The Aegre* and offering a bit of sailing and swimming for both officers and crew. I don't know what they thought of us, sailing the world in a vessel smaller than their own little cutter, but we all had a good time. Then, at their insistence, we were back in the officer's mess for dinner. By then, they knew we were in St Vincent to pick up the last of our funds, to buy supplies for our next long passage halfway across the Pacific. Then Barry Baker took over

'Come this way' he said, 'We carry enough food for two hundred people for two years. I think we could let you have a few essentials.'

Down we went into the bowels of the ship, through one watertight hatch after another, down and down into what seemed like a vast warehouse, a sort of Aladdin's cave, to our astonished eyes.

'What would you like?' he asked.

Totally unprepared for the largesse that was to follow, we suggested maybe some dried biscuit, perhaps some canned meat if they could spare it?

The officer took over, directing some ratings. 'OK, four cases of this, three cases of that, a big box of the other', on and on. His selections were passed back by a line of men, up the companionways to form a massive pile just below open deck level.

'We're not supposed to do this', he said conspiratorially, 'The locals don't like it. We'll bring it around to you later tonight when it's dark and a bit quieter.'

We were wide-eyed in shock. There was surely enough food here for us for half a year, at least.

Back on *The Aegre* in the dusk, we wondered where we could possibly stow all the supplies which were about to arrive. Some hard decisions had to be made to free up space. Bags of winter clothes from Scotland, a spare duvet, and more, all in good condition, would have to go. We hoped the Canadians would take some of them.

Much later, when it was completely dark, we heard the chug chug chug of the diesel engine of a small boat quietly approaching. Then the blacked-out open cutter from the warship nosed up alongside us. It was the Bosun and his mate, who had visited and been swimming with us earlier that day. We quickly formed a chain to pass the boxes. They just kept on coming as Julie and I stacked them all over the deck.

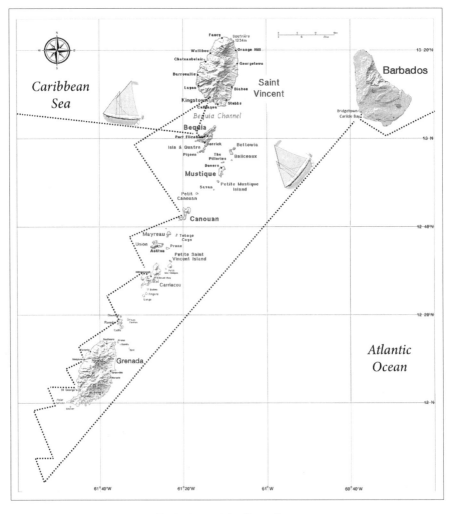

Barbados and the Grenadines

'There are a few extra things we thought you might need,' said the Bosun. 'A case of honey, a couple of cases of lime juice, oh and some paint brushes, thinners, line, we're sure you can use them. Good luck!'

And then they were gone, quietly chugging off into the blackness.

Julie and I hardly knew where to turn. The deck and the whole of our cabin were full of boxes of food. There wasn't even space to sleep. Somehow, we would have to get it all below before daylight.

And when the dawn did come, the warship was gone.

It took a few days to stow all the food properly, filling every cranny in the boat. And then there was the problem of discreetly getting rid of all the cardboard boxes. Amidst it all was a marine chart: 'Approaches to Colon.'

Our thanks to the officers and crew, who should probably remain nameless, and the unwitting taxpayers of Canada. We were overwhelmed by your friendship, support and generosity.

Now fully reprovisioned and with the absolute last of our funds on board, we set sail for nearby Bequia to complete our final preparations for the voyage across the Caribbean to Panama. Lovely Bequia was an easy sail of a few hours in the warm wind and light sea. Entering the sheltered natural harbour of Admiralty Bay, we picked our way through the anchored boats to anchor close to the beach just off the small town of Port Elizabeth. After the busy anchorage in St Vincent, a terminal for charter boats and cruise ships, it was delightfully tranquil.

We'd heard Bequia had a good sailmaker, and wanted a number of the seams in our tan Dacron sails re-stitched before heading off on the next big voyage. This was soon underway while we repackaged our food and stowed it in the right order for easy access at sea. We clearly again had enough for 100 days or more.

It was a lovely place to be anchored and to prepare the boat. Amongst the vessels around us were a few tubby 70ft gaff-rigged trading schooners. In 1974 they still provided regular services between the islands carrying everything from livestock to mail.

February 18th 1974 was our third wedding anniversary and a long way from our second anniversary in the snowbound cabin in NW Scotland. On this day a year before John had told us to leave the Adventure School and with it our work, board and lodging, and to focus on preparing for the voyage. Only a year ago, we reflected as we enjoyed a rare meal out in Daphne Cooks It, the 'in' place for a simple (but rather expensive) dinner with some other voyagers above the beach. Julie was wearing her best (oh-so-locally fashionable) faded flour sack dress, also from Daphne's, I in my grey/blue and white striped trousers I'd bought in Barbados (where else might you buy such trousers in 1973?), with no salt stains, rust, or oil marks. Well dressed, confident and happy, we ate soup, fish curry with ginger wine, ice cream and coconut. It was a fitting last night in the West Indies. The next day we'd sail for Panama, 1,100 nautical miles to the west. Except we were delayed as Julie explained in her diary: *Off at last. Spent most of the morning waiting for Daphne to finish my [new] bikini. When she'd done it, the bottom was too small. So she put on an extra piece, like a belt tie. A bit queer but not too bad. She wasn't too happy about it being only $20.*

Chapter 14
Across the Caribbean to Panama

'There is nothing more enticing, disenchanting, and enslaving than the life at sea.' — Joseph Conrad in Typhoon, 1899

Readying *The Aegre* for sea, the Caribbean to Panama, then the Pacific, I was excited, challenged and nervous. Back in Scotland, our seemingly ambitious plan had been to do the Atlantic cruise; Madeira, Barbados, north through the West Indies, then probably back across the Atlantic to England via the Azores, over about twelve months. It was a course travelled by many yachts every year, even back in the early 1970s. We'd equipped the boat for this. The most demanding passage had been from Scotland to Madeira, as expected, but since Madeira, I'd felt we were in a relatively benign environment, meeting some of the same yachts in port along the way. The ports themselves had been highly westernised and seemed relatively safe.

Now we were leaving all that behind us. Across the Caribbean we would be

Caribbean Crossing

sailing far off the coast of Venezuela and Colombia to Panama. Then after the Panama Canal, we'd be heading out into the Pacific. But where in the Pacific? Aboard an engineless yacht the wind calls the tune, but exiting the Canal we'd find little of it in the Gulf of Panama, a near windless zone for much of the year. However, a few hundred miles to the south blows one of the ocean's great winds, the south-east trade. If we could somehow make our way south to it, we could ride it westward for thousands of miles, near all the way across the Pacific. In the south-east trade, the first land we'd come to would be the remote Marquesas Islands, but they were more than 3,600 miles out from Panama, and I could hardly imagine sailing that far. Nor would there be any possibility of help along the way and little support beyond there until Tahiti, a further 1,000 miles.

Once we departed from the West Indies for Panama, there would be no turning back with the strong tailwinds we expected across the Caribbean and then Eastern Pacific. By going on, we were committing ourselves and *The Aegre* to at least sailing across the Pacific to New Zealand or Australia. It was hard to imagine taking her so far. Were we, the boat and the rig really up to it?

I wondered if the stitching on the sails and the fibreglass on the mast wearing out was symptomatic of more extensive problems. Our main compass had a slowly enlarging air bubble, and I worried if any of our polythene water tanks might be wearing thin where they pressed on the nail roves holding the hull planks together. And still, with no accurate chronometer, we were reliant on short-wave radio time signals coming in on our little transistor radio.

But we'd worked through all the potential problems we could think of. They sounded frightening when casually listed, but when we examined each one, it seemed to diminish, and we regained the confidence to press on.

Julie and I were united in our decision. I don't recall giving any thought to heading back to the UK. We seemed comfortable together, alone on *The Aegre*, heading out yet further into the unknown. There was no going back, only onwards.

There were no farewells as we tacked out of Admiralty Bay. We were on our way once more, an empty ocean ahead.

Emerging from the island's shelter, we quickly felt the full force of the Atlantic's north-east trade wind behind us and progressively reduced sail. Soon *The Aegre* was ploughing her way west at her maximum hull speed, leaving Bequia, the charter boats and Daphne's far astern.

The wind continued to strengthen, almost dead astern. In an hour or two, we were down to our gaff stormsail and the tiny storm jib. With sheets, booms, guys and vangs holding both sails firmly in place, *The Aegre* powered westward under the control of the wind vane. A white rolling bow wave swept out on either side of us.

Down below, we quickly adapted to a very different style of living from that in Bequia. It was like being on an express train, rocketing along on rails, swaying from side to side, but regularly crossing a rough patch. With a roar, the boat would lurch, catch herself, lurch again, pause momentarily, then sweep off again, accelerating down the next wave. It was a rude re-introduction to the way of the sea. Julie wrote of going into *a haze of being sick, 6 times so far. Even N has been sick 3 times which is unusual for him.*

All night we stormed along. The dawn showed us to be far out in a wild, windswept empty sea with no easing of the conditions looking likely. We settled in for the voyage. It wouldn't take long at this speed.

I steadily tracked our course westward across the northern coast of Venezuela, a few hundred miles to our south. We were now doing 100 nm a day, the boat roaring along hour after hour. At night we continued to take four-hour watches, although it wasn't necessary to be on the helm. We resumed the most comfortable position on watch, lying curled up on the cabin floor beneath the open hatch, facing aft. A compass now mounted in the cabin enabled us to watch the course without moving, and the small radio receiver at ear level allowed us to listen to world radio news via the aerial up a side stay, without disturbing the person asleep.

Every so often, we would stand up and look around outside. Huge swells were coming up from astern and often partly breaking as they swept past. It was usually dry on the deck astern, but now an occasional breaking top would come roaring down and across our stern, water pouring into the tiny cockpit. We put half the washboards in across the forward side of the cockpit, kept pumping the bilges, and held our course and speed.

We should have put all the washboards in. That might have saved the radio, which drowned one black night when a bigger than usual wave came flooding in from aft. We didn't miss the news much, but we did miss our regular time checks with WWV, and without them we were forced to rely on our not-to-be-trusted old watch and dead reckoning position fixes. But we were nearly there, a bit off the coast of Colombia, with only about 100 miles to go to Panama. By now we could also see a growing number of ships around us, all on a parallel course to ourselves.

The stress of the wild conditions and speed of the boat wore us down, Julie writing on 25 February, after a 120 nm day said; *How I hate it all. Everything wet. Well, the bed's only damp so far. I cried and cried which made N be kind and cheery whereas he was cross before. The self-steering isn't working too well and the compass is 15° off. Things aren't looking too good.*

If anything, the wind freshened as we headed south-west to close with the Panama coast in the dark. First the loom, then the light itself of the Toro Point lighthouse off Christobal/Colon, the city at the northern end of the Panama Canal. We were on course.

Having the chart 'Approaches to Christobal/Colon', I could plot our progress carefully. We sailed along the jungle-clad north coast of Panama all day, eventually turning south into the relative calm of Limon Bay, the natural harbour at the northern end of the Canal. We had sailed 1,200 nautical miles in 11 days. It was the fastest and wettest passage *The Aegre* would make.

Soon an industrial-looking US Coastguard Harbour Authority launch was towering over us in the grey dusk, rolling in the steep swell, with instructions from their loudspeaker system to follow them. They guided us to a dreadful anchorage, totally unprotected from the wind with ominous-looking mangrove swamps immediately to leeward, a heavy cross-swell, and half a mile downwind of the Yacht Club and marina. In the twilight, we anchored close to a solitary yacht, *Lute Song II*, which we knew from Bequia. It was a welcome friendly presence in this bleak anchorage.

Feeling very uneasy and worrying about everything, we made dinner. Would the anchor drag before the morning? If it did, would we be able to get under sail again before we hit the mangrove swamp? I rowed out a second anchor. Would we be able to row upwind against the steep chop the mile or more to the Yacht Club, Port Authority and (semi) civilisation the next day? How were we going to get through the Canal without an engine? How quickly could we get out of this terrible place? Thoughts to sleep on as we prepared to leave the Atlantic for the Pacific.

All night the boat pitched to the steep short chop, the strong onshore wind whistling in the rigging. I kept waking up to look out of the hatch into the night, using the hand-bearing compass to check our position. Were our anchors dragging? Every sailor's nightmare. The mangrove swamp directly downwind seemed ever closer in the darkness.

A grey morning revealed a vast grey-brown featureless anchorage. Cursing, I checked my canvas serving on the anchor warps for chafe before lowering our lovely Avon dinghy back into the water. Then, with Julie in the stern, I set out to row the mile or more dead upwind across Limon Bay to the far distant city of Colon, the waterside yacht club and hopefully some form of civilisation.

It was hot and humid when we eventually arrived at the dock to be confronted by an armed, heavily built security guard with reflecting sunglasses. He was deeply suspicious of us, as we seemed to have rowed from over the distant horizon. Nor did we look our best, spray having soaked our one set of smarter shore-going clothes.

'Whatdaya got in the bag?' he wanted to know. We showed him our wet oilskin tops.

I don't think it was my smooth-talking that won the day, but probably Julie's, possibly aided by her wet T-shirt. He allowed us to land.

Fortunately, the Yacht Club bar was nearby and packed, even though it was only mid-morning. Here we quickly met up with a few other cruising yachties who delighted in telling us horror stories of small yachts breaking loose in the lock turbulence and being smashed against the lock walls or crushed by a freighter in the confines of a lock. But we found some friendly faces, other yachtsmen we had met along the way. One of these was particularly pleased to see us too. Singlehander Tom Blackwell, whom we had met in Funchal, had recently arrived aboard his 55ft ketch *Islander* and immediately invited us to transit the Canal lashed alongside his boat. It would suit him, as he needed four line handlers when passing through the locks (to help hold the yacht still in each lock).

His transit of the Canal was scheduled for a week later. It was a deal, and with his help, we arranged for *The Aegre* to be 'measured' by the canal authorities to determine the fee for transit. Soon an official came on board to measure *The Aegre*, and he estimated us as 2 tons displacement. At 72 cents a ton, our passage would cost just $1.44.

We had a few more days to wait and put the time to good use, first moving *The Aegre* to a mooring adjacent to the marina close to the Yacht Club. From there we went grocery shopping, adding 70 lbs (32 kg) of rice to our stores for the Pacific and I rescued a parrot from drowning.

Julie wrote about it in her diary: *We had just returned exhausted from shopping and were unloading the dinghy to the boat when Nick noticed a strange commotion in the water. It seemed to be something green, and alive, which was desperately trying to stop itself drowning. The buzzards were circling overhead in the midday sun.*

Being a true Englishman, and not liking to see animals suffer, Nick grabbed the oars and went to investigate. As he drew near, he ascertained it was a parrot, and it was indeed struggling for its life. It was really grateful for Nick coming to rescue it and immediately that Nick got near enough, climbed up the paddle and squatted on Nick's shoulder, real Long John Silver style.

Nick has always been keen to have a parrot on board, as he is a great talker, and would enjoy being able to talk without my constant interjections. However, I am rather afraid of birds, and always insisted that The Aegre *was too small and too wet to carry any pets on. Now it looked as though Nick had God on his side.*

'He seems a pretty tame sort of parrot' I ventured, 'Perhaps it's escaped from one of the other yachts.' We both vaguely remembered seeing a couple of parrots on board a Brazilian schooner that we had tied up to while being measured [for the Canal]. Reluctantly Nick rowed off with the parrot and very quietly tapped on the side of the schooner. 'You haven't by any chance lost a parrot have you?' the swarthy chap cast a glance up forward to where the parrot cages were. 'Oh yes dammit! He's undone his cage again! Thanks very much for returning him.'

I breathed a sigh of relief when Nick returned alone, wishing that he hadn't been born with a conscience.

Apart from being on-hand to save drowning parrots, we used the yacht club's showers and washing machines and collected our mail waiting for us there. We were so grateful. Feeling wonderfully clean and refreshed, we sat in the Club's bar, drinking coffee and reading our letters aloud to each other, excitedly hearing all the news from our families and friends in faraway England and Scotland.

More seriously, we needed to address our navigation equipment problems. Firstly, we needed to get our little radio receiver repaired. It required seven new transistors. With no chronometer, the radio's failure had highlighted our dependence on it for time signals and thus longitude. The radio would be critical for our long westward trans-Pacific passage. But what if it got wet again? Should we carry a spare? Tom Blackwell suggested we look for an accurate Bulova Accutron wristwatch like his to serve as a chronometer. This was the most accurate watch of the time, and he was pretty sure we'd get one at a reasonable price in the Panama duty-free zone.

We had a problem with our main compass as well. This had been given to us by the Ridgways back in Scotland, but it had leaked much of the alcohol the compass plate floated in and become nearly unusable. We refilled it, but something went wrong and the screen became near opaque. It would have to be replaced. Again, our best hope seemed to be in the duty-free zone of Panama City. With a few days spare before transiting the Canal, we nervously planned a shopping trip there. Its dangers were legendary. Fortunately, Tom Blackwell, an ex-Navy man, knew his way around the city and needed to visit the city for some business of his own, With him, feeling fresh-faced and naïve, we took a train from Colon to Panama and found the duty-free zone with his guidance and advice. There we did buy both an Accutron watch (US$80) and a second-hand small boat compass ($72). Navigationally, now, I felt equipped for the Pacific. Somehow, we got back on the train without being mugged, but even Tom couldn't shield us from the approaches of the many 'ladies of the night'.

Back aboard *The Aegre*, we prepared for the Canal transit, borrowing fenders, sorting out all our spare lines, stowing everything securely and generally making her shipshape. Then it was off for the passage through the Canal. We lashed *The Aegre* alongside *Islander* and met the canal company pilot assigned to us and some additional 'line handlers' Tom had recruited, comprising three American couples living in the Canal Zone who welcomed the opportunity to pass through.

Two line handlers are required at each end of the boat to keep taut the line between their part of the vessel, and the side of the lock, as the water level rises or falls. There are giant whirlpools, back eddies and even standing waves in these 33 metre (108-ft) wide by 320 metre (1,050-ft) long locks as they rapidly fill and empty. If a boat is not held firmly on each side and fore and aft, it can crash uncontrollably around the lock. The danger is complicated by other vessels in the lock, usually huge ships which tower over a yacht. We'd all heard stories of boats being crushed and lost.

Soon we were off and headed for the entrance to the first huge Gatun lock, three of which would raise us to the height of Gatun Lake. We would be sharing it with a large freighter.

Once inside the lock, strong ropes from each corner of *Islander* were secured to the dock. The gates behind us closed, and then approximately 101,000 cubic metres of water rushed into the lock in 8 minutes, raising us 70ft. There was wild turbulence all around us. Each line handler continually tightened their line as we rapidly rose up the black stone walls of the lock, keeping the yacht securely in place. Then the gates ahead were opening, and we motored forward a short distance into the next lock. And so on, passing through three locks to reach the level of Gatun Lake.

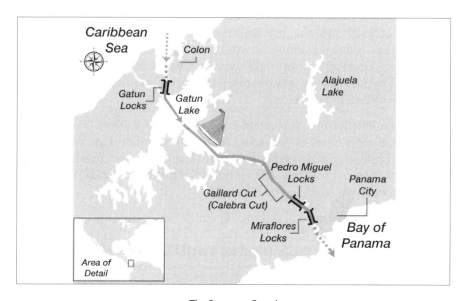

The Panama Canal

Motoring across Gatun Lake (a flooded jungle), our line handler friends unpacked and served a sumptuous picnic lunch of cold meats, chicken, salads, home-made cakes, soft drinks, ice and cold beer. What a feast after our diet of protoveg curry, crackers and cheese. Life was good.

Then we passed out of Gatun Lake into the narrower Chagres River, and on into the infamous 12.6 km (6.8 nm) Gaillard Cut. This artificial valley cuts through Panama's Culebra Mountain ridge (the continental divide). The Cut was a French venture led by Ferdinand de Lesseps (who had developed the Suez Canal) in 1881. It was an attempt to build a sea-level canal linking the Atlantic and Pacific. However, disease, underestimation of the problem and financial difficulties led to its abandonment in 1904. The US took over and redesigned the Canal to be elevated and use locks, thus enabling the Cut to be shallower. It was eventually completed and opened in 1914.

Aboard *Islander*, we passed through the Cut in less than an hour to reach the Pedro Miguel lock, which lowered us 31ft (9.5-m) to the Miraflores Lake. A short passage, then through the two Miraflores locks, which dropped us a further 54ft to the level of the Pacific. Then we motored out under the great Las Americas Bridge and into the Pacific, or at least to the Balboa Yacht Club. A Club launch was expecting us and guided *Islander* and *The Aegre* to separate moorings off the Club. We'd made it. *The Aegre* was in the Pacific. Suddenly Scotland seemed an awfully long way away.

The sea was different. On the Caribbean side, there was minimal tidal rise and fall and the water was warm at 27°C (80.6°F). However, over on the Pacific side, it was the opposite, with 18ft tides and very chilly water (sometimes as low as 16°C (61°F) due to the Humboldt current bringing cold water from Antarctica up the west coast of South America. It was also quite calm (after the constant wind of the Caribbean). There was almost no wind at all. That would make our departure tricky. From our mooring, we could see a long narrowish channel marked by stakes, leading out of the bay southwards, disappearing into a hazy horizon. It was glass-like, with hardly a ripple on it.

There was little further preparation needed aboard *The Aegre*. We noted the high and low water times in the Yacht Club for the next few days. We'd need to leave at the beginning of the ebb tide if we were to get clear of the coast by nightfall. We planned to leave a few days later, on the 14th March 1974. The ebb would start to flow at about 6 am. We'd need to be on it.

We sent a final postcard and an aerogram to our parents, giving them our next destination to which they could write: 'Poste Restante, Taiohae, Nuku Hiva, Marquesas Islands, South Pacific (expected arrival May 1974 — please hold)'.

Then we set about preparing *The Aegre* for the sea.

Chapter 15
4,000 miles in 21 feet

*'To know the laws that govern the winds, and to know that you know them,
will give you an easy mind on your voyage round the world; otherwise
you may tremble at the appearance of every cloud'* — Joshua Slocum

Singlehander Tom Blackwell sailed from Balboa two days before us, on the 12th of March, heading out west into the Pacific aboard his big ketch *Islander*. Julie and I waved him off; he had become a great friend.

'Good luck, Tom. See you in Nuku Hiva. We should be there some time in May.'

He too was headed to the Marquesas, 4,000 nm to the WSW. Conservatively, he expected to make the passage within 30 days in his large, powerful yacht.

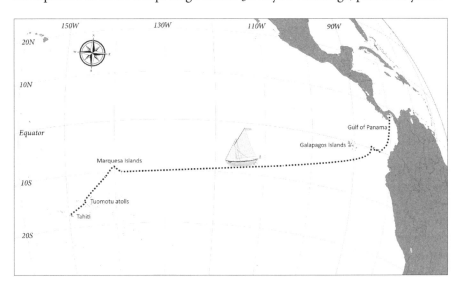

The South Pacific

At first light on Thursday, 14 March 1974, we let go of the mooring off the Balboa Yacht Club ourselves, off on a longer passage than we could possibly have imagined back in Scotland.

I was in awe of the voyage ahead of us. This was no cruise down to the south of England, nor a winter's outing to the West Indies and back. Ahead of us, the Pacific seemed almost boundless. The only land was tiny specks on the chart. Anticipating the long voyage, every tank, bottle and saucepan we had was full of fresh water, and every cranny in the boat was filled with supplies. We had food for a hundred days, spare line, sailcloth, paint, kerosene, lime juice, fishhooks, charts, torch batteries, extra timber, and more. We had little room to move below.

With an almost imperceptible breath of wind in our sails giving us steerage, we edged away from the yacht club anchorage and into the adjacent channel to the open sea, where the tide was starting to ebb. Then, with just enough steerage to hold ourselves in the marked channel, the tide slowly swept us out. One by one, we laboriously counted down the numbered poles marking the channel, some capped by a watching pelican. Finally, the last pair, No. 1 and 2. Ahead the horizon shimmered in the near windless heat. It had taken hours. Our only companion was a small freighter that slowly passed us, heading out. It was as if we were already in the vast and lonely Pacific.

The distance to the Marquesas wasn't the only problem. As already mentioned, for most of the year, there is little or no wind in the Gulf of Panama. Moreover, the north-going Humboldt current sweeps up the west coast of South America, bringing cold water from the south through and past the Gulf of Panama, pushing a vessel north.

Far to the south-west of Panama lies the band of south-easterly trade winds. These could blow us all the way to the Marquesas. But first we had to reach them, traversing this windless area and stemming the current that would inexorably push us north, the opposite of the direction we needed to go.

A further complication was the Galapagos Islands, 907 nm (1680 km) south-west from Panama, but still in the near windless zone. We'd like to have gone there to see the wildlife and top up our food and water, but the controlling Ecuadorian Government was discouraging yachting visitors with costly and long-delayed visas and rumours of confiscating visa-less yachts. We abandoned the idea of deliberately going there, but worried that the current might sweep us into the islands anyway in the windless conditions.

Drawing on the pilot charts given to us by Alex Bell in Grenada and showing winds and currents by month, we put together a plan and course to reach the SE trade winds far to the south-west, aiming to pass south of the Galapagos. We initially picked up a light northerly, making reasonable speed south. Six days later, we were just 30 miles north of the Equator, almost due south of Panama and about the same latitude as the Galapagos Islands out to the west. No problem, we thought.

Then edging out to the south-west, out of the shelter of the South American continent, we met the north-going Humboldt current. Despite sailing a south-south-westerly course, we could not make any more way south. The wind fell away, and we had to use every little flutter to keep the boat moving across a mirror-flat sea. Each day I checked our latitude, only to find we were still about 30 miles north of the Equator but were being steadily pushed west, towards the Galapagos.

Then the wind died altogether, and we were left moving in fits and starts, unwillingly crabbing our way westward towards the Galapagos Islands.

A whole week passed. Day after day, our situation worsened. Near stationary in the water in the blazing heat as the sun passed directly overhead, there was no shade on deck. The one on watch wore our large straw sunhat and a shirt soaked in seawater. Meanwhile, the Humboldt current was sweeping us towards the Galapagos. Was it our fate to be wrecked there? Fined for illegally landing, our boat confiscated, and us deported? It would be an inglorious ending to *The Aegre* voyage.

Mostly there was no discernable breeze, and we greeted the slightest ripple from the bow as a godsend. Now far offshore, I would shoot the sun every noon and then announce if we had made any effective way south over the last 24 hours. We crossed the Equator at least three times, only for the current to push us back north as the faint breeze fell overnight.

Periodically the eerie silence of the still ocean was broken by the sound of breaking water, like the rapids in a river. It was most disturbing, and we'd look all around and out to the flat horizon for the cause. Then we'd notice an area of disturbed water, quite distinct in the oily flat ocean. If we were creeping forward, we would sometimes slowly pass by or through such a patch of small waves breaking on each other. We believe they resulted from an upwelling of the north-going cold Humboldt Current water meeting with the warm water of the weakly opposing south-going warm equatorial current.

Mostly the water seemed icy cold, but it was full of brown jelly-like blobs of life, an ocean of minestrone soup. With just nine inches of freeboard, we observed it closely.

My light-weather sailing skills improved. Leaning over the side, I would dip my finger in the water, looking for the slightest ripple. Fortune favours the brave, as Ridgway would say. We held our nerve and our course to pass south of the Galapagos. It paid off, and inch by inch, we worked our way out of the windless Gulf of Panama.

It took us three weeks of night and day attention. Then, slowly but unmistakably, we started to feel the gentle cooling arms of a breeze. Firstly from the north-east, gathering us up, easing into our mainsail, and gently heeling *The Aegre*, the bow lifting a little and then the first gentle *shhhhh* as we eased through a wave, breaking the silence of the almost still ocean. We were on our way again and soon crossed the Equator for the last time, sailing south-west.

In her diary Julie wrote of it: *Wondering how to celebrate Crossing the Line, obviously shaving of heads and tarring is out — We could trim our hair a bit though. We celebrated by having tin of apricot juice — Delicious! — corned beef, potatoes (last) and tin of peas followed by peaches. Not so bad!*

Over hours, then days, the breeze slowly strengthened; ripples turned to wavelets, then to waves, and the wind moved slowly to the south-east. We hardly spoke lest we frighten it away. We set a course to head well south of the Galapagos, to the heart of the trade wind belt that we hoped would take us thousands of miles west. But then, most strangely, we found *The Aegre* wouldn't, or couldn't, sail on that course. Even with the rudder as far over as possible, she just wouldn't turn off the wind. Not only that, but she was sailing so slowly. There was something awfully wrong with the boat, and we still had thousands of miles to go.

Maybe we had snagged some fishing nets or lines and were dragging them through the water? Maybe a huge thick plastic bag was snagged on the rudder? Strapping a diving mask on, I leant over each side as far as I could and scanned the boat underwater. I saw, and felt, a thick growth of gooseneck barnacles below the waterline. We'd only been out for three weeks from Panama, but already they were long and luxuriant, growing by the day, encouraged, I guessed, by the nutrient-rich cold Humboldt Current in which we'd been drifting. So much for the expensive anti-fouling paint applied in Grenada.

The rapidly growing long-necked barnacles slowed us down in the light breeze to about 60 nm a day or less and made it most difficult to steer the boat. Even with the rudder hard over, *The Aegre* would now only sail across the wind, basically north or south, while we needed to sail west.

What could be causing this? Thinking long and hard, I decided that the barnacles, probably combined with all our stores aboard for this very long passage, had changed the fore and aft trim of the boat (how the boat floats in the water), which had put it out of balance with the trim of the sails (how the sails drive the boat). This was making the boat turn continually towards the wind. If so, we could retrim the boat by moving more weight towards the back and retrim the sails by adding a second headsail in front of the mast (on a makeshift bowsprit). Then, theoretically, the rudder would be able to turn the boat to sail away from the wind, rather than just across it. Then we'd be able to sail the course we needed to reach the Marquesas.

Much to our relief, my solution worked, and we could now sail in the right direction, though still slowly, due to all the barnacles. But the self-steering found it hard to hold the boat on course, particularly as the wind had become light and variable again. Increasingly we had to help the self-steering to hold the boat on course, which soon became very onerous for the watchkeeper.

Could I scrub off the barnacles? That would surely help both the steering and our speed. When we were next becalmed, I went over the side with a scrubbing brush to give the hull a clean-up. With Julie on shark watch, I donned a face mask and snorkel and set to. The water was incredibly blue and clear, and large metre-long dorado circled me menacingly. Scrub, scrub scrub. The boat was rolling a bit, and it wasn't easy. I noticed the lengthening trail of barnacle particles extending deeper and deeper out astern, disappearing into the vast blue depths, the white particles glinting in the sun as they slowly sank. Scrub scrub scrub. It was hard to concentrate with all those dorado eyes peering at me. The barnacle trail now disappeared into the distance far astern and below. Scrub scrub scrub… What if something a lot bigger than me chanced across it, opened its mouth and swam up it? Was I to be the cherry on the top of the cake?

Getting to the Marquesas slowly, suddenly seemed the more attractive option.

'I'm coming back on-board Julie!' I shouted. She was relieved to have me back on deck.

About twenty minutes later, three large whales did appear close by, quickly spotted after we heard their distinctive blow: 'Bpuffffffff.'

So most of the barnacles stayed.

Then the weather deteriorated, not into days of gales as in the North Atlantic, but short, vicious squalls. Our nights became battles with flogging sails as the squalls came sweeping in out of the blackness, forcing us to take in a reef, and then were gone. Their frequency increased, and grey skies and heavy grey seas became the norm for a week or more. At least it was warm, and a bonus was rainwater, which we collected from a polythene sheet strung across the cockpit at a gallon an hour. Together with plentiful fish, it eased the pressure on our stores.

And then I got sick. Up to now, we'd always been healthy at sea, but when we were more than 1,000 miles out from Balboa, violent spasms of pain in my stomach came on shortly after dinner one evening. I doubled over, speechless. There was no apparent cause. Julie started to monitor my pulse and leafed through our Ship Captain's Medical Manual. She eliminated appendicitis, the cruising yachtsman's nightmare, and then began to think it might be food poisoning. But Julie felt fine, and we'd eaten the same food for dinner. She made me sip seawater, and I soon vomited and felt near death. But then I started to feel better and recovered within an hour or two.

It shocked us; it was the first time either of us had been unwell. Julie decided it was food poisoning and gave everything below a thorough clean the next day. I wasn't so sure and thought the source was an insecticide spray we had on board (thanks to the Canadian Navy) which I had used below the previous afternoon to try and kill a minor infestation of little black flies that had suddenly developed below. Now I wondered if I had adequately covered the dinner plates and had eaten from the top one a few hours later, with its coating of overspray.

It was a nasty scare. We had thought we were careful with hygiene before; now we were even more so.

On Saturday 20 April, in 105° W 6° south, we celebrated reaching halfway to the Marquesas. We'd been out 38 days and sailed 2,100 miles (3,890 km). But now we had the SE trade wind and expected to complete the remaining 2,100 miles in 25 to 30 days, even with the barnacles slowing us down.

As in the NE trade winds in the Atlantic, we were now usually surrounded by fish (the barnacles probably helped). There were flying fish ahead of us, being hunted by dorado swimming alongside us, and almost a wall of skipjack tuna in the leading edge of the big blue swells sweeping up from astern. I'd learnt to spear the dorado from the cockpit, but they were almost family, and

I hated doing so. I had no such feelings for the skipjack off the stern. I'd also learnt how to catch them with a big hook and a strong line with a section of strong rubber to take the shock of these powerful fish taking the piece of a flying fish (from the deck) I used as bait. They were easy to catch but so strong they could pull the boat off course before I landed them. For weeks I caught one every other day for dinner, alternating with corned beef and rice, our favourite, alternating with Protoveg curry.

Dinner was a time for chatting and watching the sunset, one of us sitting in the cockpit helping the self-steering, the other standing in the hatch. As the light faded and the sun slowly sank into the sea, we'd watch for the mythical 'green flash' the instant it disappeared (we never saw it). We'd always chat, often reflecting on our lives and discussing the future.

'I reckon we should try and make Brisbane, Australia, by November,' I proposed, outlining my latest plan, cooked up on my watch while looking at a world chart showing world winds and sailing routes. I thought we would be able to find work in Brisbane, and then five months later, when the wind became right in April, sail north up the Great Barrier Reef, then west through Torres Strait into the Indian Ocean. We could aim to make Cape Town by November '75 and then sail north through the South Atlantic to the Azores in the middle of the North Atlantic. Then on, to be back in Britain in the summer of 1976.

It was an ambitious idea. But rolling gently across the Eastern Pacific, it seemed that the cruise from Australia onwards would be more complex and dangerous than everything so far. And at the end of it all, where would we be? Back in Britain, with its strikes, high unemployment, and energy crises. Why would we fight so hard to get back to all that?

Well, all of that was far ahead. Right now on *The Aegre*, it was dark, dinner was finished, and there was the washing up to do. Not hard with the ocean lapping at the lee rail within hand's reach. Except at night, we weren't too keen on putting our hands in the water. There were often torpedo-like phosphorescent wakes rocketing along beside us: the night presence of the large dorado fish, or maybe something larger? We kept our pinkies well inboard.

Later Julie reflected in her diary: *I've been thinking I should do some creative writing, but I don't know what and anyway I've never been very good at it. Perhaps I should try though… If I was going to write something I think it would have to be a factual thing, either about food or recipes… or perhaps I should write about something completely different, a book on love or education or how to pass the time.*

She was certainly loved, well educated, and had some practice of the latter as another night, another day, another week, another month, all passed

Slowly the weather improved as the fresh SE trade wind prevailed. Our daily averages picked up to 75 or 80 miles per day, Bob's trusty log spinning out the miles astern.

And so we sailed on.

I put the new Bulova Accutron watch chronometer and some calm, clear evenings and nights to good use by teaching myself to take and plot accurate star sights. I found it surprisingly easy in these favourable conditions. I could take consecutive sights on five stars, and with Julie recording the exact Greenwich Mean Time of each with the Bulova, I could draw five intersecting position lines on the chart. Increasingly these would cross to give me a 'cocked hat' less than 3 miles across, giving me confidence at least in my consistency, if not accuracy.

As we progressed, I showed Julie how to work out the sextant sights and plot the resultant position lines on the chart. She was good at it, of course. Next was how to use the sextant, and she was good at that too.

Looking back now, it seems extraordinary that from the beginning, I had taken responsibility for learning how to use the sextant to take sights to calculate our position at sea. I had always been poor at maths at school. It would surely have been better if Julie, who had recently studied mathematics at Warwick University, had taken this on. But this was the early 1970s. Maybe it was just a man thing? I wanted to be competent at everything — self-reliant, as it were.

But Julie had become very capable and was now quite the ocean voyager. Discussing what we might do after *The Aegre* voyage, she wondered about trying to become the first woman to sail singlehanded around the world non-stop. I was impressed by her ambition and by how capable she'd become. I thought she could do it too, but she'd need an easier boat to manage than *The Aegre*, with its awkward rigs. In truth, despite my quest for simplicity, the rig of nearly every modern yacht was probably easier to manage than that of *The Aegre*.

The stronger winds of the south-east trades and the faster speed of *The Aegre* added stress to the boat, to us and to all our equipment. We'd never imagined sailing on to the Pacific, and now things began to wear out. The seats of both our oilskins split within two days of each other, and even with gaffer tape repairs, it was impossible to remain dry in a fresh breeze or heavy rain. Salt sores developed on our buttocks, making sitting quite uncomfortable, which was mostly what we did. Rubbing in Vaseline helped, but keeping dry was the only real answer, and that was impossible. It was a sign of things to come.

Our butane blowlamp burner, used for lighting the kerosene Primus stove, failed due to unexpected (hidden) corrosion. This was a failure we hadn't anticipated. There seemed so little to go wrong with it. We had spare gas cartridges but no spare blowlamp. We switched to lighting the Primus the conventional way, preheating the vaporiser with methylated spirit, but we had very little of the latter and wanted to save it for lighting our ultra-bright Tilley lamp in case of some emergency. We searched the boat for alcohol and found a small bottle of paint thinner, a bottle of an evil vodka-like spirit someone had given us in Panama and a bottle of something else pretty strong from the Canaries. After that, it was Glenmorangie whisky from Scotland or Bob Macinnes's rum from the West Indies. We hoped it wouldn't come to that.

We reduced the use of the cooker to just once a day to make dinner. There were no more welcome cups of tea at the change of night watch. But then things got worse; on the Primus, the jet above the vaporiser started to block up so that even with alcohol preheating it, there was no guarantee it would light at all. I stripped and cleaned everything carefully, but it seemed to no avail. It became more and more unreliable. Perhaps the kerosene was dirty.

The quality of our daily life was deteriorating.

I was even having bad dreams as Julie noted; *Poor N woke up with moans and a jump last night — he was dreaming he was lying on the deck and something was going over his body poisoning him but he couldn't call out to me.*

I wasn't alone, a bit over three weeks out, Julie wrote: *Queer last night, I thought I saw a monster, head and shoulders like a man stand up out of the waves just close to the boat. Horrible. Woke N up straight away but it had gone. Also a black bird flying around the boat trying to land. Woke up N who got up but it went away. N really good not getting cross with me getting scared so easily. Birds really put me in a tizz wizz.*

The Aegre was showing signs of wear too. The fibreglass reinforcements of the mast where the boom jaws rested and where the lug spar passed across the mast showed lots of wear, as did the leather servings on the spars. The tiller and rudder seemed to have more movement than I remembered, and I worried about wear in the pintles holding it onto the hull. Around the companionway and cockpit, the paint had worn off, and bare wood was showing through. I worried that our polythene water tanks resting on the copper roves on the hull planking might develop wear and, unknown to us, start to leak. I checked them, and they seemed to be holding up well with little sign of wear, but there were traces of algae starting to grow in some of them. We dosed them with water purification tablets, courtesy of the Canadian Navy, which halted the growth but gave the water a chlorinated taint which ruined a cup of tea. Another disappointment was the chocolate bars we had bought somewhere to replace our late at night half a Mars bar treat at the change of watch. We found them mildewed, not just on the surface but inside the block. They tasted horrible. I think we threw them all away.

But the essential things seemed to be okay. The hull planking was still tight with no leaks, and the sails were showing little wear since the repairs in Bequia.

What about our own spirits and our relationship? How were they holding up? We were confined together in a living space about 3 metres long and 2 metres at its widest, 24 hours a day. We never slept for more than three hours 45 minutes at a time (separately), keeping the boat safe and sailing 24 hrs a day in all weathers. There was absolutely no privacy, and we had high daytime temperatures with little shade on deck. Our food and water were adequate but limited in variety and quantity. Underlying it all was the constant uncertainty about our security. And the passage went on and on — nine weeks, in this case.

The contributors to this stress are a given for ocean voyagers on small yachts, but are they more or less on a larger vessel with more crew and space?

Aboard *The Aegre,* we generally got on well. We had learnt that on the passage from Scotland to Madeira. If not, we'd have stopped there. We joked that we saw less of each other than a couple with 9–5 jobs. But the environment was so hostile, and there were so many dangers every day that we seemed to know we had to look after each other. We had to be kind and considerate to each other all the time and I think we were. Keeping the boat and ourselves safe at sea seemed to take all my attention and energy. Following our principle of always having one of us on watch, we almost never slept together, nor was the bunk at sea big enough for two. Somehow the boat and keeping it going, consumed everything I had.

By now, we had been living together aboard *The Aegre* for a year, the longest we had ever lived together in one place, as if this was the only life together we knew. We tried to live to John Ridgway's three principles of thinking positively, being self-reliant, and leaving things better than we found them. In general, they stood us well as a recipe for living together on the boat.

Unfortunately, I was not always as successful as I wanted to be, particularly in the thinking positively department. Increasingly, on this long passage, I wondered why we were doing it. Then I would start worrying about all the things that were going wrong or could go wrong. Accumulative exhaustion was probably a significant contributor, plus having to hand-steer much of the time and make frequent sail changes night and day to cope with recurrent squalls. I never slept for long. Trying to cope, I would retreat into myself, mumbling and distancing myself from Julie. But there was nowhere else to go.

Looking back, it seemed that the whole thing had been an enormous challenge to me up to the West Indies. Could we put together and fund an ocean-going sailing boat? Could we sail it across the Atlantic? But having done that, we had become different people. No longer adventurers sailing into the unknown, now we were (just) another couple on a boat sailing across the ocean from one port to another. I knew we could do it, even be reasonably competent at it, but it didn't seem enough. The boat was good, but too small for any comfort, and not only that, it was wearing out around us.

Exhausted, on watch alone, staring at the sea for hours or just gazing up at the stars, I would wonder what the point of it all was and where it might lead. What could we do next? Sometimes just being on the boat for weeks and weeks seemed such a waste of time.

I have never been a good actor; my emotions are always on show. Julie became lonely and felt rejected by my behaviour. She saw me on the edge of depression with all my complaining and dark looks. While I was saying the weeks at sea were pointless, she regarded them as mentally valuable. But trying to cheer me up exhausted her.

Julie took my retreat into myself personally, as a rejection of her, writing in her diary; *I got a bit weepy last night when N wanted me to hurry off to bed, didn't seem to want or enjoy my company, [he] just wanted to get back to bed himself as soon as possible.*

It came to a head when she spent most of a watch crying, which shocked us into a closer discussion than we had had for a while. She knew I was exhausted, but she needed my attention. She confronted me with the effect my behaviour had on her, which woke me up to the way I was behaving. I resolved to do better, and she promised to help me get more undisturbed sleep. We hove-to and spent a rare night together.

The next day we were both much happier. Our relationship may have become the stronger for it. Talking out about a problem always helps me, as if my brain is fed by my voice. It's the way I think about things. With the air clearing a little between us, we started to talk more about what we wanted to do next. Australia, Brisbane by November was one idea already discussed, to possibly try and complete a circumnavigation. Back to Britain? But then what?

We both had such happy memories of Ardmore that we wondered if we could return to live there and help run the Adventure School. Julie loved the place and wrote about it in her diary: *I wish there was some way we could live and work at Ardmore, that is my dream, to live in the Blue House, have children there perhaps, the atmosphere is so good there, I think we would be very happy.* But I wasn't so sure. Intuitively I wanted to go forward, not back.

I had my own ideas, which were much more bizarre, such as furthering my optics study by specialising in optical instruments and setting up a business in London to service sextants. Or maybe to stay in the Pacific and collect seashells on remote islands, package them up and ship them to my mother in Cottenham, who would start a business to distribute and sell them to flower shops all over Britain. I had even more wacky ideas that I won't embarrass myself more by sharing.

The backdrop to all our discussions was *The Aegre*, sailing steadily along, day and night, lifting up and over the swell, with a *shhhhhssss* from the forefoot, heeling a little more, then a little less, Bob's log spinning in our wake, the empty horizon of the sea all around.

About two months out from Balboa, and (we hoped) three hundred miles out from the Marquesas, we saw frigate birds, a sure sign of nearing land after the vastness of the ocean. We had been 62 days at sea since leaving Panama and had become very aware that the normal surface of this planet is not land but ocean, and of how empty of shipping much of it is.

Despite keeping a constant 24-hour lookout, we had seen only four ships since leaving Balboa. One of these had seen us and altered course, signaling us and asking if we needed help. It slowed and came steaming along parallel and quite close to us early one evening. We signaled back that we were OK and to (please) keep clear. The crew and apparently some passengers lined the rail and gave us a resounding cheer as they accelerated past and on into the distance, their light finally disappearing in the gloom of the evening. As we finished preparing for another black night, we imagined them sitting down to a three-course dinner, perhaps the only other people for a thousand miles.

Our navigation plots crawled slowly across our chart of the eastern Pacific. We were inching closer to the tiny specks that were the Marquesas. The Marquesas comprise about fifteen small islands. They are of volcanic origin and high, a number extending over 1000 metres (3,280 ft) above sea level. They are amongst the most remote islands in the world, being 2,590 nautical miles west of Mexico and 740 nm north of Tahiti. Today they are part of French Polynesia, but according to our Pilot book, the Spanish are considered the first Europeans to have visited them in their galleons en route to Manila and the Spice Islands.

Describing the islands, the Pilot Book told us: 'The islands rise abruptly from the deep ocean; there are few or no outlying coral reefs; the mountainous interior of all these islands is extremely steep, with knife-edge ridges falling away precipitously to deep, narrow, inaccessible ravines'.

Back in Grenada, Alex Bell had given us charts of the islands. They looked like props for a *Treasure Island* movie. They had been issued by the US Hydrographic Office, and most stated that they were based on 'a French survey of 1882.' They showed the outline of the coast and soundings but nothing inland except an indication of deep, narrow ravines running down to the sea. Nothing else seemed to have been surveyed. Inside the coastline, there was a complete blank.

Now approaching the island group after more than 60 days at sea and 4,000 nm, we were worried about making landfall, as there were few reliable lights or radio beacons among the islands. Just how accurate was our navigation? To maximise our chances of finding the islands we decided to head for the island of Hiva Oa, the second largest island, on the eastern side of the group and roughly in the middle from a north/south perspective, but it had no lights and no radio beacon. However it did have one safe anchorage, Taha Uku Bay, within Atuona Bay, adjacent to the largest settlement, Atuona. But this was at the western end, on the south (leeward) side of the island. If we were to sail into this, the best anchorage, in daylight, we thought we should be close to the unlit eastern end of the island, on the southern side, before dawn. Our navigation would need to be spot on.

A series of sun, star and planet sights showed that our progress matched that indicated by Bob Macinnes's ancient log, still spinning away on the end of the line, now more than 9,000 nm out from Scotland. According to my plots on the chart, we were closing with this small but still invisible island. We were experiencing little current and progressing as expected.

At midnight I confirmed the course to pass a few miles to the south of the eastern end of the island before dawn. But was it really there? There was nothing to be seen. Julie came up for her 4-hour watch, and I showed her our estimated position on the chart. We were making a consistent speed in a light sea, the boat holding a steady course. There was no moon, and it was very black, the only light coming from the sparkling phosphorescence briefly flashing from the bow wave. Projected on the chart, this course and speed would put us a mile or two south of the island's eastern end in another couple of hours. It was both exciting and nerve-racking. But I needed sleep. I lay down on the bunk, the bow wave swishing past a quarter of an inch from my ear. It sent me to sleep, as it always did.

At about 3 am, Julie called me and coming on deck, I was immediately aware of a deeper shade of blackness on our starboard (right-hand) bow. There was something there. I could just sense it in my peripheral vision. Julie could too. So, the island really did exist.

The wind was holding; the sea state was as before. We slowly sailed to the southern side of the deeper patch of darkness, which slowly turned to grey and then to green in the early dawn. Gradually, detail of the coastline emerged. At 06:30, in a methodical way that belied my excitement, I fixed our position using hand compass bearings on prominent points on Hiva Oa and the nearby island of Tahuata, now clearly visible to the south-west. We were just 1.5 miles off the southern coast of Hiva Oa. It was Sunday 19 May 1974.

It had been a long slow passage from Panama. We had been out 65 days, more than two months, during which we had sailed 4,200 nautical miles (7,779 km).

The dawn crept up to reveal a heavily forested island with sharp peaks and deep valleys just a few miles to starboard. It looked like a Disney set for a lost world. There was no sign of any life. I thought about Herman Melville's account of living on nearby Nuka Hiva Island, 'among the cannibals' in the 1840s, described in his first book, *Typee*.

We slowly sailed along the southern coast, and then, about midday turned north into Taha Huku Bay, the best anchorage adjacent to Atuona Bay, and Atuona, the main village on the island. As the bay opened up, we saw another yacht anchored there, which turned out to be *Marluva* from Grenville, USA. We sailed deeper into the bay, looking for signs of life, but there was none except for a short stone quay in the north-east corner. All around the thick forest, palms came down to the water's edge.

Now within the bay, the wind was flukey, little gusts sweeping across the water as if birds were running on the surface. Tacking *The Aegre* like the dinghy she was, we worked our way upwind to the most sheltered spot to anchor, not far from the beach, which looked like the best place to land. Then we ran out of wind completely. I paddled the boat the final metres, then let go the anchor, and eased her astern with the paddle to lay out the anchor chain.

We were still. Julie was in the cockpit, I was on the bow. We looked at each other from opposite ends of the boat, smiling, and shaking our heads a little in wonder at it all.

Julie was still holding the tiller, as we'd done for months, but then realising there was no need now, she turned and lashed it amidships while I lowered the sails to the deck, both somehow final statements that the passage was over.

After two months at sea, the silence and tranquility were like the first deep breaths a runner draws when they finally stop. We'd made it. We were safe; we could relax.

Chapter 16
The Marquesas to Tahiti

'The first experience can never be repeated. The first love, the first sunrise, the first South Sea island, are memories apart and touched a virginity of sense.' — Robert Louis Stevenson, 1896

For most travellers today, the first experience of a South Sea island will be through a busy international airport, sadly far from the experience that Stephenson wrote about between 1888–9 in an account of his travels by sea to the Marquesas, Tuomoto and Gilbert Islands.

In 1974 the Marquesas were still largely inaccessible. The only way to them was by yacht or on a small ship that visited every few months. Sailing into Hiva Oa in 1974, our first South Sea island, eighty-five years after the Stephensons, we didn't imagine Taha Huku Bay had changed all that much; its remoteness and feeling of isolation from the rest of the world remained. There were no signs of habitation in the forest coming down to the water's edge, just an isolated, empty small stone quay and one modest yacht anchored nearby.

After so long at sea, with an ever-present vast horizon, the near encircling shoreline was almost claustrophobic, the rocks frighteningly close. But its remoteness and emptiness were enchanting too. It had taken us two months of non-stop travel to get here. Few others made it this far.

It was unnatural to be so still and peaceful and surrounded by green forest. *The Aegre* gently swung to her anchor. No need to worry about the course or the wind. A wave of relief ran through me.

Bob and Sharon, the crew of *Marluva*, the other yacht anchored in the bay paddled over to welcome us, bringing fresh bananas. They were on their way to the beach to wash in a (freshwater) stream.

You might think we'd be desperate to go ashore after so long at sea. But no, rather the reverse. It seemed so comfortable lying quietly on the bunk or on the deck, dozing a little or a lot. We both seemed reluctant to leave our small world on *The Aegre*, so we justified staying aboard by agreeing that we should wait and see that the anchor was holding in the flukey wind and watch where the boat might swing. Too close to the shore, too close to Marluva? So we stayed aboard. After so long at sea, we felt nervous about leaving our precious boat and home, as if it was disloyal to leave her.

The peace was soon broken. Three happy, laughing young men came paddling out to visit us in a colourful pirogue. They enthusiastically sang to the accompaniment of a long-necked rosewood ukulele and brought bananas, coconuts, mangoes, limes, pamplemousse (huge yellow to pink-fleshed grapefruit-like but sweeter), wood carvings, conch shells and the tusks of wild pigs to trade. Had the Stephensons experienced this? Maybe, but times had changed a little.

In excited French, they wanted to trade anything we had, particularly Levi jeans, .22 shells, cosmetics and condoms. We found some spare jeans and swapped them for fruit and the uke. They pointed out where to land with our dinghy beside a stream flowing from the forest across the deserted shingle beach. Nearby, they said, was a path leading over the small ridge to the village of Atuona, where the Gendarme had an office and there was a bakery. A bakery? That sounded wonderful.

But while they talked, an onshore wind sprang up, swinging *The Aegre* around on her anchor line. Now we seemed too close to the rocks. Ever fearful, I moved our anchor and added a second. Eternal vigilance is the price the cruising yachtsman must pay for freedom.

Later that afternoon we finally ventured ashore, paddling our dinghy to the shingle beach by the stream. As to be expected, after two months on the ever-moving *Aegre*, the beach came up to meet our bare feet. We walked unsteadily through coconut palms and banana plants, alive with chirping birds and mosquitoes. Hidden a little back from the beach, we found a few small houses with hens pecking around them and smelled woodsmoke. An aging Land Drover came cruising along a track driven by a young woman, who looked over and gave us a gentle smile.

That night for only the second time since Balboa, we removed the leeboard, which narrowed the bunk at sea and held the sleeper in place, thus expanding the bunk so we could sleep together. *The Aegre* was unnaturally still and quiet. Almost too quiet to sleep. I tried to relax, the prospect of sleeping an entire night before me.

But a few hours later, at about midnight, there was pandemonium. I woke to bright lights shining around us, people shouting, and the boat rocking wildly. Was it a nightmare? No, simply the arrival of a coastal trading boat, surging into the bay, searchlights ablaze, to tie up at the small stone quay near us. But there was plenty of room for us all. Soon they were secure, the lights were turned down, and we were back asleep.

Waking on an anchored yacht, the sunlight slowly moving around the cabin as the boat gently rocks, is one of the great pleasures I know. With a cup of tea, a gentle offshore breeze, all was well with the world. Julie was up already, sitting on deck facing the island in the sunshine, writing her diary: *I'm sitting in the sunshine on the foredeck, the sun has just come up from behind the hill... the mountain is quite stunning, one very sharp ridge, a spine, running up the whole length of it. I don't think we've seen the top yet, always covered in cloud.*

Going ashore that next day, we were alone on the beach. We took the beaten earth track over the low ridge into the village of Atuona feeling conspicuously tall, blonde, and obviously strangers. We soon found the Gendarme's little office and were quickly cleared through the formalities, thanks to Julie's French.

Atuona was relatively undeveloped: smiling, friendly people, a shop that sold everything, a tiny bakery, a school, a church, and a scattering of small wooden houses. No hotels, cafés, restaurants, fast food or bars, just dirt tracks with one or two vehicles, but it was the largest settlement on the island and had the essentials we needed: fresh bread, fruit, onions, a new bowl, methylated spirit and prickers for the Primus. With Julie's French, we quickly found everyone welcoming and friendly. They didn't get many visitors, and time didn't matter much.

Julie has the knack of being able to talk with anyone anywhere. Soon she was chatting to Antoinette, who had a baby and lived with her husband Maurice and their hens in a little thatched cottage in the trees at the back of the beach we were anchored off. Antoinette invited us for lunch the next day to meet Maurice.

That afternoon we gorged on fruit and fresh bread, then followed a twisty path rising through the forest, past women in a clearing laying out coffee beans to dry in the sun, to Gauguin's burial place, high above Atuona.

We sat peacefully and alone in the small cemetery, looking out to the south in the silence, over the vast empty Pacific, disappearing into blueness, the sea and the sky becoming one.

Sitting quietly, I reflected that out of all the places in the world, Gauguin chose to stay here, in Hiva Oa, for the rest of his life and remain forever. It was ethereal, even to us.

I turned to Julie. 'How about we stay here forever?' I don't recall her answer, but I suspect she wasn't so keen.

The next day we visited Antoinette and met Maurice and his brother Adrian, the local carpenters. We noticed they had more modern woodworking equipment in their workshop than Bob Macinnes back in Scotland.

Lunch was a feast of delicious wild boar stew, fish, rice, oranges and bananas. They told us of going pig hunting in the forest every week and showered us with fresh fruit: bananas, limes, mangoes, pamplemousse, the large and wonderfully refreshing grapefruit of French Polynesia, and more.

Julie gave Antoinette some perfume and received coconut oil scented with put-a-te flowers for her mosquito bites, she had more than a hundred, forty on one foot.

We enjoyed the foreignness of being ashore, but as ocean cruising people, our eyes were often out to sea and quick to spot another vessel even in the far distance, particularly out here, where there were so few. One such vessel to appear on the horizon turned out to be a black replica Chinese junk about 45ft (14m) long, called simply *Junk*. She motored into our little anchorage one day flying a British Red Ensign, so of course, we went to visit. An Australian woman, Terry, and her US partner Tom had built *Junk* out of ferro-cement in the late sixties and had lived aboard for nearly three years. Down below, where the hold might have been, was an enormous open saloon with a deep carpet and big soft cushions. The floor featured a large glass window to the ocean below. The engine room was bigger than the entire *Aegre*. The only drawback, they said, was that it was hard work steering when sailing and that the boat wouldn't steer herself, so at sea, they hove to every night. We envied them rather like cycle tourers might envy a giant Winnebago. Or not.

Only one other yacht came into the bay while we were there, and she was very different. *Sartori* was a Cal 46, glossy white and modern. Owned and sailed by Cal Yachts owner Jack Jensen, we heard from the crew of *Marluva*, who couldn't believe we'd never heard of either. Apparently he was the premier glass fibre yacht manufacturer in California, and Cal Yachts' founder. They spoke of him in hushed tones.

We met Jack, his wife Nancy and crew David Samuelson (English) and Doreen (French) outside the Chinese bakery the next day. We were sitting in the shade, whiling away the time until the bread finished baking, as you might do on a remote South Sea island. Having worked out that we were from the little *Aegre* anchored near them, Jack and Nancy were full of questions about our voyage and quickly invited us to *Sartori* for dinner. There was something to be said for having the most unlikely boat in the bay.

And then the bread was ready. We bought ten small loaves for 200 francs (which wasn't much), and they were so delicious we ate most of them walking back over the ridge to *The Aegre*.

Jack, Nancy, David and Doreen were most welcoming that evening. I pretended ignorance. After all, we came from the north of Scotland, perhaps the Nova Scotia of North America.

'Lovely yacht, Jack,' I said over dinner. 'And how do you earn a crust?'

'Nick, I sell people what they want, not what they need. They need a new washing machine, but they want a new yacht. I help them with that.' A response I've always remembered.

Enough of the socialising. There was work to be done on *The Aegre*. First, I had to scrub off all the long goose-necked barnacles growing on the bottom. There was no slipway here, so I went over the side with a face mask and snorkel and scrubbed. At least there were no dorado watching me here, and we hoped no sharks. But the barnacles were big, healthy and firmly attached. It was hard work. Meanwhile, Julie did an inventory of all our stores.

Next was a more permanent bowsprit to replace the temporary one I'd built south of the Galapagos. Antoinette's husband, the carpenter, had a most suitable piece of timber, and his price was reasonable, but our cash was almost gone, and there'd be no more until we reached Tahiti and a bank, 770 nautical miles away. At least we still had lots of food on *The Aegre*.

Perhaps Hiva Oa was just too quiet and peaceful for us, for the itch to sail on came back, to visit Nuku Hiva, the main island of the Marquesas, 148 nm to the north-west. That was where we'd told our parents and friends to send letters. We said goodbye to Antoinette, who gave us 18 mangoes and a letter for her friend in Nuku Hiva and another for her mother on the island of Ua Pou, and then headed out.

Back at sea, everything seemed wonderful to me. The sea was blue, the wind firm, steady and warm. Here we were, sailing in the Marquesas in the sunshine. *The Aegre*, relieved of her barnacle colony, was heeling in the wind, riding up and over the swells, the first spray coming over the bow, the self-steering holding us on a steady course. Receding astern was the ever-changing view of Hiva Oa.

But Julie didn't share my enthusiasm. In her diary she wrote: *Hated every minute of it at first but am now getting used to it again.* Maybe I was a little over-enthusiastic and carrying perhaps too much sail, as the boat was heeling a bit more than usual, and the motion was a bit much for her as we crested the big swells of the south-east trades. Julie just wanted to be somewhere else, anywhere but here. She went below to have a sleep. Slowly she got used to it again, but I wondered if this was the beginning of her disillusionment with it all.

With the clean hull, we made good speed and sailed into Taiohae Bay, Nuku Hiva, late the next afternoon, Sunday 26th May. Quickly out to meet us sailing in was Tom Blackwell, the solo sailor, aboard *Islander*. Tom said he'd been watching for *The Aegre*'s tan sails every day for weeks. We soon learnt the sorry tale of his passage from Panama, how a midnight rigging failure 1,000 miles out into the Pacific had broken his topmast and some of his ribs and led to his subsequent unexpectedly slow 57-day sail to Nuku Hiva. He'd expected to find us already there and became increasingly worried by our non-appearance. He thought we must surely be in trouble somewhere, out there in the tens of thousands of square miles of the Eastern Pacific.

The anchorage off Taiohae was wide open and rather unsheltered. It was bleak compared to our Atuona anchorage, and relatively crowded with eleven yachts. Apart from Tom, there were two other voyagers from England, a middle-aged couple, Jeff and Frankie Clarkson, on *Pilecap*, perhaps one of the most misplaced yachts ever. She was a 28ft hard chine twin keel Yachting World design, that would have been completely happy bobbing on a mooring off Bideford in Devon and used twice a year, once for a fishing competition and once on the kid's birthday. But here she was anchored in Taiohae Bay, Nuku Hiva, a faded Red Ensign proclaiming her nationality. Jeff and Frankie had sailed from Appledore in Devon by way of Panama and Alaska. 'Alaska?' we said, surveying the unambitious yacht and elderly couple. They had taken the direct route from Panama, via San Diego ignoring the usual sailing ship route out into the Pacific. They agreed there had been little wind and that the 100 day voyage had dragged on a bit. And the name? '*Pilecap*?' we said, 'That's an unusual name for a yacht.'

'Yes, well, we publish technical manuals, and we've just finished a rather large and lucrative set for a nuclear reactor pilecap. We're having a little break.'

A little break? Sailing across the Atlantic and Pacific via Alaska? Not surprisingly, they were doing a 'little' fishing from their boat while at anchor and had just caught a hammerhead shark. So there was no swimming there for the moment.

We were soon off ashore to visit the post office. Taiohae seemed like a frontier town, scratching out a living from visiting boats since the whalers of Herman Melville's day, with bars and tourist prices. Unlike gentle Atuona, it had a main street, a prominent general store, a post office and a gendarmerie. We quickly cleared again at the latter and headed for the post office. Would there be any mail waiting for us in the poste restante? Hurray, there was including a letter from Julie's mother enclosing a pound note for coffee and cakes, but as Julie noted *there were no cafés here*. We quickly sent a telegram to our parents saying we'd arrived safely and bought envelopes and stamps for the long diary-like letters we'd written on the passage across the Eastern Pacific.

Perhaps it's difficult for sailing voyagers today to imagine an ocean sailing world without email or satellite phones, one where the only communication with family and friends is via expensive, short and cryptic telegrams or mail sent to distant poste restante counters in remote post offices which, due to the vagaries of the weather, may never actually be visited. A letter can take many weeks to be delivered, if it's delivered at all. It was a time when an ocean voyager was truly alone once they set sail on an ocean passage. If difficulties arose, well, you just had to cope with them yourself.

Whilst long looked forward to, visiting the post office was often an anticlimax. Hoped-for letters from home would be missing, and those waiting for us often seemed to disappoint me somehow. Half the message would be about how bad the mail service was, how long letters took, and letters lost. I'd want news from home, only to find I wasn't interested in how the garden was growing and realised that nothing much had happened there at all. Perhaps because I felt that so much had happened to us, lots should have happened at home too, but of course, it hadn't. As if I was homesick for a place I didn't want to go back to anyway.

So it was now, my disappointment at the post office feeding a general sense of disillusionment. Here we were in Nuku Hiva, the dream destination of the Pacific for sailing voyagers, and all I could see was a dusty frontier town only interested in taking our money. I wondered why I couldn't be satisfied and enjoy the moment. It seemed ironic that Julie was disillusioned on going back to sea, I on returning to land.

But part of our reality was that we had exhausted our cash. We still had the remains of the Barbados gift from my parents, but this was in our bank in Scotland. We planned to have it sent to us via a bank in Tahiti but had misjudged how much we needed along the way, particularly in Panama, where we had bought the Accutron and replacement compass. Now we had little money left on the boat.

Nevertheless, I'm disappointed we didn't make more of being there. Now I've come to understand that visits to out-of-the-way places like this are never repeated, that I'll never be back and should use the opportunity, but at 23, that idea wasn't in my mind. How could it be?

As before, our focus was still on the journey, not the destination or the stops along the way. Taiohae was like other popular yacht cruising stopovers where it seemed the local people knew the yacht people wouldn't be around for long. Their only interest was in selling them something or buying something from them otherwise unobtainable locally.

By now, I understood that for the cruising sailor living out on the harbour, the neighbours are not locals but other voyagers, with whom they share some kinship. They are different from land people. They've seen the dark days, the violent squalls at 2 am, the whales spouting. Some have seen the albatross and the southern or northern lights. All have known the solitude of the deep ocean, the freedom of 1,000 miles of open sea ahead. And that's where they feel at home.

So Nuku Hiva went unexplored by us, and with Antoinette's letter delivered, we sailed on to one last stop in the Marquesas, Ua Pou, to deliver a second letter from Antoinette, this one to her mother.

Ua Pou is a small island only 35 nm south of Nuku Hiva, hardly far enough for Julie to get seasick. Soon we could see the mountain spires of the island ahead. It didn't look far, so we kept the full rig up, and *The Aegre* was hard pressed. By late morning, we were into the shelter of the cliffs on the island's western side and then sailed into Haka Hetau Bay at about noon.

The hills around the bay were completely forested like Hiva Oa, but rather than rising to steep ridges, the backdrop on Ua Pou is a series of spectacular perpendicular basalt pillars that rise almost sheer to more than 1,000 metres (3,280 ft), the highest in the Marquesas.

We anchored, dropped the sails to the deck and were soon visited by cheerful local boys in another colourful pirogue, wanting to trade, just as in Hiva Oa. In those days, few yachts called there. We didn't have much left to trade, and the boys really wanted alcohol, which we neither had much of nor were happy about supplying.

But the boys were friendly and invited me to come spearfishing with them on a nearby reef. Julie didn't want to come. She wasn't much of a swimmer, but nor was she happy about my going off with them and taking our precious dinghy, being worried about my safety and the dinghy's. Unsurprising, as we'd hardly been out of each other's sight for a year.

The boys took me to the most fantastically coloured coral reef, with many fish of every imaginable colour, shape and size. I had never seen anything like it, nor have I since.

Part of the deal with the boys was playing on their side in a soccer game the next day. Everyone, including me, was barefoot on the rough pitch. They soon discovered I was hopeless, being quite unfit after a year on *The Aegre*. Having no soccer skills didn't help. I was far outclassed and I'm sure a great disappointment to them. In hindsight, I was lucky not to injure myself.

Meanwhile, Julie delivered Antoinette's letter via the local primary school teacher, who invited her back to his house to meet his wife and have a shower. She returned to the boat, bringing beautifully juicy oranges and pamplemousse from their garden.

We'd only visited three of the Marquesas Islands and now talked about sailing north to the uninhabited island of Eiao, 50 nm north of Nuku Hiva. There are legends of Spanish treasure buried there. But our Pilot Book wasn't encouraging, warning of unsheltered anchorages and changeable conditions. Ashore the landscape seemed steep and uninviting, though there were thousands of wild sheep. It seemed like one of the few remaining 'desert islands' left in the world, and a part of me wanted the challenge of going there. But common sense, or laziness, or perhaps just the mythical allure of Tahiti led us to decide to sail south from Ua Pou, not north.

Tahiti was just 700 nautical miles to the south-west. After the long passage across the eastern Pacific, it seemed almost like a short hop, but it had a new set of hazards for us.

The direct course meant sailing through the north-western end of the Tuomoto Archipelago, a maze of coral reefs and strong currents, the final resting place of many a vessel. They comprise approximately 80 islands, mostly atolls and are the largest chain of atolls in the world, spread out over an area roughly the size of western Europe. But the actual landmass and population are tiny. Most of the atolls are uninhabited, comprising just sand bars on coral reefs. Some have palm trees growing on them. There is no natural freshwater except rain. Many of the reefs are rarely above the surface of the sea. The reefs and atolls are merely the tip of massive undersea mounts that rise from the deep ocean floor. They thus present a long underwater barrier to natural water flows caused by tides, trade winds, and the earth's rotation. As a result, strong currents flow up and down and through the reefs. These currents are known and mapped to some extent, but are known to be inconsistent and unreliable.

We faced the choice of sailing around the north-western end (the longer, safer route) or picking a course through them. Well, I wanted to see the atolls. To me, they were emblematic of the South Pacific. The tiny sandy island with a single palm tree and a shipwrecked mariner sitting forlornly beneath it, a familiar cartoon image. Did they exist? Apparently so in the Tuamotus. How could I come this far and not see one? I'm not sure if Julie was so keen, but we agreed we'd head towards the western end of the group and see how the weather was, keeping the option open of ducking through between some of the atolls.

I'd love to have had the option of visiting one of the larger atolls with both a navigable pass into the lagoon and a settlement, but it was very hazardous, and few yachts attempted it. A strong engine, a steel hull and a brave heart seemed essential prerequisites, and unfortunately, we were missing at least two of these.

We sailed out of Haka Hetau on Tuesday 4th June 1974, and headed south. Soon we felt the full force of the SE trade wind and were down to our small gaff stormsail and jib, and settling back into our sea-going routine.

We made good speed all day Wednesday and with clear skies I could fix our position with sights on the sun and stars, but then on the next day, Thursday 6th, it clouded over and the wind further increased. More spray came aboard, seeming to pass straight through our worn-out oilskins. Now with no astro sights, we were relying just on Bob's log for distance run through the water to fix our position and thought about turning more to the west to avoid the Tuamotus altogether. But a few days later, the sky cleared, and once more, I could fix our position with the sun and stars. With renewed confidence, the plan to sail through the Tuamotus was on again.

Our plan was to make a landfall on the large outlying atoll, Manihi, and positively fix our position. Then we could sail on south, aiming for the sizeable gap between the large Rangiroa atoll and the smaller Arutua. Once through the gap, we could set a course directly for Tahiti. Julie agreed it was a good plan.

Now 400 miles out from Ua Pou, we approached Manihi. It comprises a lengthy, nearly submerged coral reef, its highest point being palm trees growing at sea level. They aren't too visible from far away, especially when your eye is just 6.5 ft at best above sea level, as on *The Aegre*.

We hove-to for half the night so as not to be too close before it became light, then started sailing again with the dawn. Manihi slowly appeared on our horizon precisely as expected, the palms looking like a line of distant pinheads on the horizon. It was Sunday 9th June. We slowly approached and then sailed along its south-eastern edge, close enough to see the sandy shore and the thin line of palms, sometimes with glimpses of the lagoon behind. It was just as we imagined but somehow more remote, wild and desolate.

Then we pressed on for the gap between the Rangiora and Arutua atolls, 60 nm ahead. In the bright sunshine, I spent all my time taking sights, working them out and plotting them on the chart. The stress was exhausting me, but I couldn't sleep.

We'd found Manihi, but picking out the atoll on the horizon had been difficult. Even at a few miles, it was like a tiny 1 mm high row of short black hair-thin lines on the horizon. Now I could see it, now I couldn't. Did I imagine it? No, there it was again.

Rangiora and Arutua were 60 miles ahead, more than 12 hours sailing at our current speed. Studying the chart, I was confident we would still be well outside the gap between them at dawn the next day. But I needed to allow for both tidal flow and the current which, according to my calculation, would be flowing towards the north-west, so I carefully offset our course so although heading towards the northern end of Arutua, it would carry us into the middle of the channel.

Nervously we sailed all night. It was a cloudy evening, and disappointingly I couldn't fix our position with star sights. The wind was from the east, even with a bit of northerly in it. Behind us was a moderate swell travelling faster than the boat. Looking ahead at the backs of the swells, there was nothing to be seen of the tops of the waves breaking forward in a lazy way. In the darkness and in such a sea, I imagined being swept onto a reef without even seeing it until too late.

During my 1–5 am watch there was a little grey moonlight, but it revealed nothing to the horizon in any direction except the grey hurrying waves quietly sweeping us onward.

Annoyingly that early morning, our self-steering system wouldn't consistently hold *The Aegre* on course. I had to continually adjust the setting and watch the effect on our compass course. Then a little before 5 am and the watch changeover, it seemed to stabilise, and I ducked below and made a coffee for each of us. Then sitting on the cockpit floor by the cooker, my head below deck level, I chatted to Julie, who was waking up on the bunk.

Coffee time over, I stood up in the hatchway to wash my coffee cup over the side. Straightening up, I turned to look forward and was shocked to see a line of palm trees right ahead. What?! We were making good speed on a port tack, with a strong breeze astern and an almost following sea. How many minutes did we have before we were in the breakers on the reef and escape was impossible?

Frantically I shouted to Julie as I disengaged the self-steering and then, pushing the helm down, I brought *The Aegre* around, first across the wind, then tightening the main sheet, bringing the mainsail in hard and pointing the boat as close to the wind as she would sail. She started to make her way back against the wind and oncoming waves and away from the reef. Now we

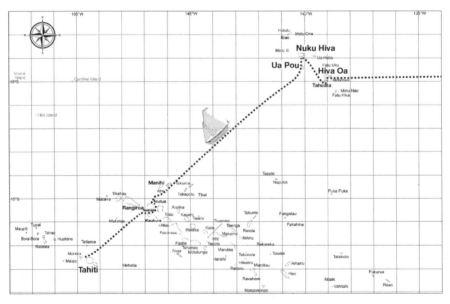

The Marquesas to Tahiti

were heeled hard over, feeling the full force of the wind. The gunwale was underwater. The sails were drum-tight and vibrating. Slowly we clawed our way back over the top of the first big swell, gathering a little speed on its back, then over the top of the next. We desperately needed to reduce sail but couldn't afford the time to stop and reef. Instead, we just had to drag ourselves offshore with the sails we had up, spilling wind to stay upright. We just had to make a bit more distance away from the reef.

One swell at a time, we did it. Dawn was breaking, giving us more perspective. We slowly realised we were probably now a good mile off and could relax a little. I tied a reef in the mainsail to bring *The Aegre* back to normal sailing. The stress on the boat and ourselves slowly diminished.

But where were we, and how had this happened?

Julie was now on the helm holding us on a steady course south-east, parallel to the reef and palm trees. The big swells were rolling in, lifting *The Aegre* high before sweeping on inwards to the coral. Ashore we could see the narrow sandy cays, with a thin line of coconut palms, and the still silvery lagoon beyond.

Far ahead of us to the south-east I could see another tiny line of palm trees extending a little to the north. I sat down on the cockpit floor, the chart board on my knees, again studying it minutely, willing it to help me see where we must be.

I went over our course of the last twelve hours and my logic in setting it. Gradually I concluded that since my last astro fix the night before we'd experienced a current diametrically opposite that which I'd predicted from the chart, so rather than sailing into the channel between the two atolls we'd sailed directly towards Aratua atoll on the eastern side of the channel.

If so, continuing to sail south-east would bring us to a channel between Aratua and the next atoll that would take us through to the open ocean on the other side of the atolls in a matter of hours. The most important thing was to be through before darkness fell. We just needed the wind to hold.

The wind eased a bit, the sun came out, and the sea and the sky turned blue. We were making good speed south-east parallel to the reef. Our spirits were lifting, but it was as if our hearts were still beating too fast, our minds still full of the disaster so narrowly averted. A lightly built wooden boat sailing at speed onto a coral reef would be quickly destroyed as the breakers swept it across the sharp coral. It would soon come to a stop, each successive wave pounding it into smaller pieces. For the crew, there would be no protection from the hard, sharp coral. In the best case, they might make it to the sandy cay, if there was one. Often there was no land above the high-water mark at all. Survival might then depend on finding a wrecked ship on the reef and scratching out some sort of a living on it until attracting the attention of another passing vessel, which might be weeks or months in the coming, if ever.

But for us now aboard *The Aegre*, the channel to the south was opening up. To the south-east we could now see growing out of the sea another low line of palm trees, which we decided was surely Apataki atoll, and if so, this must be the pass between them. We followed the reef around, sailing into the channel. In the distance ahead, we could see more tiny sticks on the horizon. We hoped this was Kaukura atoll, which marked the south-western edge of the islands.

Slowly our confidence returned as we sailed down the narrowish channel, which was bounded by small sandy islets on the reefs on either side. I must have been more relaxed because I sat on the deck eating the last of our pamplemousse and watching the little sandy islets on the reef pass by. We imagined ourselves on the 'Desert Island Discs' radio show and speculated on what music we would like to be played.

Soon we were through the channel, then past Kaukura atoll and finally out into the open Pacific. With relief in our hearts, we set a course for Tahiti, a few hundred miles to the south.

With the crisis past, we reflected on what had happened, Julie writing in her diary: *N hadn't been keeping a proper lookout after having had to steer for the first 2 hours of his watch. He was rather casual about it though, and thought it was fore-ordained that we wouldn't hit the reef that night. After the success with Manihi he had become too complacent with his navigation. Instead of being 10/11 miles off as he thought we were nearer 1 mile off!*

I thought this a little harsh, although there was some truth to it. But I didn't take it casually and, for years after, I had occasional nightmares when I relived that early morning, mainly with a different, tragic outcome.

Julie had been taking more interest in the navigation for a while and the next day she took morning sights with the sextant just after I had. Maybe she no longer fully trusted me. We plotted both, and they agreed. Julie was proud of herself, as I was, of course.

Now, with the Tuamotus behind us, it seemed that tiredness and the stress of it all had caught up with me. I became irritable, accused Julie of nagging, and withdrew into myself, mumbling and generally being objectionable. I was trying to catch fish, but the line became caught up with Bob's logline, leading to a huge tangle that tested my patience. At the same time, the wind was falling, and at dusk I had to change rigs, during which our best torch stopped working. Things weren't going well.

Julie tried to cheer me up by producing a tin of haggis from her special store, which we had with rice and peas. A pretty good effort by Julie, but it didn't help my mood much. As she wrote in her diary, *Couldn't sleep last night for crying, fed up with N getting angry at sails and torch. He wouldn't come to comfort me and eventually I was nearly hysterical. Then he did come to me till I calmed down. He let me sleep longer that night.*

Her crying shocked me out of my introspective gloom. She was just as exhausted as I with the stress of the last 36 hours when we'd come the closest yet to losing the boat.

The Aegre was sailing smoothly now, the self-steering holding her on course, and there were no hazards close by. We took some rest and comfort together, then I gave Julie a longer sleep off watch and later slept well myself, which helped my mood, and soon we were best friends again.

We sighted Tahiti's Mt Orohena, the highest peak at 2,241 metres (7,350 ft), when we were still 50 miles away, but the wind was light, and we were making only 2 knots. Painfully slow progress. But by any standard, it was delightful. *The Aegre* was sailing gently along, steering herself beneath a blue sky and warm sun, and ahead was Tahiti, the mecca of the South Pacific

We came in, guided by the powerful light on Venus Point. It was the first strong light we'd seen since leaving Balboa in March, and its bright light somehow giving an air of modernity and civilisation. It seemed like we'd been out at sea a long time.

As we neared the island that night, I felt I was coming under its spell. I was entranced to be approaching this island at the centre of the South Pacific, made so famous by Cook, Bligh and the Bounty Mutineers and so many voyagers since.

We planned to go into the main port of Papeete, which is about 8 miles to the west of Venus Point, but its harbour lies behind a coral reef with just a single narrow pass. I didn't want to try and sail through it and into the harbour in the dark, but rather to make the most of sailing in, to savour the moment of *The Aegre*'s arrival in Tahiti, the emotional and cultural centre of the South Pacific.

So instead, we closed to a few miles off the reef, where we could see street and house lights and the headlights of cars, more people than we'd seen since Balboa months before, all just going about their business. Then we turned north-west to follow the coast and lights of civilisation around towards Papeete. Soon we identified the leading lights which guided vessels through the pass in the reef and then hove to, waiting for the dawn.

As the sky in the east started to lighten that Friday, 14th June 1974, we kept a careful watch on the two leading light beacons, flashing red in the darkness. Gradually, as it became light, we could make out their red and white superstructure and fix their position relative to the town and hills.

Soon it was light. The small, low-rise town of Papeete revealed itself before us. The only sign of the outlying reef was the lazy breaking of the low swell over the coral just beneath the surface. With an eye on the leading light beacons and in a fresh morning breeze, I set the full mainsail, jib and flying jib. Then I raised the yellow quarantine flag and courtesy French flag on the side stays and set our big Red Ensign flying from the peak of the mainsail.

Thus it was, with *The Aegre* appropriately dressed, that we turned and sailed at full speed down the 85 metre-wide pass in the reef towards the harbour. Julie, wrapped in a patterned blue-and-white pareu, stood on the bow like a blonde Viking princess figurehead as we made as triumphant an entrance into Papeete, Tahiti, as any 21-ft sailing boat 11 months out of Scotland possibly could.

Chapter 17
Tahiti sojourn

'*At the pass in the barrier reef of Papeete, a genial French pilot took charge, and he secured us the best berth in the harbour. Here the coral wall that forms the beach is so sheer that it is possible to make fast to the trunk of a flamboyant [tree], as though to a bollard on a quay, and walk ashore on a gangplank- which we promptly did and dined in splendour at the best hotel.'*
— Ralph Stock, *The Voyage of the Dreamship*, Heinemann, London, 1921

S ailing in aboard *The Aegre* 55 years later, things were a little different from the way Ralph Stock found them. There was no genial French pilot to guide us through the reef (though we would have liked one and were

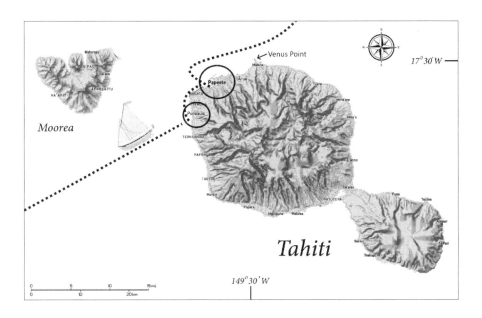

subsequently charged for one we did not have, as entering without one we found was illegal). Visiting yachts were still being berthed at right angles to the coral wall, 'stern to', with an anchor out off the bow and a gangplank off the stern to the shore; it was very convenient. But for us that day, it was a line of expensive cruising yachts, despite a busy boulevard into the city just a few metres away, making it insecure and noisy. We missed out on dinner at the best hotel too.

It was after 9 am when we made our own grand entrance. With all sails set and pulling strongly, we came in through the gap in the reef into the harbour and then along a line of about thirty cruising yachts, anchored stern to on the coral wall. With Julie on lookout on the bow, we did a smart little turn at the end of the line like the dinghy we were and came back along the line of yachts, making the most of it. We were only ever going to sail into Tahiti once. We were also looking for familiar yachts from the Marquesas, Panama, the West Indies, the Canaries and even Madeira, but there was only one, *Tahia*, a 45′ catamaran we knew from Barbados, sailed by Jim and Wendy from the UK, so we rounded up and anchored close by her.

Soon we were aboard *Tahia*, exchanging hugs all around and then sitting on their deck in the shade from the hot sun and exchanging tall tales of derring-do since Barbados. They gave us fresh pineapple, and the sweet juice ran down my chin. Suddenly the trauma of our near loss on the Tuomotu reef was far behind us. Such socialising was strictly against quarantine and immigration rules, but no one seemed to worry too much.

Then we were off to the Port Captain's office to clear. As Britain had recently joined the European Common Market, we expected clearing here to be easy and inexpensive. But no, no one had told officialdom in Tahiti, and they denied all knowledge of such a thing. Clearing proved neither easy nor inexpensive. But hey, we were in Tahiti!

Emerging, we sighed and headed for a boulangerie (bread shop). It was a shock to suddenly be immersed in a small city after three months of the quiet of the ocean and then the rural tranquility of Hiva Oa and Ua Pou, as if we had been out in space and travelled to a different time and world. The noise of the traffic was overwhelming. Citroen, Renault and Peugeot cars were everywhere, all driving so quickly, scooters whizzing about every which way, often with a beautiful wahine on the back (sitting sideways), their long dark hair blowing in the wind. There were people, people, people everywhere, beautifully dressed, all so chic, and rushing along. The noise, the colour, the bright sunlight, the heat reflecting off the concrete. It was both wonderful and daunting.

Tahiti has been a tourism hotspot since at least 1767, when Samuel Wallis advertised it as having a perfect climate, the island being 'one of the healthiest as well as most delightful spots in the world.' Not that he saw much of it, as he spent the entire two weeks his ship was there sick in his cabin. Had he gone ashore, he might have mentioned other delights. Wallis was the British Naval Officer commanding HMS *Dolphin,* making the first recorded visit by a European navigator. He named it 'King George the Third's Island' (in honour of the current King of England), taking possession in the name of His Majesty.

Of course, the Tahitian people, who had been there since at least 500 BC, already knew how pleasant it was and were not happy at Wallis's intrusion. His sailors exchanged fresh fruit and other pleasures ashore for disease, guns, and drunkenness. Later, visitors brought alien values such as the need to worship a foreign god, wear clothes, and ostensibly practise monogamy. Then the French took over, and some sort of paradise gradually faded.

The big flat deck of Tahia was a natural gathering point for discussion on everything, where we quickly met the crews of some of the nearby yachts. For these people, their stay in Tahiti was mainly a holiday, a time to pause and recharge, to enjoy French Polynesian life and the delicacies of France in the middle of the South Pacific, whilst waiting for the winds to be at their best to sail on or back. But for us it wasn't, firstly because we had little money and would need to work to sustain ourselves, and secondly because, unlike just about every other yacht that sailed into Papeete, *The Aegre* was worn out, and to go on would need a lot of restorative work.

All around us, the yacht owners were ten to thirty years older with considerable assets (compared to us), on larger yachts, mostly built of steel or fibreglass, with efficient low-maintenance hulls and rigs. Their voyage was planned and prepared for over many more years than ours. Not that these voyagers and their yachts were trouble-free. We noticed the older and apparently wealthier took cocktails of pills every morning, had bad backs, couldn't find their glasses, and worried if their outboard motor failed and they had to row their dinghy. Their yachts usually had problems somewhere, be it in the engine, plumbing, refrigeration, generator(s), radio(s), or cooker. Sometimes in all.

We were young enough to be their grandchildren and had the health, fitness and energy to go with it. And while *The Aegre* had no systems to go wrong, she was travel-worn, and the closer you looked, the worse she was.

Most obviously, the varnish above the waterline had been completely washed off one side leaving bare, unprotected timber. The wooden mast and other spars showed even worse wear. I hadn't decided yet what to do about these but at the very least, we believed we needed to strip and repaint the whole hull exterior.

Also, whilst sailing for thousands of miles, we had continuously discussed how *The Aegre* could be improved so that her rig was less challenging to handle and her light weather performance improved (even further). We had many ideas for improvement both above and below the deck that we wanted to put in place here.

Two months in Tahiti improving *The Aegre* sounded like fun to me, and neither of us enjoyed just lying in the sun. I didn't see it as a chore. I loved working on *The Aegre* and looked forward to it, seeing it as part of the whole adventure.

In retrospect, having come this far, we had no choice. Sailing on was our only option, and to go on safely, we needed to give *The Aegre* essential maintenance. To fully protect the timber of the hull the varnish would have to be replaced with paint, multiple coats of sealer, primer, undercoat, and topcoat. Each one would have to be rubbed back, hard work and time-consuming. It would take weeks to complete if we were both working elsewhere and could only work on it in our spare time, far longer than the few days we might have on a small slipway. And how much would it cost in boatyard fees? Someone said that just the haulage on a slip was £20-£30.

Someone suggested we haul *The Aegre* out onto a sheltered beach, and a neighboring yachtsman knew just the place. The next afternoon he took me there on his yacht to have a look while Julie tidied up *The Aegre* and went shopping for food.

The reef at Papeete extends around the coast to the island's west, past the airport at Fa'a'a', with a navigable lagoon inside. We followed it for about 10 miles to where the reef joined the island and the lagoon ended in a broader, deeper pool where a few yachts were anchored. Ashore was no development, just a few small cottages and a little restaurant, Auberge du Pacifique, just above the beach. The beach itself was sandy, gently shelving, sheltered and peaceful, perfect for us. The only sound was the booming of the surf on the outlying reef. Beyond the reef in the blue near distance were the spires on the island of Moorea. This was Puna'auia.

Back aboard *The Aegre* in noisy Papeete harbour, I excitedly told Julie all about it, how sheltered, quiet and secure it was, and free. How it would be a wonderful place to live and work on *The Aegre*. There was a downside: it was 8 km (4.3-miles) from Papeete by road, 20 minutes and 30 F on the truck. And it seemed unlikely we'd find any paid work there, so we might have to commute to Papeete. Julie wasn't convinced at first, but we talked it back and forth, eventually deciding to pull *The Aegre* out there and commute to Papeete if necessary. The friend who'd taken me there offered to tow *The Aegre* to the beach the following weekend.

That evening we heard someone calling from the shore and waving. A reporter from *La Dépéche de Tahiti*, a newspaper, wanted to do a story on us. Would they buy the story? Sadly not, but we told him about our voyage anyway, hoping the publicity might make it easier to find work or get some discount on materials for the refit.

We spent the next day exploring the town, asking people about work, and becoming depressed by the high prices of everything. We picked up mail from England at the post office, and the last of our money arrived at the bank.

Expecting to leave Papeete at the weekend and with the last of our money, we gathered the things we would need for the refit: sandpaper, filler, brushes, solvent, primer paint, undercoat, and topcoat. The newspaper story helped, and a yachting supplies shop gave us a good discount.

Food was expensive, apart from locally grown fresh fruit. Dinner became a small piece of tuna, rice and onion cooked on our little stove aboard *The Aegre*. We badly needed paid work.

Sometimes luck fell our way, and it certainly did when we met Pierre, a local resident who was a pilot with Air Polynesie. Pierre excitedly told us that he had seen *The Aegre* in the Marquesas. Apparently, he flew the weekly mail plane from Tahiti to Hiva Oa and had spotted us from the air when we were sailing along the coast on the day we arrived. In an extraordinary coincidence, Pierre lived with his wife Denise in one of the small cottages above the beach at Puna'auia, where we planned to pull *The Aegre* out. Moreover, he was building a steel cruising yacht nearby and would employ me to work on it.

Everything seemed to be falling into place. Well, not quite. Julie was preparing for job interviews. She needed her smarter clothes, which were stored up forward on *The Aegre* somewhere. But stylish clothes do not survive very well scrunched up, perpetually damp for months on end, squashed under spare anchor lines, a big bag of woodworking tools and boxes of food. Even washed and laid out flat to dry on the deck, they looked bleached, rust-marked, and travel-worn, far short of the chic look she would need in Papeete for job interviews. I encouraged her to go clothes shopping, but the months of scrimping and saving, and her disappointment at the prices, resulted in her coming home empty-handed. Denise lent her some, but even with them and her now well-remembered French, hopeful work opportunities in local tourism gradually disappeared, leaving her dispirited and feeling inadequate.

Meanwhile I went to the Port Captain's offices and told them we would be leaving Papeete harbour for the Puna'auia lagoon, where we would haul out and live on the beach for a while. Actually, I may have forgotten to mention that last part—no need for officialdom to know more than necessary.

But amongst our ship's papers, one issue did concern me; our vessel registration, which was shortly to expire. The previous owner, Andy Bryce, had her registered as a fishing boat in Lerwick in the Shetland Islands as LK92, and we had simply maintained that for the last two years. Now it needed to be renewed. From Papeete, I mailed a renewal application to the Fishing Boat Licensing Office in Lerwick, Shetland, wryly wondering just how many other Lerwick registered fishing boats there were in the South Pacific and how long it might take to get a reply.

Then we were off to Puna'auia.

As planned, our friend towed *The Aegre* with us aboard around to Puna'auia on Saturday, and then on Sunday, with the promise of beer to follow, a dozen friends from other yachts in Papeete arrived to help pull her up onto the beach as the tide approached high water. Soon she was secure with a 44-gallon drum under each bilge, well above the high water mark and under the shade of some trees. Now it was party time. Everyone had brought drinks and food. The sun set over Moorea, the surf boomed on the distant reef, and here we all were on a beach in Tahiti, celebrating — being truly alive.

We lived on the Puna'auia beach aboard *The Aegre* for the next three weeks. The small beachside restaurant nearby allowed us to use their toilet and gave us freshwater. Life fell into a pattern. I would work on Pierre's boat nearby from 8–4 most days, then on *The Aegre* till dark. Julie looked for work guiding with Tahiti Tours, Tahiti Nui, Club Med Voyages and Pacifique Tours, but the island's economy was still largely based on supporting the French nuclear testing on Tuomoto atolls at the far end of the chain, and tourism was relatively small and no work came her way. Teaching English, even contract sewing proved unattainable. Dispirited and feeling inadequate she eventually gave up and worked on *The Aegre* with periodic trips to town to buy food, and bits for the boat, collect our mail and catch up on news and gossip aboard the other yachts.

Pierre's boat on which I worked was a few hundred metres away in a clearing in the forest, a 38ft (11.58m) hard-chine steel yacht. It was still at the bare empty rusty hull stage, and my job was to chip mill scale inside the hull. It was hard work, hot, noisy, and boring. I stuck with it, working in a pair of old swimming trunks, sandals and safety glasses. By the end of the day, I was hot, thirsty, and covered in red dust and mosquito bites, whilst my toes on both feet were bandaged from tripping on coral and banging them on Pierre's boat. Returning to the beach and the boat at 4pm, Julie would hose me down, washing off the red dust while telling me about her day. One time, Julie surprised me at 4 pm with a carton of ice-cold chocolate milk. 'Here, try this', she said, passing the cold carton to me as I stood on the beach facing Moorea. Chocolate milk? This was a luxury unknown to me. Starting to drink the sweet icy chocolate, I wondered if I had died and gone to heaven.

Every week Pierre paid me in cash. It wasn't a lot, but our living costs were low, just the cost of daily fruit and vegetables. We spent nearly all of it on the boat, paint, brushes, snap shackles, rigging screws, wire rigging, the new mast and the like.

Aboard *The Aegre*, we had stripped the old varnish. It was so soft we could have just used our fingernails. Soon we were down to the bare wood and filling the imperfections. The refit was underway.

As darkness fell, we'd climb back aboard *The Aegre* to cook today's version of our one-pot ratatouille and muse on the future. Sitting on the cockpit sides in our open air saloon under the big canvas sunshade as the sun set over Moorea, we'd discuss whether to sail to New Zealand or Australia or here's a wild idea, what about selling *The Aegre* here? She was just too small. Then we could fly to New Zealand or back to England and work to build a larger boat. Would someone pay GBP2,000 for her? Unlikely. But it wasn't really a serious question. Even camping ashore, here we were in Tahiti and having too much fun to not continue the adventure.

Together we progressively gave the boat multiple coats of primer, undercoat and topcoat. The bottom got the full treatment, too, with a sealing paint, primer, undercoat, and expensive antifouling paint. The words of Lance Bell, the elderly handyman at Ardmore were ringing in my ears, to do it once, do it right, and never fight the weather. We also turned many of our improvement ideas into reality, such as more strongly securing the bowsprit and designing and building a metal horse fitted across the stern of the cockpit to securely support the boom when reefing at sea. We serviced the Primus cooker, bought a new blowlamp to start it and repainted the surrounding cooker can. We removed the existing rudder pintle fastenings and replaced them with stainless through bolts. Gradually the very worn-out *Aegre* emerged from a sort of chrysalis, being reborn as a small but sharp-looking go-anywhere boat.

Unable to find paid work Julie worked on the re-painting, took the truck to Papeete to the market, Post Office and visit our friends on yachts there, but she often felt dissatisfied, inadequate and listless, writing in her diary on the 21st July; *Getting bored as I have very little to get on with. Sometimes I just sit on the dinghy and read a book. Once I just lay still on the bed and fell asleep! And that was before lunch. It's difficult not to get depressed and feel inadequate. I started to write a piece about the trip from Panama, but I got bogged down in details and it's not exciting enough. N seems to have the knack of it.*

Eventually, we re-launched *The Aegre* at high water with the help again of a band of other voyagers and locals. With rollers and lots of willing hands, we ran *The Aegre* back into the placid water of the lagoon. I was a little worried about the effect of the sun on the hull timber whilst we were out on the beach. Had any seams opened? No, not really. She initially took a little water, but within 24 hrs, we took no water, and then the bilges were as dry as they usually were.

Then we started on stage two of the refit, the rig. The spars were all badly worn, and I used a hand plane to thin each down into a smaller spar. This left me looking for a new mast. I wanted solid Oregon Pine, but that was unobtainable in Tahiti. I toured the timber yards looking to see what timber was available. Famed circumnavigator Bernard Moitoisser had done this not many years before me, looking for a new mast for his sloop *Joshua*. The most suitable timber he could find was old telegraph poles. These were still for sale. I wondered about their weight and flexibility, but had little choice. At least they were very well seasoned. I would just have to plane one down to size and then carefully support it with new rigging. They were 30ft long and cost 1,000 francs (about £10 in 1974, £52 in 2021).

I selected the straightest one with the fewest shakes (surface splits) and arranged delivery to our beachside workshop. There I set it up on trestles in a vacant lot just above *The Aegre*. Nearby was a small beachside restaurant. I then spent many hours with a hand plane, gradually bringing it down to size. Around me was a growing pile of shavings as I progressively brought it into shape, giving it a fine taper.

It was not all hard work. One of the vessels anchored in the lagoon was *Varua*, a famous brigantine, now showing her age. Her owner, William Albert Robinson, who lived ashore nearby, agreed to give me a guided tour. The day came, and I rowed him out to his beautiful white boat. Robinson must have been about 70 then, white-haired, with a wiry light build. He seemed happy to show his lovely boat to this enthusiastic kid, who seemed to know something of her history, but he was reserved too, and I was a bit shy of this famous sailor.

On the surface, *Varua* was every inch the sea-worn brigantine. I stood at the wheel and pretended we were ploughing our way across big rolling swells on a broad reach at 10 knots, with 1,000 miles of sea room ahead. But Robinson went on to show me the reality below, where electrolysis between the steel framing, galvanised bolts and wooden planking had weakened her enormously. She would never sail far again without a complete rebuild.

Soon I was back hammering on Pierre's boat and planing the mast after work. It was slowly coming along. In the evenings after dinner, we'd read aloud the latest letters Julie had picked up from the Papeete post office and discuss the news. But it was bittersweet. I longed to keep in touch, but increasingly I didn't want to return to the world the letters described. Britain had gone into recession. A three-day week had been introduced between January and March to conserve electricity because of an extended miner's strike. The IRA had exploded a bomb in the Houses of Parliament and another in the Tower of London.

But it wasn't just these disturbances that put me off returning. I loved the sense of freedom I had found since leaving Britain. I felt I could be whoever I wanted to be. I could do anything, if I wanted to badly enough, as if I'd thrown off some invisible constraint, and it no longer mattered where I came from, how I spoke, or what school I went to. These seemed important in Britain, and I found the release invigorating. I didn't want to go back.

We'd drift off to sleep to the roar of the surf on the reef. It was always there, reminding us of where we were.

But overall, things were going well; the mast was almost finished, and I started to mount the fittings on it.

Then one day, I returned from working on Pierre's yacht mid-afternoon to find the nearly finished mast had disappeared. How could that be? It was extraordinary. It was nowhere to be seen. It was as if I was in some fourth dimension of the world. Where could it have gone? What possible use could it be to anyone else?

Then Julie came running over from the beach, looking horror-struck and near crying, to tell me what had happened. Apparently, the elderly woman who every day swept up around the outside of the nearby little restaurant had earlier made a big pile of rubbish, then set it alight to burn it. But it was (as always) a bit windy. The next minute all my wood shavings nearby had suddenly caught fire, and then the new mast, the old mast and the spars. It was as if the whole vacant lot suddenly caught fire.

The old lady was panic-stricken. Somehow, she and some passers-by had grabbed one end of the mast and each spar and dragged them down the beach into the surf to put them out.

When Julie returned from town, there was no sign of the mast or any of the spars. They seemed to have just disappeared. But then she found their blackened remains rolling in the surf. And that's where I found them now.

In disbelief, I dragged the partially burnt timbers out of the shallows and put them back on the cradles I'd made for them. They seemed severely burnt and unrecoverable. I would just have to start again. But did we have time before the strong winds of the hurricane season began to sweep across our planned course to Rarotonga and on to New Zealand? It was August 9th 1974. Should we abandon our plan to leave this year and wait another nine months?

Word of our disaster quickly spread amongst our cruising friends, and with their strong encouragement and help, we went back to the timber yard in Papeete to look for a replacement. Previously I had selected the best piece of timber, but now I had to choose one of the remaining poles. Reluctantly I decided on the best I could see, and the next day it was delivered to us. Most generously, some neighbours at Puna'auia, the Sylvains, who we had come to know and who lived in a beautiful house above the lagoon near us, offered to pay for the new mast and the hire of an electric planer.

Soon, grim-faced, I was back working on the new mast and making fast progress with the electric plane. However, as I brought it down to size, I became more and more worried by how deep some of the surface splits went. Should I look for a third possible mast? Or have a closer look at the original one that had been burnt? It seemed a terrible quandary, but eventually I decided that a slightly thinner mast (the burnt timber planed off) would be a better bet than a split one, so I abandoned the second one the Sylvains had paid for and concentrated on recovering the first one. I tried planing off the thin charred layer to see how it looked. It had been a lovely piece of timber, and beneath the blackened surface it still looked surprisingly good.

The new mast was a bit higher than the original, as part of our plan to make the rig easier to handle and to allow for an increase in sail area. To support the higher mast, I set up two sets of mast stays, one to two-thirds of the way up the mast, the other to the top, all in strong galvanised wire, and rather than swaging the ends around eyes, I used cable clamps, a fortunate choice as it turned out.

The recovered mast was almost finished when we learned that Alain Colas, the celebrated French yachtsman, and his Tahitian wife had moved into one of the beachside cottages. The following morning, while Julie and I were having a breakfast pamplemousse aboard *The Aegre* out in the lagoon, we recognised him swimming past. 'Bonjour, would you like to join us?' we called to him.

Soon he was aboard, eating pamplemousse with us and telling us about his latest exploit, the building of a huge 236 ft (72m) four-masted monohull for the 1976 Trans-Atlantic Single-Handed Race. It was just beyond our imagination. But he seemed to like our little boat too and asked all about our refit and sailing plans. That day I planned to step (set up) our new mast. It's a tricky operation even on our little boat, requiring a strong person (or two) on deck to hold the mast vertically and then lower it carefully through the hole in the deck, while someone below guides the foot into a notch cut in the keel. Maybe Alain could help, if he wasn't too busy? *Oui, bien sûr*, yes of course!

Later, with Alain's help, we brought the new mast out from the shore to *The Aegre*. Then, with big Alain lowering it gently through the hole in the deck, I guided it down below into the mast step slot in the keel, where it fitted perfectly over a gold half-sovereign for luck. I thought our new mast looked rather good.

Every morning after that Alain joined us for a chat and *un petit déjeuner* as part of his morning swim. He was quite charming—a lovely man.

Alain was just one of the many visitors we had in Puna'auia. Julie was particularly sociable and through her we knew the crew of every yacht not just in Puna'auia, but many in Papeete too. Some we'd known since Madeira. As ever we'd often get together, for instance as Julie wrote on 21st August: *Around 6pm we went on to* Daddy's Dream *and swapped some books, and 10 gallons of dried mushroom soup for a Primus, which we thought a good bargain as the Canadian Navy had given us the soup in the first place. Stayed quite a long time and N showed the skipper how to take star sights. When we came back*

N couldn't sleep and jumped up and wrote an article to send to the Cambridge News.

It seemed we were almost ready to go, and not before time. The season had been changing for a few weeks. Increasingly the days were windy, chilly and overcast. We knew we would never be ready to leave, but all the big jobs were done, and like migrating birds, we knew it was time to go. Many yachts had already left Papeete, and around us, people were saying we should leave as soon as possible before the weather worsened.

The question of whether we would go to Australia or New Zealand had been simmering in our conversations for weeks. We had gradually settled on New Zealand via Rarotonga. At the time, New Zealand seemed almost close, as if one final passage would take us there. But despite our months of sailing, we'd only reached the middle of the Pacific. It was still far to NZ, 4,100 km (2,200 nm), and the voyage would need planning and care. But first, we'd have a pleasant sail to the small island of Rarotonga on the way, a convenient place to pause. After that, we'd head south for the cooler climes of NZ.

Rarotonga is the capital of the Cook Islands, a group of fifteen mostly low coral atolls, tiny, widely spread specks in the ocean. It lies at the southern end of the Cook Islands, 1,176 km (730 miles) to the west-south-west of Tahiti. Its origin is volcanic, and it has a high central peak, rather like Tahiti but smaller, with an encircling coral reef. The Cook Islands are self-governing, and were reputedly much less expensive than Tahiti. We planned to replenish our food stocks there. They were low, as we'd been dipping into them in Tahiti, where food was expensive. In Rarotonga we would restock our food for the remaining 3,000 km (1,860 miles) voyage on to New Zealand.

So we did a stocktake of the food left on *The Aegre* and decided we had more than enough for 14 days, double the time we expected to take for the 730-mile (1,352-km) passage. But we filled all the water tanks just in case.

While we were planning our departure, we received in the mail a reply from Scotland about our application to renew the registration of *The Aegre* as a fishing boat. It was disappointing. Our tongue-in-cheek claim to be undertaking 'exploratory fishing in the South Pacific' was rejected. Clearly, the official in Lerwick had no sense of adventure or humour. But we wondered just how officialdom in Papeete and all points further west would react to *The Aegre* no longer being registered anywhere.

We had been in Tahiti for 80 days, far longer than we had intended, but we had given our little vessel a substantial refit. The ideas brewed over thousands of miles on the boat had matured into physical improvements all over her.

It was time. We felt we could and must leave. First, we'd need to clear at the Port Captain's office. We planned to catch the truck to Papeete on Tuesday morning, September 3rd, to clear, then return and sail that afternoon.

Our last night in Tahiti was a progressive farewell with the many friends we'd made amongst our neighbours in Puna'auia. The next morning we did not feel quite so sparky, but we were still up first thing to take a truck into Papeete to start on the round of departure officialdom at 9 am sharp. One office after another. It was even hotter than usual. Just on 11 am, we arrived back at the starting point office for the final payment of fees and a clearance stamp, but the shutters were just coming down. 'Fermé', we were told in unsympathetic terms. It would only have taken minutes. We were furious, because the office would now be closed for the traditionally long lunch break until mid-afternoon. The official knew we were doing the rounds to clear, and he seemed almost deliberately obstructive.

We were hot, cross, and impatient to leave. We looked at each other, shaking our heads. Exasperated, I turned to Julie and said, 'I've had it for today. Let's just go back to *The Aegre*. In fact, let's just sail this afternoon anyway.'

Would they send a gunboat out after us? I doubted it. Would it be a problem arriving in Rarotonga with no clearance papers since the Marquesas? Well, it wasn't French, so probably not. We stood in the busy, noisy street, looking at each other.

'Yes, let's just go,' agreed Julie.

Back aboard, we excitedly readied the boat for sea. As we set the mainsail on our new mast, the familiar routine was coming back, and I started to haul in the anchor warp. 'All ok Julie?' I called back to her in the cockpit in the familiar way. Then the anchor was clear of the bottom, and once more, *The Aegre* was starting to heel to the light breeze. With the jib set, we picked up speed and were quickly joined by Bob and Sharon from the yacht *Marluva*, out in their dinghy to see us off. Then it was out past *Varua*, heading for the narrow Puna'auia pass through the reef.

No French gunboats appeared as we swept out through the narrow pass. I was back on the helm and smiling, feeling the wind in the sails, the boat picking up speed. Bob and Sharon gave a final wave and blast on their air horn and then turned back.

Emerging from the shelter of Tahiti, we were alone again, heading out. I loved this moment of leaving, off on another adventure. Where would this one take us? What lay ahead, beyond the empty horizon? Everywhere I looked, *The Aegre* around me was improved. She was the best she'd ever been. It was a bit like leaving Scotland, and I wanted to sing:

> *Oh come by the hills to the land where fancy is free*
> *And stand where the peaks meet the sky and the lochs meet the sea*
> *Where the rivers run clear and the bracken is gold in the sun*
> *And the cares of tomorrow can wait till this day is done*

Astern, the little blue world of Tahiti became smaller and smaller. The harbour officials would be back at work now, demanding this form and that, a stamp here and a stamp there. Ahead of us, the open sea.

Chapter 18
Disaster

'The best bilge pump of all is a bucket in the
hands of a frightened man'. — Anon

Back on the helm of *The Aegre*, smiling, feeling the boat heeling to the wind in her sails, the boat lifting and falling over a gentle sea, the familiar rhythmic *shisssh* of the bow wave. This was where *The Aegre* was at home, not on a beach, even a Tahitian one, not on a mooring, even if under the skirts of *Varua*. The Cook Islands and New Zealand, here we come!

As we crept out of the shelter of Tahiti and then Moorea, the wind developed a hardness to it, and the waves became higher, the swell longer. It became chilly on deck with the dusk. Now *The Aegre* was powering along, sometimes dipping her lee rail, spray from the bow coming aft to the cockpit, the sea rushing by. Ahead were dark clouds. I'd need to reef the mainsail before the night set in. I'd forgotten how tough it was out at sea on our little boat. I was soft after three months of island life in Tahiti.

We'd brought easy food for dinner, but Julie was feeling seasick, had no appetite and was understandably miserable. She retired to the bunk while I took the first watch, progressively reducing sail over the evening as the wind strengthened. Then at midnight, by the light of our little oil lamp, I gently woke her with a cup of tea. Strong-willed, she soon got up to take over in the middle of the wild, windy night. After the relaxing months in Tahiti, I really admired her fortitude. There's just no romance in some parts of ocean voyaging.

The next day we were in a full gale by lunchtime, and I'd taken the mainsail down and lashed it on deck while we sailed on under the tan Dacron jib, still making good speed. The weather continued to worsen, and by dusk even that little sail was too big, and I changed it for the tiny flax jib. We slowed down.

Now we were sailing across the direction of the waves. But *The Aegre* handled the strengthening wind and the building seas without much trouble.

I took the first-night watch again and sat in my oilskins, hunched on the floor of the little cockpit where I was out of the worst of the weather. We were running diagonally before what was now a full-on south-easterly gale. It was black and stormy, the wind blowing the tops off the waves and howling in the rigging. The calm lagoon in Tahiti seemed very far away. I was tense, checking everything in my mind. Was everything tied down properly on deck? Was everything secure down below? We hadn't been in seas like this for months.

Fortunately, the self-steering was working well and holding us on a steady course. I watched the compass and the hands of the clock. Midnight came, then 00:20, changeover time this night. 'Wakey wakey!' I called down to Julie. Now, as ever, she struggled out of the warm bunk, pulled on her oilskins and life harness and stood up in the companionway to face the miserable night.

'Gosh, do you think we're all right?' she shouted, feeling the full weight of the wind. A nearby breaking wave top roared behind us, and in the pitch darkness the water surrounded the stern with white phosphorescence, which slowly faded in our wake. No light was needed to tell it was very rough.

I shouted back, 'Well, yes, I reckon so. We're only making a couple of knots, and it's in the right direction. We should be OK.' I thought we'd had weather as bad as this before and had no real problem. The boat would swoop and dive, in and out, up and over every wave, giving a violent motion. But unlike bigger boats, solid water rarely came on deck.

Julie joined me in the cockpit, the little two-foot-square well in the deck, clipping her life harness into a deck eyebolt and closing the hatch behind her. We sat on the side deck, our feet in the well, fully exposed to the wind and spray. In awe, we stared out into the darkness as spray battered our oilskins. *The Aegre* just moving slowly under the tiny flax jib, as safe as could be. I waited for a lull between big waves and then, opening the hatch, stepped into the cabin, slipping off my life harness and oilskins. Then, giving Julie a smile, I ducked down into the cabin, sliding the hatch shut behind me. Oh, the relief to be out of the wind and into the haven of our cosy cabin, its small oil light giving a sense of security and calm. I crawled forward and sprawled onto our damp but comfortable bunk. Sliding out of my thermal underwear, I pulled the duvet up, checked the time, about 00:30 am, and quickly fell asleep.

It was Thursday 5th September 1974.

I was woken by a sudden roaring. The next moment I was turning head

Disaster! (John Quirk)

over heels. My eyes were clenched shut. I managed to open them, but it made no difference to the blackness. Where was I? I'd been asleep in the oil-lamp-lit cabin. Where was I now? I was lying in water, but breathing air. What the hell was going on? Were we sinking? Where was Julie?

'Julie! Julie!' I shouted, but there was no reply.

Threshing around with my hands and arms, I felt for the cabin sides around me, but everything was in the wrong place. Then I felt the deck beams beneath me. My mind raced. We must be upside down.

It was eerily quiet. Were we below the surface, sinking into oblivion?

I had to get out, but how? Where was the hatch? Could I get to it? My way seemed blocked by the lockers and shelving. My hands found a passage aft beneath them. Now I could feel the closed hatch underwater beneath me. What would happen if I opened it? But I had to open it — it was the only way out. Would it jam?

I wrenched it back and plunged down into the ocean beneath. With my hands I felt the boat above me and pulled myself to one side, then up. Would I make it to the surface?

Almost instantly I did and was gulping air. It was still dark, but in front of me I could make out the shape of *The Aegre*, floating upside down. I couldn't see Julie anywhere. In dread, I screamed into the wind and darkness, 'Julie! Julie!'

'I'm here,' came back faintly over the wind from the other side of the boat. Pulling myself around the boat to the other side, I found her clinging on, gasping for breath as wave after wave swept over her. Relief that she was alive flooded through me. Together, we were strong.

'We have to get out of the water!' I yelled, pulling myself up onto the upturned hull. The edges of the clinker-laid planks gave narrow hand and footholds. Soon I was clear of the water and sitting astride the shallow keel.

Julie, in her thick oilskins and boots, couldn't get a grip. I leaned over, grabbed her hand and pulled her up. As I did so, *The Aegre* tipped violently towards her and turned over again, throwing us both back underwater. I came back to the surface, my eyes full of water, to dimly see that the boat was now the right way up but almost flush with the sea.

But Julie had gone. Our hands had been dragged apart as we had hit the water. Where was she? Under the boat snarled in the mast and rigging, fighting for her life?

'Julie!' I screamed, pushing myself back under the boat to feel around wildly for her. There were just rope and wires. I burst back to the surface for a breath and heard a faint cry from the other side of the boat. I pulled myself back around the boat to find her, shocked, gasping, and spluttering. In the dim light of the night I could see *The Aegre* had just a little freeboard, perhaps two inches, but she wasn't lifting to the seas, and colossal breaking waves were sweeping right over her, pouring through the hatch into the cabin. Within seconds the deck was flush with the sea. Now she was only floating because of the polystyrene foam buoyancy we'd built into either end. I pulled myself aboard, into the flooded cockpit, and helped Julie to roll back on board too. She crawled along the deck to the base of the broken mast and clasped her arms around it to avoid being swept back overboard as waves swept across the deck and in and out of the cabin. Everything from below swirled in and out in the gloom, polythene food containers, books, pieces of wood, papers, everything.

I stood in the cockpit as if I were standing in the ocean, terrified that the boat might break up under the stress of the buoyancy lifting either end and the lead weight in the middle. I thought of our inflatable Avon dinghy, our last resort if the boat should break up.

Full of water, *The Aegre* had no stability and tipped to port. Would she roll over again? If she did, that might be the end of us. Julie sat on the deck, trying to balance the boat as waves swept over us.

'I'm going to blow up the Avon,' I yelled, unlashing the green bag we kept it in, but the pump — the pump? I couldn't see it. Desperately I set about blowing it up by mouth. Julie blew up the seat bolster. With just enough pressure, Julie took the line to the dinghy. 'Don't tie it on, we might sink!' I shouted.

It was getting lighter, and now I dimly saw the Avon dinghy floating high and dry and just downwind of us, above the maelstrom of the sea. A last resort. But I knew *The Aegre* herself offered us the best chance, not the Avon. I just had to get the water out.

Standing in the cockpit, up to my thighs in the sea, I frantically bailed with a basin that came to hand. Could I just get a fraction ahead of the waves sweeping over us? If I could, the stern might lift enough for less of the next wave to flood in.

I began bailing like a madman in the semi-darkness. Everything in the cabin was washing in and out through the hatchway. I grabbed things that might be useful to our survival, passing them to Julie at the base of the mast to put into the Avon for safe keeping: a jerrican of water, our waterproof canister of emergency things, a sharp knife wrapped in a sheet, the wooden box containing the sextant, a string bag of onions that floated out, whatever, before they were washed away and lost downwind.

I kept bailing but was getting nowhere. Breaking wave tops kept sweeping over the boat. Water was pouring into the cockpit and flowing straight into the cabin — the washboards separating the cockpit from the cabin were gone. How could I stop it? Could I protect the cockpit itself from the water that was rushing in with every wave?

I lashed the boom and gaff trysail to protect the cockpit and hatchway and tried again, frantically throwing water out with the big basin, struggling to get ahead of the incoming water. Just as I thought I was getting ahead, Julie screamed, 'Look out!' Her shout was instantly followed by a crashing wall of green and white seawater which exploded over me.

It looked hopeless. Worse, I was now feeling the cold, having gone to sleep naked. There was no sign of my clothes.

Julie screamed another warning and I clung to the boat, but was knocked over again by a wall of water. I thought we were going over but the boat surfaced in the wake of the wave, still the right way up, but Julie had gone, the deck bare where she'd been sitting. Swept overboard, her life harness attached to the base of the mast saved her, and I grabbed it to pull her back aboard, but the Avon was gone, torn from Julie's hands, leaving them raw and bleeding.

In horror, I saw the Avon's shape on the crest of a wave, already a boat's length downwind. I paused. Should I dive after it? Could I catch it? Would I ever get back to The Aegre if I tried? Better together than apart, and better on The Aegre even if it was swamped than on a barren inflatable.

I saw the fear in Julie's eyes now that our last resort was almost gone. But no, I wasn't going after it. And then the chance had passed. The dinghy's outline quickly fading into the greyness of the wave crests downwind, and then was gone.

Had I made the right choice? I was tormented, briefly thinking not just of the security it offered but the things we'd put in it, particularly our precious sextant. But it was done. Too late for regrets. Now there were no options. We'd have to stay on The Aegre, which was how we'd always planned it anyway. She had everything we needed to survive. She just happened to be underwater right now.

I had to save *The Aegre*, had to somehow get the water out. I attacked the bailing again. Whatever came floating into the basin, I flung over the side with the water. Nothing else mattered. My oilskin top swept out of the cabin on a wave, and I did grab it, throwing it on. Cold and clammy, but it kept the wind off. Maybe it helped my brain to work.

'We can use the water jerricans as extra buoyancy,' I shouted to Julie.

From the hatch, I felt around underwater in the cabin to find the fresh water jerricans stowed under the sides of the cockpit and pulled two out, wrenched off their caps and poured the water out over the side deck into the sea. Each contained ten litres, five days of water. Was I bleeding an already sick patient? Would the extra buoyancy save us now, only for lack of water to ultimately kill us?

I stuffed the jerricans, now containing nothing but air, back under the sides of the cockpit, displacing water, but the boat's movement seemed unchanged. I grabbed two more. Julie, trying to balance the boat, looked on in horror. Still there was no change in the boat's movement. Waves were still sweeping over us. Now I'd dumped 20 days' worth of water. I went back underwater into the cabin to extract two more jerricans. Perhaps the boat was holed underwater and would only ever lift a little until I found and patched the holes? Now I'd dumped 30 days' worth of water. The back of the boat seemed to be just starting to lift a little to each wave.

We'd started with 22 10-litre polythene jerricans of freshwater, but we'd lost one in the Avon dinghy. Now I was keeping a careful count.

'We won't need all this fresh water if we're dead from exposure,' I shouted to Julie as I emptied jerricans 7 and 8. 40 days of water now were gone, 60 days left.

It was now almost light, and I could see what I was doing. I'd started with the easily accessible jerricans stowed around and beneath the cockpit. The boat was definitely lifting to the waves now, but still we needed more buoyancy to prevent waves sweeping over and into the boat.

The jerricans I wanted now were under the floorboards where access was more difficult. I dived underwater to find my tools and a screwdriver in the wreckage of the cabin. Working desperately in the gloom and chaos and frightened we might roll over again, I unscrewed the floorboards and pulled out more jerricans, keeping a careful count. Now, with every empty jerrican I stuffed under the decking around the cockpit, we rose a little. Finally, with just 7 full ones left (water for 35 days), *The Aegre* was lifting to most of the oncoming waves.

Desperately I tried bailing, only to be swamped again, but now I knew it was possible. *The Aegre* was starting to lift to the waves. I tried again, only to be swamped again and then again. And then there was a longer gap between big waves. I threw water out like a maniac; whatever came into the basin went out with the water. Nothing was more important than getting ahead of the next wave.

All manner of stuff was swilling in and out of the cabin. Filling the basin as quickly as possible, I scanned the contents in the early dawn light; everything we owned had been reduced to a slurry of paper. Anything important, I wondered, looking down at another basin load of water and sodden paper. No, just a few books. I hurled the lot over the side and quickly refilled the basin. What's this now? No time to be picky, whatever, it's not that important, over the side with it, next load, and so on. Gone, over the side, next load... Nothing much mattered compared with getting more buoyancy before the next big wave hit. Our lives depended on it.

And I did get ahead of it. With the water down to the cockpit floor, we rose to the next big breaking wave. This time the white water surged around us, not over us.

It was light, perhaps 7 or 8am, when finally I paused, exhausted, my chest heaving, and looked up at Julie by the mast. We smiled at each other. Now there was hope. Back to bailing with the basin, and soon the water was down to the floorboards, and using the bilge pump became practical.

I'd saved the boat, for the moment at least, but, we progressively realised, I'd thrown over the side most of our library, all our sailing records of the voyage, our passports, money, and more, all gone.

By late morning the immediate survival crisis was past. *The Aegre* was buoyantly rising and falling as the big grey seas passed beneath us, rather than over us. Looking up and around, as if for the first time, all that was to be seen was a vast windswept seascape. Looking down, I surveyed our poor broken boat and tried to assess our situation.

I guessed we were about 150 miles south-west of Tahiti and being blown further away every moment. Above me, the mast was broken about 8.5-ft up from the deck. The top section, still attached by the rigging, was lying in the sea alongside the boat, knocking against the hull but not posing any immediate danger.

There were gaping holes in the upper starboard strakes (planks) where the mast side stay plates had been torn out of the planking. We were taking in water there every time we rolled, the water pouring onto our bunk. Some plywood patches would fix that, a high priority. But there was no other observable hull damage above the waterline.

Lost was our main steering compass, missing from its square box set into the rear deck just aft of the cockpit. Lashing and all had gone. But we had other compasses on board, so this wasn't a disaster.

The self-steering wind vane was cracked, and the steering lines detached. It looked fixable.

Missing from the top of the hatch was a large red cork life-ring we kept there, and the flax sea-anchor lashed beneath.

We seemed lucky not to be more damaged. Bob Macinnes's strong flush deck had saved us.

Below deck, in the cabin, there was chaos: polythene food boxes, clothes, tins, torches, lines, bottles, and spare parts for the rig, cooker, tools, spare lines and everything else, all covered in a mass of saturated paper, a mixture of the remains of our charts, personal documents and library.

Missing from the cabin floor was our heavy main anchor and most of the chain. I'd dumped it all (unwillingly) over the side in my desperate attempts to get more buoyancy when the boat was full of water. But right now, no anchor and the chaos below were far less important than the safety of the boat.

On deck, the wind was howling. The sea was piling up into monstrous waves, the tops being blown off to create a near fog of spray that zig-zagged across the surface like dry sand on a wind-blown beach. The waves were running across another even larger swell coming from a different direction. Periodically two of these waves would meet and join, rising together to create a single mega-wave which would build, then momentarily tower menacingly, then break with a roar. Watching them wide-eyed, I wondered if one of these had turned *The Aegre* over.

Now *The Aegre* was lying sideways to the huge threatening waves, and we were in danger of being rolled over again by the high breaking crests sweeping down on us. Our sea-anchor had been torn from the hatch top, but I hastily made another using the jib (foresail), an oar to spread it and some remaining anchor chain as a weighted spring and then trailed it from our stern. We quickly swung around, so the waves were striking us somewhere on our pointed stern. It seemed safer. *The Aegre* was rolling less, rising to the waves that now broke around us, not over us. We were still moving downwind, but slowly. Sometimes the sea-anchor stopped the boat abruptly, with a sudden jerk, which meant it needed a longer cable and more chain, but there was no more to be found.

Julie crouched out of the wind on the cockpit floor, just above the cabin water level, urgently working the bilge pump handle back and forth. Water was gushing over the side from the pump outlet, but already the flow was slowing, the pump's inlet pipe in the bilge getting blocked by the detritus from the cabin.

Scrabbling in the cabin, I lifted the floorboards to clear the bilge pump intake, then found my tool bag and some spare plywood to patch the holes in the side of the hull where the starboard mast stay plates had been torn out, splintering the timber around them. The damage was a few inches above the waterline, but water was pouring in when we rolled.

Roughly measuring the splintered part of each plank, I cut the plywood and coated it with sealing mastic on one side. Then, back up on deck, I lay down to lean over the side and used a hand-drill to make pilot holes in the planks for the first few screws. How I hated to drill into our perfect paintwork! Every time the boat rolled everything went underwater. Then I had one plank patched, then the second. It was the best I could do. Thankfully I hadn't dropped the drill, screwdriver or screws over the side. Back inside the cabin, the previous torrent coming in every time we rolled had reduced to a drip. I was still running on adrenalin.

Next was the broken top part of the mast, still attached by the rigging but now in the sea lying beside us and bashing into the hull with every wave. We couldn't afford to lose it, so I had to get it on deck and lashed down. With all the rigging still attached, it was a massive tangle. Piece by piece I took the rigging apart, desperately trying not to drop any shackles or lines. I knew I would need everything to eventually get sailing again.

Meanwhile, Julie was relentlessly pumping, switching arms every 20 strokes, but she was winning. The water level inside was dropping. That meant any leaks we had were slower than the pump.

With the broken mast section securely lashed on deck, I paused, breathing deeply, trying to calm down. Then I took over pumping while Julie ventured further into the cabin and the chaos. First, she cleared a pathway to our storage area forward of the mast. There she discovered that most of our food was wet despite being wrapped in polythene and inside polythene boxes. Practically everything that could be affected by seawater was wet.

With no possibility of drying anything until the weather improved, it all looked like being ruined—all our rice, biscuit, flour, dried curries, Protoveg, everything. We'd planned to restock in Rarotonga and had departed from Tahiti with theoretically about 14 days of food, double the expected length of the passage. Now we had just a fraction of that. A few small squares of chocolate kept us going that day.

But things are never quite as bad as they at first seem. After fifteen months of cruising, we knew *The Aegre* was like a family pantry. Tucked away here and there all over the boat were the remnants of food we had accumulated along the way; food from Scotland, food bought in Madeira and the Canaries, and food from the Canadian Navy. Water had got into everything, unless it was in a tin or bottle, so we would just have to check everywhere to work out what we had.

But not today. Starvation was still some time away, but then so was land.

Freshwater was less of a problem. We still had seven 10-litre jerricans, easily enough for 35 days, plus, with any luck, we'd catch rainwater.

By mid-afternoon of the first day after the capsize, *The Aegre* was riding relatively easily to the makeshift sea anchor, the obvious hole in the hull was patched, and the broken mast section had been secured. We seemed to be still taking in water somewhere, but we could keep the level below the floorboards with the bilge pump with twenty strokes an hour.

We could now get to the bunk and lie down in the cabin. Everything was still soaking, but being out of the driving wind and spray was a relief. By 3 pm, Julie was totally exhausted, but she was terrified of sleeping on the bunk in case we rolled again. However she had no choice. She finally slept in her oilskins under the sodden duvet until 3am the following day.

Lying to the sea anchor, *The Aegre* was handling the conditions quite well, with the waves coming onto one side of the stern. Little water was coming on deck, and she wasn't surfing off down the waves. The boat's movement was quick and sometimes violent, but we were used to that.

I kept a lookout as best I could, although it was almost impossible to look upwind through the driving spray. But ships are often easier to see at night with their lights. Fortunately, both our French 'La Spirotechnique' diving torches had survived. I hoped that if I saw a ship, they'd see our torch signal. But neither seemed likely. We had also found our pack of emergency flares, triple wrapped in polythene. Were they wet or dry inside? I wasn't game to unwrap them unless we definitely saw a ship.

At first sight, the Primus cooker in its swinging can seemed to have survived. It looked undamaged. I found our new blowlamp from Tahiti, but with no dry matches I couldn't light it. I knew matches were stored in a few plastic boxes in different places and hoped we'd find dry ones before too long. Until we did, there would be nothing warm to eat or drink.

On the day after the capsize, Friday 6th September, Julie took my place at 3am, huddling on the cockpit floor. She checked on the sea anchor lines to ensure they weren't chafing on the fairleads, watched for the possible light of a ship and pumped out the bilges every hour. I slept on the sodden foam mattress under the soaking quilt in my oilskins. I suddenly woke up thinking we had rolled over again, but then I saw Julie's shape in the cockpit, and slowly calmed down and went back to sleep.

On the Saturday I woke again with the dawn and could feel *The Aegre* buoyantly riding the big seas. On deck, the wind was still howling, and mountainous waves rose around us, their tops breaking with a roar, often surrounding us in white waters. Over the day, we took turns on watch and clearing up below

I was in the cabin about mid-morning when we were suddenly hit violently by a mammoth wave which knocked *The Aegre* completely over onto her side. I thought we were going right over again, but she slowly righted herself, water pouring from the deck. I pulled the hatch open enough to stand up and look out. Water from the deck was still pouring into the cockpit.

Julie, crouching outside on the floor of the cockpit, lashed in with her lifeline, looked up at me with fear in her eyes and shouted over the wind, 'The sea anchor's gone!'

I looked down at the massive oak cleat to which the sea anchor line had been attached, but only a few wood splinters remained. One of the sea anchor's sudden jerks must have been too much for it. Thankfully the broken hardwood cleat hadn't hit Julie on its way past her at head level.

Without the sea anchor holding her, *The Aegre* had swung round broadside to the huge oncoming waves. Our situation was desperate. We could be rolled right over by the next big breaking wave. What could I use to make another temporary sea anchor? The best I could think of was to use the broken piece of the mast. I quickly secured another section of anchor chain I'd found to each end of it to hold it underwater, and then a line to each end, bringing each line back onto the boat through a block (pulley) to minimise chafe, one on each side of the back of the boat (the quarter), then secured the end of each line around the base of the mast stub. Surely that couldn't break? We'd be pulling the piece of mast sideways through the water. Would that hold the boat with the pointed stern facing the waves and reduce the likelihood of us being rolled over again?

It worked. *The Aegre* swung round to a safer position where she was slowly making way downwind, the big breaking waves building behind us and then sweeping down on either side as she lifted to them. No longer lying broadside to them, the motion aboard diminished.

I breathed deeply. A disaster narrowly averted

We relaxed a little as *The Aegre* settled into her previous safer motion. For a time, I watched carefully to check the lines weren't chafing anywhere, but they were not. Soon we reinstated our regular watch on/watch off 4-hour routine. On-watch meant keeping a lookout and pumping and tidying the chaos below. Off-watch meant sorting out the mess below or trying to sleep.

'Look what I found!' shouted Julie. On her hands and knees in the middle of the cabin and bracing herself against *The Aegre*'s continuing violent motion, she had lifted the floorboards to clean out the bilge, covered in a layer of sodden paper and small bits and pieces from all over the boat. They constantly blocked the bilge-pump intake pipe as we pumped to keep the water from rising above the floorboards.

Triumphantly she held up our beautiful Accutron watch-chronometer. Like everything, it had been missing since the capsize. But here it was, in the bilges and still going.

What a relief. A wonderful moment. Badly needed good news. Knowing accurate GMT (Greenwich Mean Time) could help us work out where we were, even without the sextant lost in the Avon dinghy.

But like any clock, even the Accutron didn't keep perfect time. Across the eastern Pacific, we'd checked it every day against the time signal broadcast continuously on the shortwave station WWV. Consistently it would lose a second a day (known as its 'rate'). We didn't adjust the watch, but each day we knew to add another second to calculate the exact GMT. (The cumulative difference to GMT, known as its error). We recorded this accumulative error daily on a rating card, kept carefully beside the watch.

But the rating card was missing, lost somewhere in the sticky mass of papier-mâché covering everything, or maybe I'd bailed it out in my frantic efforts to save the boat the day before. Without it or the radio to check WWV (the latter had drowned), the watch was useless.

I went from elation to despair as the realisation sank in, but Julie came to the rescue. With her eyes squeezed shut, she concentrated, then, opening them, looked at me and smiled. 'Remember we checked the Accutron against WWV on the day we left Tahiti?' she said. 'Well, I updated the rating card, and the error was …'

I was open-mouthed. She'd remembered it! We could calculate accurate GMT after all, vital to determine our position.

On Saturday 7th September, day 3 after the capsize, the storm blew on all night. Our makeshift sea anchor kept us safe, mainly stern-on to the big seas, while we slowly eased forward downwind. The relentless driving wind, spray and noise of it all on deck was exhausting and in sharp contrast to our tiny cabin's peacefulness and quiet.

It was like the worst gales in the North Atlantic, but on a different scale. The size of the waves and swell, the depth and power of the wind, all seemed in a different order of magnitude. I felt we were terribly alone out in the vastness of the Pacific. Could we survive this?

We rotated watches during the night, pumping every hour to keep the water inside from rising above the floorboards. It eventually became light, revealing that in the big seas and driving wind, the surface spray was immersing us as if in a deep white streaming mist, through which we could see little, and nothing upwind at all.

We knew we weren't on a shipping route to anywhere. The chances of there being any shipping here were negligible. But we had to try and make ourselves visible. Could we raise some sort of emergency flag? Desperate to be seen, we braved the conditions on deck to thread the end of the 12ft boom through the arms of a spare bright orange oilskin jacket and then, lifting the boom vertically on the rolling deck, lashed it to the remnants of the mast. A square of orange 12 ft above the deck, flapping wildly, wasn't much, but it was something. Then we collapsed below to recover from the physical effort and stress.

Above us on deck, the noise of the furiously flapping oilskin at the top of the temporary mast added to the wildness. Catching the wind, it was helping to keep us facing straight downwind. But the sound and vibration of its incessant shaking came down the mast to the person off watch lying on the bunk at its foot, bringing stress into the heart of the boat.

Sunday 8th September: Day 4 after the capsize

We spent another long night lying to the sea anchor, the boat swooping and diving as large breaking swells roared around and under us while the wind in the flapping oilskin jacket flag was shaking the whole boat. We were alive, but I lay there wishing I had set the radar reflector on the top of the mast too.

As soon as it was light, I lowered the temporary mast, attached two blocks (pulleys) to the top and, rove lines through them, then we raised it again and re-lashed it to the remains of the old mast. Now I could haul our radar reflector and the spare orange jacket to the top. It was only about 12ft above sea level, but it was the best we could do. I was exhausted by it all as we'd eaten little since the capsize.

Sitting back on the floor of the cockpit, I looked up at our slightly improved makeshift mast. We had to move on from thinking about being found and rescued. We'd always considered that unlikely. Rather we had to work out a way of sailing to land by ourselves. For that, we'd need a more robust mast that we could set sails on.

I looked up again at my current attempt. To make it stronger, it needed to be supported on the deck with chocks to hold the base securely and wire stays to its top. I could modify the existing wire rigging to fit the shorter mast by undoing the cable clamps and resetting them to give the required length of stay. An eyebolt through a deck beam could replace the torn-out starboard (right side) attachment plates. The mast would be shorter than before but could be quite strong.

What about sails? We still had our flying jib, and I thought about how to shorten the luff (leading edge) to fit the shorter mast. We wouldn't be able to set our old mainsail, but we could set the gaff trisail with a single halyard, using a wire span to lift the gaff. We'd need a boom to run along the foot. We'd used the old boom for the jury mast, but I could make a new one lashing together an oar, and the old jib boom (which we'd used when running before the wind) which had leather-served jaws that would fit around the mast.

All day I thought about it, envisioning how it would work and gathering the pieces together.

Monday 9th September: Day 5

Another long night on the sea anchor, but the wind eased a little, so at dawn, we had yet another go at the mast. It had to come down again so I could attach my revised forestay and two side stays to it and seat the base between wooden chocks on the deck. Now with the additional weight of the rigging and the howling wind on the violently rolling deck, it seemed near-impossible to set the mast back in place. Crying with frustration and exhaustion, I all but gave up, but somehow, we did it.

We were exhausted. Lack of food, lack of sleep, the wild conditions, the near loss of the boat, and our lives. Five days of trauma. And I thought it would only get worse as we became weaker. Any job requiring strength had to be done now. I was confident that we could set the sails on the 'new' mast when the wind went down, but which way should we sail? Where were we? Even with the sea anchor, we'd been swept along before the wind and seas for five days. Critical to sailing on was knowing where we were and the course we'd need to sail to reach land.

Knowing we'd eventually need this if we survived the capsize, we'd kept an hourly record of the direction and estimated speed of our drift since Day 2. Most of our charts had disintegrated into papier-mâché, but we still had an Atlas of American Pilot Charts (thanks to Alex Bell in Grenada) up forward, and somehow this had remained relatively undamaged. With the Americas on one side and Australia on the other, the scale was relatively small, but with nothing else, it would have to do.

Now I spread one out to work out where we might be. We'd capsized about 150 nm (277 kilometres) south-west of Tahiti. Now adding in the estimated direction and speed of our drift and the strength of the probable current from the chart, I estimated we might be about 270 miles north-east of the Cook Islands. If so, we needed to start sailing soon to get the best angle on the wind to reach Rarotonga, the largest of the Cook Islands.

North of Rarotonga were fifteen atolls that make up the northern Cook Islands. They are tiny dots on the chart, but each has razor-sharp coral reefs that could destroy *The Aegre* and probably us. If we were further west than I estimated, we would sail right into them. With no lighthouses, they would be invisible at night. The first sign would be when the boat hit the coral, and then it would all be over. Another worry.

You can get used to anything. We'd progressed from thinking we might not survive the night to planning how we could sail on to land, but now we were struggling with the difficulties that would arise with that. Our ultimate survival seemed uncertain, so we started to keep a diary. If we didn't live to tell the tale, we hoped it would survive us, so that ultimately our parents would learn what had happened. The only dryish paper was inside the cover of the Nautical Almanac. This, together with the other books of navigational tables, had survived immersion quite well and were now dry enough to write on.

We wrote describing the capsize and days since, each taking it in turn. It became apparent that I was becoming more optimistic as we improved the boat bit by bit, Julie less so.

Tuesday 10th September: Day 6

The wind was down a little at dawn, so we pulled in the sea anchor and set the flying jib on our makeshift mast for the first time. The Aegre started to make way, and we were sailing again, back on our way to Rarotonga. Our little boat had come back to life, and I was full of hope.

Reaching across, up and over the long high swells required the utmost concentration to steer the boat. Julie couldn't bear to look at the big seas and wouldn't steer, and the self-steering was still out of action, but I was happy to be on the helm all day, I was so pleased to be actually going somewhere, to be able to take some action to get ourselves out of this situation. It gave me more courage and determination.

By 5 pm, the wind was back to its previous strength, howling in the rigging. I was exhausted and becoming wide-eyed at the monstrous swells that seemed to be becoming ever taller and steeper with the increasing wind.

Soon I dropped the small jib to the deck and lashed it down, and we continued sailing with just the bare mast. Before long I could barely control the boat, and fearing we might be pushed sideways across one of the huge breaking wave tops and rolled over again, I reset the sea anchor to slow us down and hold our stern to the oncoming waves. Despite this, we were twice nearly rolled over again.

We were still making way downwind, which gave us steerage, so I tried steering the boat downwind by kneeling in the cockpit and looking backwards to the oncoming breaking swells. Then, with the tiller in both hands, I steered as straight as I could down the face of each oncoming wave. It worked, but again, a big cross-sea was coming up from the south. Occasionally, waves from the east and south would meet, then impossibly quickly build to form a great wall of a wave that would break with a terrifying roar. Every time they seemed to sweep past either side of *The Aegre,* still gallantly rising to each one. But what if she ever went under one of these giant breakers? Was another capsize inevitable?

As darkness closed in, I wondered if we would survive the night. I desperately needed to sleep, and somehow, Julie overcame her fears and said she'd try steering downwind for a bit, as I had been doing, kneeling in the cockpit looking aft in the darkness to steer down the oncoming mountains of water. In the darkness, she had to do it by feel more than sight. It was terrifying.

We took turns through the night, steering, staring back into the face of walls of black water marching down on us, breaking high above us and rushing roaring towards us in a mass of white phosphorescence. In between spells on the tiller, we lay on the sodden foam mattress under a soaking wet blanket in wet clammy clothes and oilskins, wondering if the next wave that broke with a roar out of the blackness would roll us again.

This was the worst so far. We were surrounded by the biggest waves we'd ever seen.

That night Julie wrote in her diary: *Just after dinner I was terrified of the waves, and thought of committing suicide, taking some pills or something.*

Wednesday 11th September: Day 7

But somehow we and *The Aegre* survived the night.. The wind eased a little in the early morning. It seemed the worst had passed. Once more, we lay to the sea anchor, exhausted.

The following day, with the wind down a little, I set the small flying jib again, and Julie steered up and over the giant swells. It seemed easy after the previous night's drama.

While she steered, I set about repairing the self-steering system. It was mounted out on a beam in the clear air off the stern, where it had always been awkward to reach at sea. Usually there was no need to reach out to it; all the adjustments could be made with lines coming to the cockpit. But now we had to replace these lines. I had to lie out over the stern along the beam. It wasn't easy on a good day, as the boat rolled and pitched, but now as I braced myself with my legs, it was excruciatingly painful for me due to cuts on both my knees. I'd unknowingly bashed them badly getting out of the cabin after the capsize. After a week of being perpetually wet, they had become ugly open sores that were excruciatingly painful to touch. With tears in my eyes, I un-rigged the self-steering system, brought it inboard, replaced the lines and reset it, thankfully not dropping it overboard.

It worked. No longer would we be tied to steering by hand all day and night. Another small step toward normality. But I was all in from the effort.

Julie produced four little squares of chocolate from somewhere, and I quickly revived. But there weren't many little squares left. Our meagre lunch soon followed, half a pamplemousse between us, a little cheese, a small knob of butter and half a teaspoon of jam. Then we got sailing again, but now with the self-steering working.

By the evening, the wind was howling through the rigging again, and we were back running before it under the bare mast. But we knew the drill and spent another night kneeling in the cockpit (me on my poor knees), staring down the mega-waves while the wind howled and squally showers swept over us.

It seemed never-ending. Then Julie's oilskin top tore badly at the elbow as she was putting it on at our change of watch at 0220 in heavy rain. Both our oilskins were just worn out. We'd tried to replace them in Tahiti but found nothing like what we wanted. It seemed there wasn't much call for heavy-duty wet-weather sailing clothing in Tahiti. Funny that.

Thursday 12th September: Day 8

The weather again improved with the dawn, the wind falling as the sky brightened in the east. Optimistically I set the jib again and pulled in the sea anchor, and the self-steering system took over. Was our long night coming to an end?

It had been a whole week of shocking weather since we'd capsized. Our spirits lifted as the beginnings of relative normality aboard *The Aegre* started to return. We'd been wholly consumed by surviving, then just steering or sleeping for so long. Now we began to sit and chat again.

Julie told me of her experience of the capsize. Apparently it was 04:15, and she just had five minutes left on her watch when she saw a huge wave coming up from astern. She tried to shield the cabin by blocking the companionway with her body. The next thing she knew, she was breathing and swallowing seawater and thinking she had to stop doing that, or she'd drown. She struggled free, surfaced and was shocked to find *The Aegre* upside down. She knew I must be trapped, asleep inside, and it would be impossible for me to get out. She felt helpless and alone. She thought of how many times we had listed the qualities of the boat; unsinkable and self-righting. Well, now she knew one of those was wrong.

She shouted for me, then heard me calling her back from the other side of the boat, and then saw me scrambling up onto the hull. 'I realised I wasn't going to die just immediately,' she said.

She remembered how I started to pull her up onto the hull, and then it all went black again for her as she was dragged back underwater, being pulled by her life harness to the other side of the boat. She surfaced again and saw *The Aegre* was now upright. She remembered me pulling her back aboard, then clinging to the mast, gasping, having swallowed a lot of water. Then she saw me bailing like crazy to no avail, then blowing up the dinghy and passing the lines to her, then another monstrous wave crashing over the boat, sweeping her overboard again, and the dinghy lines being torn from her hands.

But here we were, a week later, still going.

With the sea and wind going down and *The Aegre* comfortably sailing herself, we escaped for a little while, Julie lying on the bunk, me sitting on the floor of the cockpit, head beneath the hatch. It was almost cosy, almost like old times, as we chatted and joked, remembering our happy times at Ardmore and the Scourie Hotel.

With *The Aegre* making progress again, I brought our position on the chart up to date. According to Bob's log (which had survived everything and seemed to be working as well as ever), we had run about 100 miles roughly towards Rarotonga, but finding the tiny island without the sextant would be difficult. From our slowly drying Nautical Almanac, I knew that the declination (the latitude on Earth over which a star passes vertically) of the bright star Antares was 26° 22′ south, and Sirius was 16° 42′ south. Rarotonga was in 21 south. So if we kept Antares to the south and Sirius to the north, we could be somewhere near the latitude of Rarotonga. But with a 9° difference between them and 60 nautical miles per degree, 'somewhere near' meant being somewhere on a north-south line 540 nautical miles long, and I didn't fancy our chances of seeing the island.

Rarotonga did have a Radio Direction Finding beacon, but our little radio had spent hours underwater and despite copiously spraying it with WD40, it never worked again.

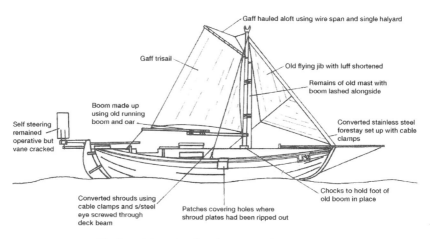

The Aegre's jury rig after the capsize (N Grainger)

We started talking about what to do if we got to where we thought Rarotonga was and there was nothing to be seen. A worrying thought to sleep on as I turned in after my watch, *The Aegre* now almost gently easing along, the self-steering in full control. I resolved to set more sail tomorrow if it stayed this way.

By the dawn of day 9, the wind had dropped considerably, and the seas were down. We even saw a little bit of hazy sun for the first time. Now I tried setting the gaff mainsail and jib together. The set-up all worked, and soon we were sailing again in a reasonably normal way towards, we hoped, Rarotonga.

In all, the terrible weather lasted only eight days, but it seemed never-ending. Unable to dry ourselves at any time during this period, we developed open salt sores on our buttocks and the cuts on my knees developed into excruciatingly painful sores.

Based on my latest estimation of our position, I thought we might see Rarotonga in two or three days' time. But what if we didn't? Or worse, sailed onto the reef of one of the Cook Island atolls?

We knew that if we could time sunrise or sunset, we could calculate our longitude and then, knowing when we had reached the same longitude as Rarotonga, we could look most carefully north and south. Rarotonga is a high volcanic cone-type island like Tahiti, so it should be visible from 10–20 miles on a good day. We just might see it. If not we'd still know it was to the south of us, or to the north. But which? Turning either way would be a gamble. We hadn't seen the sun or sunrise or sunset since we'd left Tahiti. However, the weather was improving, and that day we'd had a little hazy sunshine. Maybe tomorrow?

Without confirming our longitude, we decided there was no point in going south or north looking for Rarotonga. We could easily be too far east or west and see nothing and just sail on out into the North or South Pacific until our food was finished, and then our water came to an end. No, we agreed that wasn't an option.

Staring at the chart, I could see that if we kept going on our present course with the south-east trade wind behind us, we might possibly see some of the tiny Cook Island atolls, but probably not, and would most likely sail through or to the north of them. Continuing westward, we'd eventually reach the longitude of the larger Tonga archipelago that ran north/south ahead of us.

The Tonga group comprises 169 small islands and coral atolls spread over 800 kilometres (432 miles) from north to south, right across our projected path. We'd surely see one of these islands or atolls I optimistically thought. But there were two problems with setting a course for the Tonga group. Firstly it was 1,597 kilometres (860 miles) further west than Rarotonga, 16 days sailing at 50 miles per day under our jury rig, so another 18 days from where we were now. Would we have enough food? But almost a bigger problem was that extremely few of the tiny Tonga islands had lights, and few (only 36 apparently) were inhabited. Many were just low coral atolls. But there were several higher volcanic peaks, too, the highest being 3,389ft (1,033m), so we might see one of them.

There were also potential hazards on the way, such as the unlit Cook Island atolls to the north of Rarotonga and some other possible unmarked reefs shown by a tiny, dotted circle and 'Breakers Reported' on our chart.

Sure, we might sail all the way to the Tonga group, then be wrecked on a reef in the middle of the night. Or sail right through the group without seeing anything at all. But we might see another vessel on the way, or possibly come up with a better idea. Still, I mused, tomorrow, if we could just clearly see the sunrise or sunset, we could get a good estimation of our longitude. That might change everything.

Saturday 14th September: Day 10

The next day the weather did improve, and it became sunny during the middle part of the day, but the sunset was hazy, and I didn't trust our timing of it. Now we were worried that we might be approaching the Cook Island atolls, so at dusk I dropped the sails, and we just lay still in the water all night. There was a good breeze, and it seemed a pity to waste it, but we couldn't risk going onto an atoll in the darkness.

Sunday 15th September: Day 11

The light wind continued, which was comfortable to sail with but meant we made slower progress. We used the time to scour the boat for food. Julie went through all the rice and had to throw out about 10 lbs which had gone mouldy, but we still had 6 or 7lbs, which she spread out in bowls to dry in the sun.

Regarding the remaining food, she drew up a list. The main items were a dozen small cans of sardines, a few small blocks of cheese, some canned butter and jam, some bottles of honey and lime juice (thanks Canada), some cans with no labels, some pamplemousse and potatoes, the rice, and some mildewed chocolate

Wanting to make our food last as long as possible, our diet had been very meagre since the capsize. I estimated we'd been sharing about half of what I used to eat for breakfast over a whole day.

We thought if we didn't see Rarotonga, we should sail on towards Tonga, despite our misgivings, and we needed to plan for the food to last at least another twenty days. We reduced our daily ration further. We were less worried about water, having at least enough for twenty days, at more than two litres a day.

Ironically, after having masses of fish around us in the Eastern Pacific, now we saw none, possibly because the bottom of the boat was clean after the Tahiti repaint.

We talked about how we would enjoy toast for breakfast in our own place, coffee and tea, lovely dinners, and music one day. We decided that if we made it, we should kick each other sometimes, just to remind ourselves that we'd survived all this.

Monday 16th September: Day 12

The light wind fell right away during the night. We were becalmed and the sky cleared, the stars shining brightly. Using a hand-bearing compass, I tried to track Sirius and Antares as they rose. Antares reached its meridian (peak) altitude during our night and was definitely to the south. Sirius was still rising at our dawn but had been tracking closer and closer to due east, and seemed it would pass right overhead, putting us in a latitude of about 17°S.

I kept rechecking the bearing of Sirius. Could this be right, that we were in about 17°S? I'd estimated we were in about 20°S, 180 miles further south. If the bearing of Sirius was right, we were well north of the Cook Island atolls and more than two hundred miles north of Rarotonga.

Aghast at how far out my estimation had been, I plotted our new estimated position on the chart. To be in this position ten days after the capsize we must have been continually swept west-north-west, not west-south-west. How could I have got it so wrong?

If my logic regarding our position relative to Sirius was correct, there was no point in looking for Rarotonga. We were much too far north. So should we just press on for Tonga?

Clouds on the horizon during dawn and dusk obscured the sun and a possible longitude estimation, but as the overall weather continued to improve, maybe tomorrow?

Julie used the fine weather to dry out food on deck. I dried out the wicks in the two kerosene lights we used in the cabin at night and replaced the kerosene. They worked. It was so much more homely to have a little light below at night.

The primus cooker was next. We had two, the one in use and a spare, but neither would work. The jets were blocked, and the box of prickers and spares was missing. I'd need to make a fine wire pricker to clean the jets. Until then, no hot food or drinks.

Despite our minuscule diet for the last two weeks, we were still in good health, but we quickly became weak. We began to avoid standing up or doing anything requiring energy.

A light wind had given us some miles during the day but then fell away, and we were becalmed again by nightfall. But for the first time saw a clear sunset and were able to time it exactly with our Accutron watch. With Julie remembering its error, we could convert this to GMT, and applying a refraction error, calculate our (approximate) longitude. I'd tried this method before, in the eastern Pacific, comparing the longitude it gave with star sights. There was a constant error, I believed due to refraction. Now trusting it, I was surprised to find it put us further west than was indicated by Bob's log, which measures the distance travelled through the water. Maybe there had been a current pushing us west-north-west? Assuming this position was correct, we expected to be on the same longitude as Rarotonga in the afternoon of the next day at our current speed. But from our observations of Sirius, I doubted we'd see the island. We were surely too far north.

Even so, we kept an extra careful lookout overnight as *The Aegre* sailed on.

Tuesday 17ᵗʰ September 1974: Day 13

It was a slow night as the wind died. It would be yet another day before we reached the longitude of Rarotonga, but our spirits were improving with the calm, sunny weather. Visibility in the day was good, but there was no sign of Rarotonga.

The next morning, now two weeks since the capsize, a clear, sunny dawn brought a light wind from the south, flecking across the water and giving me yet more hope. I set the jib and mainsail, and soon we were sailing close-hauled into it and making nearly three knots under our little jury rig. But was Rarotonga ahead? I doubted it, but somehow I felt unwilling to give up the possibility. Maybe my original position was correct? Could I trust my bearing of Sirius?

Now making some miles, we expected to be in the same longitude as Rarotonga the next day.

Thursday 19ᵗʰ September 1974: Day 15

A clear sunrise gave us a firm longitude fix: we were in the same longitude as Rarotonga.

It was another beautiful day typical of the SE trade winds in the South Pacific. High volcanic islands like Rarotonga sometimes had a stationary white cloud over their peak. But all around our horizon lay puffy little white clouds, typical of the trade winds. Was one of them stationary, over an island? A skilled Polynesian navigator might have been able to say, but we couldn't tell. There just seemed to be an empty horizon in every direction. As the day wore on, our not-very-high hopes slowly fell away to nothing.

Now we had to decide whether to try and find Rarotonga by sailing for maybe 240 miles to the south or abandon looking for the island and sail westward towards the Tonga group a further 860 miles (1,600 km) to the west.

Chapter 19
Sailing on to where?

'There is a reason the remote Pacific was the last place on Earth to be settled by humans: it was the most difficult, more daunting even than the deserts or the ice.' — Christina Thompson, Sea People: The Puzzle of Polynesia

Rarotonga seemed by far the closest land, only about 240 miles to our south, so why wouldn't we head there? There were two reasons. Firstly, it wasn't the closest land. About 120 miles due south of us, on about the same longitude as Rarotonga, was the large atoll of Aitutaki, one of the fifteen Cook Island atolls to the north of Rarotonga and mostly a little more to our east. If our longitude was just a little out, we could sail straight into them, as we so nearly had in the Tuomotus. Secondly, Rarotonga is a single island, and while it has a high volcanic cone, our longitude wouldn't need to be far out for us to sail past too far away to see it. Then we'd be heading on south towards the empty ocean.

The alternative, to keep sailing west, ultimately toward the wide band of the Tonga islands, seemed the better choice. And we might see another vessel or come up with a better idea in the further two weeks it would take. We'd just have to nurse our jury rig and eat less.

A small tin of sardines became a two-day ration for the two of us, supplemented by a narrow sliver of cheese, a tiny knob of butter and half a teaspoon of jam. We had ten more tins of sardines plus two other mystery cans. It seemed possible as long as the rig held together and we didn't have too much bad weather. But quietly, we were beginning to face the possibility that we might never find land again.

A clear sunset that evening put us in longitude 160° 30′ W, a little over 30 miles west of the longitude of Rarotonga but still close to the islandless reefs and atolls to the main island's north. To avoid possibly running onto one of these atolls in the night, we again dropped the sails and hove to, stopping the boat in the water for the night. I put out our rudimentary sea anchor, which held *The Aegre* in a position where she didn't roll much. Suddenly it was silent. There was no noise from the bow wave, no howling wind—just silence. The boat rocked gently. A gentle kerplunk sound came from the edges of the hull strakes hitting the ripples on the water. Bob's log hung straight down into the depths. Meanwhile, a favourable light wind rustled over us as if going to waste. Were we being overcautious? There's no answer to that question, except we didn't sail onto a reef that night.

Sprawled on the cockpit floor of the silent boat on watch that night, looking up at the stars, I thought of the early navigators sailing these waters, knowing little of what lay ahead. How many times had they stopped sailing at night?

Now that the main crisis of the capsize had passed, and particularly with the boat still and quiet, Julie was missing the books we had amassed aboard; *Boredom is a problem,* she wrote in her diary, *with so many of our new books destroyed. I'm going to have to start learning poetry soon to pass the time.* But of course we still had each other for company. *We talk a lot,* wrote Julie, *about the future and the comforts we hope to enjoy. I think Nick misses them more than I do. I just want to get onto dry land away from the relentless sea and wind.*

We got underway again at first light, sailing with a gentle breeze. The day before we had had our best day's run under the jury rig, 80 miles. We had now sailed 350 miles with the jury rig. We just needed it to hold together for another 700-plus miles to take us to the Tonga group. But *The Aegre* was still taking in water, and now we were pumping about 30 strokes every two hours to keep the water below the floorboards. It was containable, but I couldn't find where it was coming in, which worried me a bit.

We still thought there was a possibility of being picked up by a ship, so we used the fine weather to methodically plan and prepare what we should take with us if we had to abandon *The Aegre*. We packed the items we weren't using every day into a backpack and the now-empty big green canvas Avon dinghy bag.

The best way to keep cheerful seemed to be to think about the future. To plan the good times, well, just returning to quiet everyday life, but the idea seemed luxurious to us now; a bit of security, delicious meals and listening to music.

The light ENE wind seemed to have settled in, pushing us along smoothly now to the west, with sunny days and calm seas. Easy sailing if a bit slow, but still, we averaged over 50 miles a day.

We used these easy days to try to improve our situation, and for me the next priority was the Primus cooker. Our 'impossible to go wrong' cooker hadn't worked since the capsize, now 17 days ago. The fine vaporising jet was blocked, and we'd lost the packet of prickers. Painstakingly I made a new pricker by filing down a thin strand of stainless wire, then refilled the cooker with fresh kerosene. It worked! Not perfectly, but well enough to cook rice or potatoes, or even make a cup of tea. Then it blocked again, and my makeshift pricker broke trying to clear it. So I filed down another one, which also worked.

Calm weather like this had been good for fishing in the past, and we continually scanned the water around us for dorado, but there was no sign of them, nor any other fish. With our cooker going again, fresh fish cooked in a little oil was but a dream.

Beneath us, *The Aegre* slowly sailed on westward, our progress confirmed by clear sunrise and sunset timings, our longitude and estimated latitude plotted each day on the pilot chart of the Pacific. By Day 18, we were approaching the Auckland-US west coast shipping route. We hardly expected it to be like the busy mid-Atlantic shipping route where we'd seen a near-continuous line of ships, but we kept a close look out anyway. We saw none.

On these calm days and nights, with the future so uncertain, Julie and I continued to talk a lot. We hoped our parents weren't worried about us. We'd told them we'd be in Rarotonga by about the 10th September, 11 days ago. I imagined my mother sitting by the fire in Cottenham, staring into the embers, lost in thought.

We talked about our childhood, our friends, and the future. I created a list of things I wanted to do during the rest of my life if we survived this. Julie wrote in her diary: *the future for me would be fine with a house, children, security, an interesting job, preferably in education, Nick happy in his work. I think I've had enough adventure. Nick keeps very cheery, by talking of the future. This time he'd like to go in for single handed ocean racing, like Alain Colas who we met in Tahiti. He is quite resigned to me being finished with sailing.*

Ironically, in the depths of the boat we found a collection of mouth-watering recipes. Although we had lost most of our 30–40-book library in the capsize, bits of some books had survived and come to light in unexpected places. One such was a red file of recipes that my sister Diana had given us when Julie and I married.

Now living on about a sixth of what I usually ate every day. I gorged (in my mind) on detailed instructions about roasting meat and how to make brown stews, toffee shortbread, rock cakes, Richard's birthday trifle and the date and walnut cake that never failed. Julie wrote about food too; *We think and talk about food a lot of the time, Christmas dinner, mince pies, I am going to make 50 for the two of us if we are ever spending Christmas together by ourselves, and I'll keep hundreds of jars of mince in the cupboard so I can make 50 more. Shepherd's pie, curry. Really any normal sort of food seems delicious under these circumstances. I think Nick likes main course the best. I like puddings. Apple crumble and ice cream, treacle pudding, jam tart, Mmmm!*

Inspired, we tried cooking some of the dried but rather smelly rice one evening, mixing it with some soup mix we'd found, but it was uneatable. We threw most of it away.

Then the wind died entirely, and we were becalmed once more. Making no progress was a worry, but we still had plenty of fresh water, having consumed just 20 litres in the previous 19 days. We still had 40 litres in jerricans.

Becalmed and hot, I went for a swim. We hadn't seen any sharks for days, but I checked beneath the boat before diving in this time. It was so refreshing. I inspected the hull and noticed that the antifouling was marked on the port side where I clambered over it after the capsize and also where the broken section of the mast must have hit it. But there was practically nothing growing on the hull underwater. That was probably why we had no fish swimming with us now. Even the effort of the swim exhausted me.

In time the wind returned and steadily freshened. I didn't want to stress our jury rig too much as it still had far to go, so I eventually dropped the mainsail, and we ran under the jib for a day and night. It was easier on our nerves too.

Food was always on our minds, and after the previous dinner disappointment, we decided to treat ourselves to a 'big meal'. Well, hardly. We opened a 14 oz (400 gram) mystery can, which turned out to be ravioli, and spread it over two evenings with 7 oz between us each evening. Compared to our recent 1 oz each of sardines, it was pretty filling.

Our appetites had shrunk. We had also found two small containers of curry powder, one a little damp but slowly drying out, and a tub of glacé cherries. Not counting the rice, we still had eight cans of sardines and three other evening meal cans. Enough for 22 meals, sort of. Plus, the flour, jam, butter, a can of condensed milk and some jelly crystals. Surely enough to reach the Tonga Islands?

But after 20 days, our much-reduced diet was beginning to tell. Whenever I stood up I felt dizzy, although this would quickly pass, and routine deck work such as lowering and stowing the mainsail in a squall was exhausting.

In general, Julie seemed to be surviving physically better than I was, although I think I was more confident of our survival than she was. Indeed, she was losing less weight than me. We even agreed, at her suggestion, that I should have a bigger share of our tiny daily ration of food, but we almost immediately scrapped the idea as we found it impossible not to be scrupulously fair in its division.

We would have had ample food for this voyage had not nearly all our dehydrated and dry stores been ruined by seawater despite being wrapped in polythene and inside polythene boxes.

As ever, we alternated being on watch every four hours, both to keep *The Aegre* going as best we could and in the hope of seeing a ship. In this routine, we didn't really see that much of each other. While I always enjoyed Julie's company, I liked being on watch alone too. With the self-steering freeing one from the bondage of the tiller, I had time to ensure all the little details of the rig were right (to minimise chafe), and to sit and reflect and wonder at the sea.

But I was becoming increasingly worried about our hoped-for landfall, and with the self-steering in charge, I focused on the chart. As I studied it, I couldn't help noticing how big a gap there was between some of the islands that make up the Tonga Archipelago. How easy it would be to sail right through and see nothing. And what about all those reefs that had no land nearby? If we hit one of those *The Aegre* would break up, and that would probably be the end of us.

I had been thinking for a while that there must be a better way than just blundering into this atoll-strewn area. An undefined idea in my mind was about how to use all the information in the Nautical Almanac and Sight

Reduction Tables. They were damp but still readable. Surely we could use all that information somehow?

What we needed was a more accurate way of determining our position. Well, we had our longitude from sunrise and sunset times, but our latitude was much more of a guess. Was close under Sirius in 17°S really good enough?

I knew that if I could identify a star that reached its meridian altitude (highest point, like the sun at midday) directly above me, then our latitude would be equal to its declination. But how could I tell if a star reached its meridian altitude directly overhead or slightly to the north or south? And wouldn't the star have to reach its meridian altitude in our night so I could actually see it?

I'd been thinking about this for a few weeks and on clear nights I had been identifying relatively bright stars one by one using the data in Vol 1 of the Sight Reduction Tables (Selected Stars), as I had done before in the eastern Pacific passage. My developing plan had been to record the approximate azimuths (bearings on a terrestrial scale) of two stars, one having a declination well to the north of our estimated latitude, and one well to the south. Then, having confirmed that they reached their meridian altitudes to our north and south respectively, I would gradually close in by selecting other stars with declinations north and south, closer to our estimated latitude. Finally, I hoped to find a star that reached its meridian altitude as close as I could tell to overhead. The declination of that star would be equal to our approximate latitude.

But now, I could go a step further. We'd recently found a lovely little Suunto hand-bearing compass jammed in an obscure cranny in the bilge (everything seemed to end up somewhere in the bilge). We had bought this for a song from another yacht at the ocean yacht cruising equivalent of a garage sale in Barbados, but thought it lost in the capsize. It was a beautiful instrument created inside a block of stainless steel and designed to be held to the eye, the compass scale being projected onto the horizon. It was well damped and could give an accurate bearing. It had some luminous night illumination, but that was rather dim.

To use it to accurately measure star azimuths I needed it to be well lit at night, and now discovered that if I held one of our French diving torches vertically downwards on the horizontal face, which it just fitted, it didn't deflect the bearing shown, but the compass card reading was now clearly visible projected onto the horizon. If I kept both eyes open, I could line the projection of the compass bearing reading, visible with my right eye, with the star visible with my left eye. Keeping both eyes open and integrating the two quite different images is not so hard. I learned how to do it while studying photography and later working with optical instruments in London as a student. Suddenly it was a useful skill and enabled me to measure the bearing of a star quite accurately. Seeing a star rise somewhere in the east, I could track it until it was due north or south, and therefore at its meridian altitude.

I first observed Rigel (declination 8° 14′ south) and Antares (26° 22′ south). As I could use only relatively bright stars, I was forced to take readings on some stars that did not reach their meridian altitudes during our night, but I could predict their track using my tables and their rising and setting azimuths.

I soon confirmed my previous rough observation. Sirius (declination 16° 41′ south) did indeed reach its meridian altitude almost directly overhead, so our latitude must be very close to its declination, i.e. 17° South. This further confirmed that we were much further north than we had initially estimated. I trusted it, so we had indeed been well north of Rarotonga, which was much further south at near 21° south, so we had indeed been more than 200 miles to the north of it. No wonder we hadn't seen it.

Well, it was still only an estimate. Nevertheless, I wondered how I could use this knowledge to make a safe landfall.

I was back to studying our surviving Pacific chart. The little blobs of land looked tiny. They could be only fly marks. Just reaching an island wasn't the answer either, as so many were bounded by off-lying reefs. The chances of getting over the reef and making it to the land (swimming the latter part almost certainly) were slim indeed, especially as, in many cases, the land is literally miles from the encircling coral reef.

I just had to keep thinking.

As I have already mentioned, one of the delights of ocean sailing to me on a yacht with a small crew is being on watch alone. It's a sort of forced idleness. I loved Julie's company, but I loved too the time when she slept. After the boat-keeping chores were completed and the self-steering system trimmed, I would sit on the floor of the cockpit, head at deck-level watching the sea and the way of *The Aegre*, and thinking. I thought about how the early navigators had found their way, particularly those from Europe. Quite early on, they had developed ways of measuring their approximate latitude, how far north or south they were. But longitude (how far around the world, east or west they were) was much more difficult as it needed accurate timekeeping, which they didn't have. I remembered how they got around this problem using a process known today as 'latitude sailing'.

Latitude sailing required the ship to reach the latitude of its destination long before it reached its approximate longitude. Then they sailed due east (or west), maintaining the same latitude until their destination appeared (sooner or later) ahead. On *The Aegre*, we seemed to have it the other way around. Our longitude measurements with sunrise and sunset times were more accurate than our latitude measurements with star azimuths.

So maybe we should go longitude sailing? In other words, get on the same longitude as an island, but well to the north (or south), then sail straight north (or south) while maintaining our longitude until we got there. It seemed to make sense. I'd thought a bit about this when we were north of Rarotonga but abandoned the idea because Rarotonga was a single small island, although moderately high, and the low Cook Island atolls lay between us and it. With all the possible errors in my thinking and measurements at the time, the chances of our seeing Rarotonga had seemed slim. But now, with renewed confidence in our longitude and approximate latitude, I carefully studied the chart and quickly realised that the place to head for would be the Samoa islands.

This small group of islands had several advantages. Firstly they lay in latitude 14° south, i.e. somewhere between 150 and 200 miles north of where we were, in 17° south. (At the Equator, 1 degree of latitude is 60 nautical miles). Even allowing for quite a bit of error in my estimation of our latitude, they were surely to the north of us.

Secondly, they are relatively high mountainous islands, so potentially visible from some distance.

Thirdly they lie roughly in an east-west direction, over about 150 miles. The biggest gap between any of these high and (hopefully) easily observable islands seemed only about 50 miles, so the furthest we could be from the land if we happened to sail through the biggest gap would be 25 miles. With any sort of luck, we'd see the land on one side or the other at that distance.

Fourthly, they don't have coral reefs lying many miles out from shore and, in fact, seemed relatively free of off-lying dangers. Nor were there any dangerous reefs or atolls between us and them.

Fifthly, one of the islands, Pago Pago, is a US territory, and that would mean US coastguard, aircraft, and coastal shipping. All the things we dreamed about.

To reach the Samoa group, we would need to continue sailing west on our current latitude (17°S) until we reached the longitude of the middle island of the Samoa group (Upolo). Then we would turn north and sail up that line of longitude, probably for about 180 miles, until we sighted the land.

From the chart, I could see that we would turn north just before we reached the edge of the Tonga group. We'd avoid the atolls, but we would be extending the voyage yet again—this time by a couple of hundred miles. I had a brief moment of doubt. What if I had been making a significant navigational error all along, and we saw no land where Samoa should be? Perhaps we should just sail straight on and risk the reefs of Tonga?

But no, I felt confident I was right. This was undoubtedly the best plan. I progressively explained it to Julie as it evolved in my head. I noted, too, that we would be sailing north along the Auckland-Pago Pago shipping route. Hardly likely to be busy, but it might increase our chances of seeing a ship.

It was now three weeks since the capsize, but we had the most hopeful plan yet. In fact, it seemed a good plan. Julie agreed, and to celebrate, we opened our one and only bottle of Glenmorangie whisky. We'd brought this rare malt carefully from the north of Scotland, saving it for some auspicious occasion. This seemed as good as any. We didn't have much food or water left, but we had some excellent whisky. We had also found a small tin of glacé cherries, so we had a sort of cocktail party *Aegre* style, with a sip of whisky and half a glacé cherry. Usually, we didn't drink any alcohol at all at sea. It was difficult enough aboard *The Aegre*, but a quote from one of my sailing heroes, Sir Francis Chichester, always made me smile. While loading gin aboard *Gipsy Moth IV* in London before sailing for Sydney, he reputedly said: 'Any damn fool can navigate the world sober. It takes a really good sailor to do it drunk'. It made me smile. I knew we weren't that good.

With the cocktail party over, it was time for dinner. The ravioli was finished, so it was back to half a can of sardines, between us.

A few days later, as if to encourage us with our plan, we saw lots of frigate birds and other seabirds for the first time, a good sign, although we knew frigate birds could be found up to 300 miles from land. Based on our estimated position, we believed we were now indeed within 200 miles of Samoa (to the north-west, 14° south, 171 45 west) and 120 nautical miles off the small island of Niue (to the south-west, 19° south, 169° 55' west).

Saturday 28th September was my father's birthday and our 24th day since the capsize. I was sorry not to speak to him, but we sang 'Happy Birthday' to him anyway.

A clear sunrise put us in longitude 169° west. It was our first sighting for a few days and indicated we were being pushed west about five miles a day by a current. Overnight the sky had been clear and I had plotted the rising paths of Rigel and Sirius. Rigel went marching off to the northern sky, while Sirius just kept coming straight up from due east. I was increasingly confident that we were in a latitude of 17° south.

Steadily we were creeping westward towards the point when we would have to choose between turning north for Samoa or going straight on for Tonga.

By Monday 30th September 1974, 26 days since the capsize, the sunrise longitude measurement put us due south of Pago Pago, the easternmost of the three larger islands of the Samoa group. Based on our estimated latitude of 17° S, Pago, in Latitude 14° 18' S, would be about 200 miles due north. But sailing due north, we had to allow for a current pushing us westward which would push us toward Upolo, the middle island, and in the worst case towards Savai'i, the large western island. Surely we couldn't miss all three?

Looking at the chart, it seemed we were at a crossroads. Straight on for Tonga, maybe closer, or turn north for the Samoa group. By turning north, we would be extending the voyage. But if our navigation was correct, we'd have more chance of sighting one of the islands and of making a safe landing.

Up on deck, it all looked just the same in every direction, just blue sky and fleecy white trade wind clouds.

At 8am, we agreed and committed to our thinking. I pushed the tiller hard over, and we turned 90° to start sailing due north. I looked back at our wake. The right-angle turn was as if around an invisible buoy, and it briefly marked a decisive point in the ocean and then was gone. We had come more than 1,300 miles since the capsize, and it seemed we were on the last lap, one way or another.

The next morning, we checked our longitude with the sunrise time, confirming we were maintaining our longitude and on course for Samoa. By noon we had made about 60 miles north. But the wind was shifting to the north of east and including leeway (the sideways movement of the boat due to the wind), I estimated our true course was now about 330° T or 30° off the true north (360°) course we needed to maintain. We were being pushed

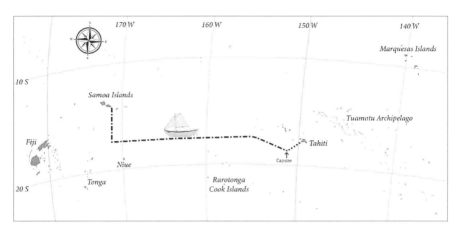

Tahiti to Samoa

further west than we intended. It seemed ironic after the prevailing wind had been from the south-east for most of the time since the capsize.

We hoped the wind would return to the south-east, then we could sail east of north to return to our target longitude, aiming for the middle of the Samoa group.

All our logic said we were on the final leg of our self-rescue from the capsize, dismasting and loss of the sextant. We were surely heading north for the middle of a high island group that extended a few hundred miles east-west and had to be to the north of us. Even with quite a bit of error in the estimation of our position, we'd see it sooner or later. Wouldn't we?

But another part of my mind questioned the logic. How accurate really was our longitude position derived from sunrise and sunset times? And our latitude estimation from star meridian azimuths (north-south direction of stars at their peak altitude)? Was I just making some fundamental mistakes in my thinking? My methods weren't in any textbooks I'd ever seen. I had explained my thinking to Julie and kept going over it, but she had left the navigation to me in the past, and now, while she supported my logic, I didn't feel reassured. We opened our last can of jam at breakfast time and a can of fruit cocktail. It contained 36 small pieces of fruit in syrup. 18 each. We would make it last two days. Then we would have just one can of peaches left. The end of our food was in sight.

The sky was still clear, and visibility good, but there was nothing to be seen on the horizon in any direction. I reminded myself that it was still a long way to the Samoa Islands, and I shouldn't expect to see anything for a day or two yet. How big the ocean is. But my optimistic mind said that if we were south and approaching Samoa, we might see a ship going to or from New Zealand, and if they saw us, we could get a position fix from them and then decide what to do. We talked through the options. If we were approaching Samoa, we agreed we might just ask for some food and then carry on, to sail in by ourselves. In hindsight, a bold choice, but *The Aegre* was sailing well by now, and we had renewed confidence in her. The alternative seemed to mean abandoning her, and after coming so far and through so much, that felt as if we were giving up, and it didn't sit well with us.

In reality, just holding the rig together took time and care. The wind vane self-steering gear had continued to go well, enabling us to stay out of the sun, but now one of the lines was chafed and needed replacing if it was to keep going. This required working on the vane gear stuck out on a beam off the back of the boat to clear our long boom. Working on it had always been tricky in rough weather. In the past, I had lain down out over the stern, partially on the beam, where I could just reach it with outstretched hands. A precarious position. The sores on my knees, still unhealed and excruciatingly painful to touch, now made it all but impossible for me. I just couldn't find a position where I could reach the gear without having to brace myself with my knees as the boat rolled. I tried and tried, but couldn't do it. With tears in my eyes, I eventually pulled myself back to slump on the floor of the cockpit, exhausted and gasping with the pain from my knees. I thought I was going to faint.

Throughout the voyage, I had looked after the boat and rig. Now, four weeks after the capsize, exhausted, hungry, with screaming pain from the sores on my knees, I felt all in, but we needed the self-steering to save us from having to steer all the time ourselves.

Julie said she'd have a go at replacing the line. It was a terrible job hanging out over the stern, and incredibly awkward. I helped her out onto the stern and hung onto her as she inched further and further out onto the bumpkin (a short spar extending from the stern) until she could just reach the self-steering system. Once there, she painstakingly threaded and tied the new lines, then carefully wriggled back onto the aft deck, the hero of the day. Now the self-steering was working again, thanks to her effort. It was a significant moment that I still think of whenever I look at the scars on my knees.

But Julie was suffering in her own way, as she describes in her diary: *I seem to feel depressed all the time now. I just want to lie on the bed, and go into a deep sleep which will last forever. Perhaps we have got the bed too comfortable now. We have a blanket underneath, then a sheet, then a dry comforting Downie. It's really bliss to get in.*

Now the wind was shifting even further to the north-east, forcing us to sail close-hauled to maintain our longitude, the most stressful point of sail for our jury rig and its least effective. The self-steering was working well again, but now we were sailing up and over and through the oncoming seas. The motion became violent, spray flying everywhere. Despite her valiant effort on the stern Julie became increasingly unwell and depressed, and was eventually seasick. I was worried about her as she could ill afford to lose any fluid. It was desperately important to maintain our bodily condition in case we did not see any of the Samoa islands and were forced to think again. But if we were to have any faith in our navigation, which indicated that the islands were to the north, then we had to maintain our longitude, which meant beating to windward regardless, so that's what we did.

But what if we didn't see any of the islands of Samoa — Pago Pago, Upolo or Savai'i? The possibility was starting to enter our thinking, and we discussed it. If we reached, say 12° N, we decided, surely to the north of Samoa, with no sight of land, we'd just have to turn west-south-west and head for the Fiji group, another 630 nautical miles (1,169 kilometres), another 12 days, the Tonga archipelago now further to the south. A daunting prospect, but at least we had a plan.

The stress was telling on both of us, as Julie wrote in her diary: *Both a bit more cheery than yesterday, but both weak and easily tired. We sat up for a while after dinner. Talking and holding hands, and it cheered me up a good deal. I had to cry in my afternoon watch to relieve my tension a bit. Poor Nick had a tiring watch. Becalmed at first, he dropped the sail, and immediately some wind came. We have been managing to make a better course since then, east of north. At change of watches, 0430, I was sick. Perhaps the beating instead of running? I took an Avomine, half, after breakfast. I can't afford to lose any body fluid or food. Nick seems very weak, I think he is worrying about his parents who must be worrying about us now. I just try not to think about it. Still we may be where we think we are, in which case we should reach Samoa in the foreseeable future I think.*

About midnight, the wind picked up from the south-east, I set the sails, and soon we were making good speed beating east of north as we had hoped, to maintain our longitude going north, but now into a rising sea. We continued to make way just east of north all the next day too. Julie took the first night watch, and I went below to sleep.

Near the end of her watch, about midnight, she woke me. She was shouting, 'Quickly, quickly, there's a light ahead!'

I sleepily scrambled on deck to look where she was pointing. Sure enough, ahead were the distant steaming lights of a small ship coming our way.

I ducked below to grab our pack of flares. They were triple wrapped in polythene, and it took some moments to unwrap them, but I soon had a red one out. Scrambling up onto the deck, I wrapped my hand in a tea towel to avoid burns and pulled the tab to ignite it. Was it wet inside? Would it light?

Suddenly it crackled and brilliant red flames and smoke billowed from the end, showering my hand with hot embers. The tea towel started to burn as I waved the flare from side to side.

The small ship appeared to slow, then stop, and we slowly sailed closer. We recognised the bright lights of a small Korean squid fishing boat. In the darkness and moderate swell, we slowly closed with her, then ground along her steel side in the swell. The crew were lined up along the ship's rail just a metre above the water, shouting, 'OK? OK?' but that seemed the full extent of their English, and we had no Korean.

I wanted to know our position, but we couldn't communicate. Were we close to Samoa? Could they radio the American Coastguard? But they understood nothing we said, nor we them.

In desperation, we passed them some empty water jerricans, saying 'Water, water.'

As we did so, *The Aegre* was swept along the side and then under the fishing boat's overhanging stern. In the moderate swell we desperately fended off, trying to avoid our hands or feet becoming trapped and crushed. Even so, in one roll, my right knee was caught between *The Aegre* and the steel bulwark. Nothing was broken, luckily, thanks to our boat being relatively light, but it was terrifying.

Suddenly the top of our jury mast swung into the stern of the ship, and there was a fearful crack. Was it broken? We were swept around to the other side of the vessel, the swell rolling us into it and smashing the low gunwale around our deck. The bowsprit caught something and cracked. Then the Korean crew were excitedly passing us back the full jerricans together with a bag containing some rice, potatoes, milk powder and sugar. 'Fishing, Fishing!' they said, pointing south, and cast us off.

It was all over in minutes. We had more food and water, but no confirmation of our position. *The Aegre* was damaged in all sorts of ways, but how badly, I didn't know. I felt both traumatised and thankful for their help.

As the ship's stern light slowly faded to the south, we hove to, alone in the darkness once more, and I lit the cooker with its half-blocked jet. We boiled some potatoes, and while they cooked, I checked the mast and side stays, but there didn't seem to be any serious damage. I thought we'd be able to raise the mainsail again. The bowsprit was broken and the port gunwale smashed, but overall *The Aegre* seemed to have stood up to the shocking encounter surprisingly well.

For so long we had wished for a ship to appear, perhaps expecting some sort of miraculous rescue. Maybe we had a cruise liner in mind. The Korean squid boat had been nothing like that, a near disaster in reality. And we still had no confirmation of our position. But the hot boiled potatoes were delicious, like nectar, and we savoured them one by one, followed by a whole cup of tea each, one of the few since the capsize four weeks before. Life seemed better already.

We hadn't noticed it clouding over, but suddenly there was a violent squall. We abandoned sailing until dawn, just keeping a lookout for the remainder of the night. We were mindful that the fishing boat might have radioed its base, perhaps Pago Pago, who just might have contacted the US Coastguard, who might just come out and look for us. That all seemed a long shot. Far too many 'mights'. Possible, but not at all probable.

Over the night the weather rapidly deteriorated, but nevertheless, we started sailing again at dawn. A wild day followed as the cloud steadily lowered and darkened and the wind freshened. I was worried about damage to our jury mast by the fishing boat, and we eventually hove to again at dusk under our fully reefed gaff mainsail.

That was a terrible night. We were constantly surrounded by wild thunder and lightning, strong wind and rapidly building seas as squall after squall passed over us.

At last a late grey dawn crept over the sea, showing a dense low bank of cloud to windward. Squalls with violent gusts of wind, heavy rain, thunder and lightning increased in number and content over the morning. At times the rain was so heavy I couldn't see the bow of the boat less than 19 feet away. We were lying hove-to under the fully reefed gaff stormsail, which was holding us so that the waves were bursting over the starboard bow, while we drifted slowly westward. It was our best hope to maintain our longitude. I carefully tracked our estimated drift.

In the late morning, the rain paused and wanting to stretch, I pushed back the hatch, stood up in the companionway and looked around. We were surrounded by dense walls of cloud and rain. Visibility was minimal. Then a little gap appeared in the grey-white clouds ahead, and through it, I suddenly realised I could see a distant rocky headland perhaps 7 miles off to the north-west.

'I can see land, I can see land!' I shouted to Julie in the cabin, and diving below, I grabbed the chart to update our estimated position. Sure enough, we had come over 170 miles due north. This must be one of the Samoan Islands!

But we weren't there yet. Julie was for closing with the land immediately. I could understand her feeling, but didn't agree. We'd thrown our anchors overboard just after the capsize, trying to reduce the boat's weight and get more freeboard, so we couldn't possibly anchor anywhere. Our only option would probably be to sail the boat ashore. If there was a coral reef or big surf, this could be suicidal unless we could find a pass in the reef. And even If we did make it safely to the shore, our problems might not be over as the area might be completely uninhabited. If it was one of the bigger islands, Upolo or Savai'i, we might have to walk miles, perhaps survive by ourselves for weeks before finding anyone.

No, I thought, we were OK on the boat for now. A better plan seemed to be to maintain visual contact with the land, keeping it abeam, and wait for the weather to improve. That way, we might see the lights of a village (and be able to signal and obtain assistance to safely land) or even see another vessel travelling along the coast. Julie reluctantly agreed.

We tried to beat eastward, to avoid being swept to the west, perhaps past the island, but found it impossible under our jury rig and in the rough sea. We were gradually being swept westward by the wind and current. From what I could see through breaks in the cloud, we were at the eastern end of a fairly large island, probably either Upolo or Savai'i. Assuming the worst, i.e. the most western island (Savai'i), then we could not afford to be swept down past it. There were no more islands to leeward, not for hundreds of miles.

We agreed to try and stay where we were overnight in the hope that we might see the lights of a settlement that we could aim for in the morning.

But we agreed that if we saw nothing during that night, then the next day we would have to close with the coast and sail along it looking for, and ultimately choosing, somewhere to put ashore. Despite my fears, it seemed the most sensible decision. I knew it would mean the end of *The Aegre*.

In the afternoon I prepared for a possible beaching the next day, collecting all the empty water jerricans together to make two emergency rafts: one to help Julie through the surf, one for me and to float a survival pack ashore. I tried to think of everything we should try and get ashore to live there, thinking it might be weeks before we met anyone.

I took the first watch that night. It was very dark due to the heavy cloud, but the wind and sea had gone down a bit. I knew it to be the sort of night when the loom of a light or the glow of a town or village would be visible for miles. I continuously scanned the horizon where I thought the land to be, but there was nothing to be seen. Not a glimmer. Just blackness.

I thought of our plan for the next day. This would be the last night I would ever spend on *The Aegre*, my beautiful boat. I knew every fastening in her. I scanned the darkness yet again. And again. And again.

Suddenly, just on the edge of my vision, I saw something. Yes, a tiny spot of light out at sea. I turned away, then back. Yes, there was a pinprick of light.

'I can see a light, Julie, quick, wake up!' I shouted to her on the bunk, 'Bring the flares!'

She hurriedly scrambled up into the hatchway with them.

I chose the biggest, a red rocket/parachute type. Trying to stay calm, I carefully read the instructions in the faint torchlight, then climbed up on deck and, holding onto the mast, wrapped my hand in a tea towel again and struck the detonator cap. Nothing happened.

Oh no, don't say this one got wet. But suddenly, WHOOSH! Up and up it went, then 'Crack!' A brilliant red flare burst and floated gently down on a parachute. It was so bright I could see a large freighter some miles away, illuminated by the flare against the horizon. Unmistakably it altered course towards us. They'd seen us!

As it slowly closed with us it was clearly a large ship. Soon its steel walls were nearby and high above us in the darkness, her searchlights illuminating everything. This time we were better prepared, and I threw a heaving line high, up to their deck far above, with a message explaining our situation and need. They closed with us carefully and sent the line back with a message saying they were going into Pago Pago, that it was very close, and they would take our boat in tow, but we would have to come aboard. They wouldn't tow *The Aegre* with us aboard.

We slowly closed with the hard steel wall of the ship's side, fearful after the experience with the Korean fishing boat. We were rising and falling a couple of metres or more on every swell and rolling wildly, soon smashing into the ship's side. It smelt of steel and diesel and safety. I threw up bow and stern lines to help secure us. I saw the top of our jury-rigged mast smashing heavily into the side of the ship above us and breaking off. Then we swung around, and the remains of the bowsprit were smashed.

They let down a rope ladder and a strong piece of line which I secured beneath Julie's arms, and then at the top of a wave, she jumped for the ladder, half scrambling up, half hauled on the line by many willing hands above. A vast wave of relief ran through me as I saw her helped over the ship's rail onto the deck. Julie was safe.

Then one of the ship's crew swarmed down the rope ladder and jumped for *The Aegre*. I caught him; he was a small man of Asian appearance. 'OK? Dai jobe?' he said urgently, and more that I didn't understand as we balanced on *The Aegre*'s precarious deck in the darkness, bashing into the ship's side with every roll. I shoved our prepacked survival pack bags at him and pointed upwards, he shouted to the deck above and they were soon hauled up, and a stout tow line sent down which we passed through the now empty bowsprit hoop and secured to the mast. Then it was my turn to jump for the ladder at the top of a wave and climb to the deck. It was a sad, sad moment, but one of relief too. Then I was over the rail and being welcomed by Julie and a group of small men in grey overalls and hard hats, bowing and smiling broadly and speaking a language I didn't understand. Below us, *The Aegre* looked so small and forlorn.

One of the crew indicated that we were to follow him, and soon we were on the bridge, where a small middle-aged Asian man in smart overalls stepped forward smiling, bowed, and said in English, 'Welcome to my ship, MS *Hokko Maru*, from Japan. I am Captain Kikuchi. Are you OK? Please come and sit down'. He led us into his small saloon adjacent to the bridge.

This was my first experience of Japanese people. I felt terribly disheveled in the relatively smart surroundings as we sat back on a couch and he served us green tea. 'I've ordered some food for you, it will be here soon,' he said. He was very friendly. 'Your parachute flare was very pretty' he said, and then 'This is where we are now'. He pointed to a chart and showed us that we were just off the eastern end of Upolo, Samoa. He had sailed from Tokyo and was going to Pago Pago (just nearby), then Puerto Rico via Panama. He said he would slow from his normal 18 knots to 9 knots to avoid damaging *The Aegre* any further.

Then a huge meal arrived for us, fried eggs, rice, soup and thick slices of toast. Afterwards we luxuriated in a large, white-tiled Japanese-style bathroom. First a hot shower, then soaking in deep hot water. It was dreamlike. He gave us a cabin with two bunks with clean white sheets. Julie seemed to go straight to sleep, but I lay awake, my mind buzzing. Soon I was up again to check on *The Aegre* and then joined the Captain on the bridge to chat. We sat in the darkness, the gentle rumble of the ship's engines beneath us. He asked about our voyage and our boat, and sitting there, rather serenely high above the ocean, in the darkness, I told him our story.

It was only a short passage to the port of Pago Pago, but as we talked, the wind was building and with it, the sea. The Captain became worried the tow line might break, so he stopped the ship and *The Aegre* was pulled back alongside. We replaced the towline with steel wire. In the now rough sea, he reduced the ship's speed to 6 knots, but even so, I could see *The Aegre* was taking on a lot of water and heeling to one side. Soon, all that could be seen in the darkness astern was a dim glow of phosphorescence on the end of the towline. At that point, I didn't expect *The Aegre* to survive as far as Pago Pago.

A bit before 4 am the next morning, Saturday 5th October 1974, 31 days after

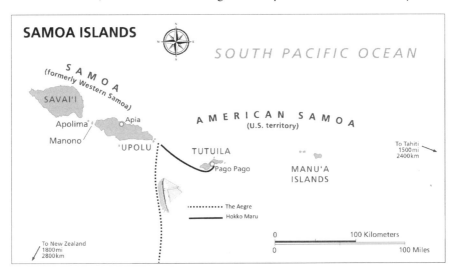

Samoa Islands

the capsize, the ship anchored in the large flooded volcanic cone that is Pago Pago harbour. Soon the ship was quiet and nearly still. Amazingly, *The Aegre* was still there, her shape just visible in the twilight on the end of the towline, like a faithful dog that won't give up following you no matter what you say or do. But she was completely swamped again, only being kept afloat once more by the buoyancy we had built into either end. The remains of her mast were still there, but all her rigging was gone. She looked a total wreck

Around us in the harbour were the lights and noise of the tuna canning plant on one side, on the other the small dim lights of the township. Everywhere in between there was dark green rain forest.

At 8 am, the Harbourmaster arrived, an American on a Harbour Authority launch, and he rather brusquely arranged for *The Aegre* to be towed to the quay. We bowed deeply to the Captain and crew of the MS *Hokku Maru*, who had been so friendly and kind, then went back down the rope ladder to the launch. The launch cast off and swung around to *The Aegre*, lying semi-submerged astern. We took and secured her bow line, and then the launch slowly towed her to the deserted dock.

It was grey and overcast in the dawn light as Julie and I scrambled up onto the concrete quay and secured our semi-submerged boat. The Harbour Authority launch turned and put-put-putted away and we stood alone on the strangely still, deserted quay. It started to rain.

Bedraggled, exhausted, and hungry, we looked at each other. I think I managed a sort of smile, almost a laugh, a near-unbelieving shake of the head. We'd made it. We gave each other a hug.

Chapter 20
High and dry on Pago Pago

*'There's nothing like a shipwreck to spark the imagination of
everyone who was not on that specific ship.' — Jon Stewart*

Somerset Maugham visited Pago Pago for six weeks from mid-December 1916, staying in a 'dilapidated lodging house with a corrugated tin roof'. It became the setting for his short story 'Rain', published in 1921. The tale depicts a psychological battle of wits between a wayward on-the-run prostitute, Sadie Thompson, and a conservative, self-righteous missionary. Maugham apparently stayed at the lodging house with a real person named Sadie Thompson, who reportedly had been driven from a red-light district in Honolulu. The lodging house that Maugham stayed in is still there in Malaloa, one of the villages of Pago Pago. Indeed, not much seemed to have changed in Pago Pago by 1974, 58 years later, when the Harbour Authority launch deposited us on the quay that October morning.

We secured *The Aegre* alongside. Again she was swamped, completely full of water, her deck almost level with the sea, barely afloat.

It was shortly after 8 am on a grey Saturday morning, and indeed raining. There were no other vessels and no one else to be seen. We felt hungry and exhausted, but there was nowhere to buy any food, not that we had any money anyway, having blindly bailed it out with our passports and all our other documents just after the capsize.

We remembered that one or two cans of food were still on *The Aegre*, so I gingerly went back aboard and felt around underwater in the cabin, looking for them. Meanwhile, Julie went off to see if she could find anyone and hopefully get some food. I couldn't find the cans but stayed aboard, having discovered the basin jammed in beside the cockpit. Thinking we'd need somewhere to sleep that night and hoping I'd find the remaining food somewhere in the chaotic washed-out cabin, I started to bail again.

A visitor came wandering along the quay and stopped to look and say hello. A bit aghast at our plight, he said he'd find a motor pump and hurried off.

Julie, meanwhile, had bumped into the Harbour Authority Chief Engineer, who jumped into action and quickly came down to the quay with a cardboard box full of cans of food and some bottles of soft drink, having broken into the Harbour Board Emergency Supplies store. But neither he nor we had a can opener. A hammer and wood chisel from *The Aegre* sufficed, and we cut open a can of Spam as a starter. Then he returned with a big paper plate of Sapa Sui (Samoan chop suey); noodles, soy sauce, meat and vegetables. We stood on the wharf in the light rain, sharing the plate, the most we'd eaten for a month. It tasted unbelievably good.

It stopped raining, and the sun came out as we finished off this memorable breakfast. Things began to look up.

Then the previous visitor arrived back, lugging a Honda motor pump, and introduced himself as Nick King, a fellow sailing voyager. He soon had it roaring away on the quay, water from its outlet pouring everywhere. Slowly *The Aegre* rose in the water, but only until she was about half empty, then she stayed at the same level while the pump roared on. Clearly the water was getting in somewhere. I went over the side into the harbour to examine the hull underwater, mainly by feel, and found a big leak where the wooden keel had moved away from the first planks. I guessed this damage had occurred during the tow. *The Aegre* would have to come out of the water to be repaired.

Nick King said there was a small slipway half a mile away. 'Ask for Stan Swerdloff,' he said, pointing further up the harbour.

Feeling a bit wobbly back on land, I set off walking, following the harbour edge. There were few people about. Now that the rain had passed and the sun was out, it felt steamy. I eventually came to it, a narrow concrete launching ramp adjacent to a small low building on the water's edge that looked as though it had only just survived the last few tropical cyclones. It was deserted and all locked up. Several small blue fishing boats were propped up ashore nearby, and amongst them, I noticed the rusty wireframe of a half-built Ferro-cement boat. Kneeling with his back to me beside it and working on the wire was a fair-haired man in a blue work shirt.

'Excuse me, do you know where I could find Stan Swerdloff?' I asked. My

Cambridge (England) accent sounded out of place, even to me, on this little American island in the middle of the South Pacific.

In silence, the kneeling man slowly turned, then stood to look me up and down in amazement. Then, peering at me more closely, he replied quizzically, 'Yer what?' in as broad a north of England accent as I've ever heard. I'd chanced upon Ken Bailey, 35, English shipwright extraordinaire, from Lancashire, now in Pago Pago on a United Nations fishing support programme. He and his wife, Jennifer, were the only English people on the island.

I explained about *The Aegre* up at the dock. Ken was almost speechless. In shock, I think, he sprang into action. A boat was dispatched to the Harbour Authority quay to pick up Julie and slowly tow *The Aegre* to the slipway. Meanwhile, Ken pulled together a bunch of helpers to gather timber and quickly build a rough wooden frame which they would guide under *The Aegre* to support her, and then to pull her up the slipway. The Fire Brigade was called to bring a strong water pump to empty *The Aegre* as she came out of the water.

Ken must have called Jennifer, because she soon arrived with many friends, bringing sandwiches, cakes and soft drinks. More and more people came to look. *The Aegre* was positioned off the end of the slipway and the wooden frame placed under her. Then, with a tow line attached to a Landcruiser and the Fire Brigade's pump gushing water out, they slowly started to pull her up the slipway.

All went according to plan as *The Aegre* was inched out of the sea, but she was heavier than expected (probably due to the water still in her), and halfway up the slipway, the framework broke and she crashed onto her side. I wanted to close my eyes, but I trusted Ken, and under his leadership, *The Aegre* continued to be slowly drawn up the slipway. She seemed a total wreck. As if it wasn't bad enough to have our entire home turned upside down and shaken about in the mid-Pacific and then towed underwater for a few hours, she was now being dragged up a rough concrete slip on her side, like a dead and broken whale. Her insides, her entrails, everything we owned, spilled out, broken. It was not a time to be houseproud. We were just thankful to be there.

Meanwhile, news of the event had spread, and a crowd had assembled. In the heat of the morning I'd stripped off my shirt and after our enforced diet over four weeks every rib stood out, my arms were like matchsticks, my face gaunt. Julie had survived a little better, but still everywhere we turned, sandwiches and drinks were pressed into our hands.

Finally, at the end of the day, *The Aegre* was propped up on land beside the slipway. The hull looked in remarkably good condition, considering. I fussed around her as if she were a sick friend, ensuring she was safe and secure. I didn't want to leave her alone, but luckily we didn't have to sleep aboard her that night. Instead, Ken and Jennifer took us back to their home and into their hearts. That night we feasted on fresh barbecued tuna. Nothing had ever tasted quite so good. Afterwards, we crawled into a lovely bed between clean sheets. It was so quiet and still. We felt secure and safe.

We'd arrived on a Saturday. The following day, Ken and Jennifer took us to a church service held outdoors on a big green lawn directly above the sea. I'm not religious, but there was something extraordinary that morning about singing hymns, saying prayers, and giving thanks under a calm blue sky, looking out over the ocean. We were thankful to be alive and safe.

Immediately following the service, I was asked to say a few words to the large congregation about the events leading up to our rather dramatic arrival the day before. It was the first of many tellings of the story. Then, over a pot-luck lunch of staggering proportion and diversity, served on the lawn, we were introduced to a Who's Who of Pago Pago: the Governor, Attorney General, Samoan Chief of Youth Development, other Samoan chiefs, senior government officials, business people and their partners, dozens of people. They took us under their wing. Visas were arranged, an empty house just like Ken and Jennifer's found for us and work in a bank arranged for Julie, while I was asked to take over teaching a navigation class at the Community College, with other work offers to be confirmed. Extraordinarily, we seemed to have landed on our feet.

Monday came, and one of our highest priorities was to let our parents know we were safe. In our last letters from Tahiti, we'd told them we would sail next to Rarotonga, 10 days maximum away, probably less. That was now nearly 40 days ago. My father had been following our voyage very keenly, plotting our positions from our letters on a large wall map of the world. We wanted to reassure them we were safe, and to reassure Julie's parents too. This proved difficult. Mail from Pago seemed likely to take a couple of weeks (at least), so we decided to try and call them on the phone. We had never called them before, the cost seeming prohibitive from every previous port. We asked the Post Office, who told us we would have to book a call some days in advance. I learnt the call would go by a single channel radiotelephone to the US and then by cable to the UK. The call could only be made between 2 am and 4 am and would cost tens of dollars a minute.

We booked the call and showed up at 2am. Ken and Jennifer must have loaned us some money. Eventually, with much static interference, I heard the phone ringing in Cottenham. My sister Diana soon answered it.

'We're OK, we're in Pago Pago', I said.

Diana hadn't seen or talked with me for more than twenty months. Much later, she told me how surprised she was to hear my voice. She remembered our next stop was to be the Cook Islands (wherever they were). Now she heard we were in Pago Pago (wherever that was). So what, she wondered, and why wouldn't we be OK? Then my mother took over the phone, and I tried to explain.

'We're OK, we capsized, but we're safe in Pago Pago.' Well, that's what I tried to say, but on the single-channel line, only one person could speak at once, so it was a chaotic mixture of both of us speaking simultaneously and then silence. My mother only got half the message, which half we never knew. It was a totally unexpected call from us, probably in the middle of the night, that included the word 'capsize' and some weird sounding place. Was it Pango Pango? La La Land? Where was that? Whatever, all her worries were confirmed.

We didn't know it, but she already had plenty to deal with. My father had had an angina attack some weeks before (unconnected to us, I like to believe) and had been told by his doctor to consider early retirement. He'd been moved to a makeshift downstairs bedroom, rarely got up, and my mother was naturally most anxious about him. Now this worrying half-message from her son somewhere in the South Pacific.

It was hopeless trying to explain. I realised I was probably making things worse, but then the line went dead before I could even hang up properly.

In desperation, we quickly sent them a telegram: SAFE AND SOUND IN PAGO PAGO LETTER FOLLOWING WRITE MARINE RESOURCES NICK AND JULIE

Today it's hard to imagine just how difficult it was to communicate across the world back in 1974, particularly from remote South Sea islands.

I later learned that the garbled news had sent my father into a downward spiral, and the doctor was called. Much later, I wished we hadn't tried to call them but simply sent a telegram saying 'All's well in American Samoa' and followed this with a postcard saying we'd decided to stay there for a while and work. But we didn't. Instead, we went on to send a letter all about the capsize and our subsequent voyage to Pago under jury rig. How we'd lost our passports and other documents and asked their help to replace them as soon as possible. We were just so tied up with ourselves and our problems. I don't think we considered for one minute that they might be facing their own crisis, or the effect our news might have on them. I learned later how my father's health had worsened with our news.

The Aegre was now propped up on the land beside the other boats and the slipway. Rather sadly, I stripped everything from her — the remains of all our belongings and everything that could be detached — and took it all to Ken's house, piling it all on the veranda.

Two days after we had arrived Julie summarized our situation in her diary: *I should be sorting out the kit, still on the veranda, but I feel too weak to do it. We are still recovering mentally and physically from the ordeal. Nick looked terrible last night, out to dinner with the Lomas's, the Minister and his wife. He looked ashen, deep sunk eyes, very dark rims, very quiet too. I feel weak all the time and difficult to get up interest in anything. Not very keen on Samoa, with all the red tape and the Govt. Nick is very keen to make a go of it here though. I expect I'll feel better when I start working. Also when we've got a place of our own, although Ken and Jennifer are wonderfully kind and thoughtful., and we don't feel in the least awkward staying here, though they only have one bedroom, one lounge, one bathroom and one kitchen. Somehow it doesn't seem crowded. I slept this morning till 8 or so. The first uninterrupted nights sleep, 12–7:30. The night before we had less than 4 hours.*

Without any plan for the future, we just got on with recovering our lives. We needed documents to prove who we were and help us find work. We needed somewhere to live, good food to recover, and to buy our own clothes. We just needed a period of calm, secure life to move on from the drama of the previous four weeks — well, the drama of the last fifteen months, really.

Julie was possibly feeling more lost initially than I, writing: *I really am leaning on Nick all the time for support, but still don't feel close to him. We're too busy to have time for each other.*

But she soon started at the bank as a savings bookkeeper and became much happier with a regular job to go out to every day, her first since Scotland. My days were quickly filled with preparing to teach navigation, looking for full-time work, and with writing letters. Letters to our parents explaining what had happened, a letter to boatbuilder Bob Macinnes telling the story and saying not to worry because his bottle of Barbados rum and his Grandad's log were safe. A letter to the British Passport Office in England asking how we could replace our passports, and more. The mail was our only link with the outside world.

One of the first to reply was Bob Macinnes. I imagined him sitting on his stool in his dusty Nissen shed workshop, unshaven, in his old blue overalls, wearing his scratched, half-broken glasses. He'd be holding our latest letter from the South Pacific in his big, gnarled hands, smiling and shaking his head as he read it. Then he'd share it with Robert McLeod and Angus Mckenzie and the village. He replied, saying how relieved he was that we had survived the capsize. He went on to say that regarding his grandfather's log, which we had trailed behind *The Aegre* for more than 12,000 nautical miles, always promising to return it to him. He wrote: 'I think you deserve to keep it. Show it to your grandchildren.'

His offer thrilled us. The log had been so valuable and precious. What a memento it would be, of Bob, *The Aegre,* the voyage, everything.

We'd told Ken Bailey all about Bob and his work on *The Aegre*, and Ken had offered to take the log and Bob's bottle of rum back to the UK on his next visit. Ken wanted to visit him, which would give him a great excuse to make the long drive north from his home in Lancaster to Scourie in Scotland. But now he'd just be taking the bottle of Mount Gay rum we'd looked after so carefully for him since Barbados, while the log would stay with us.

The UK Passport Office eventually replied that our passports would be re-issued by the British High Commission in Apia, Western Samoa, so we wrote to the High Commission in Apia. Some weeks later, they replied saying they were no longer the British High Commission but now the New Zealand High Commission. They said our passports might be re-issued by the British High Commission in Tonga. So we wrote to Tonga. Then we waited — and waited.

Back in England, I had loved watching *Monty Python* on TV. It wasn't so much fun being part of the show.

Meanwhile, I was still looking for work. There had seemed to be so many opportunities to start with, but now they were fading away one by one. Eventually I joined with a local Samoan entrepreneur and set up a sport fishing business. At the time there was no such business on the island due to no one having the required US Coastguard certification. I took the exam and, with the certificate in hand, set about battling the island bureaucracy. It took weeks as I painstakingly worked my way through it, gaining the necessary approval from the Development Planning Office, for Zoning Requirements; Public

Health, for Sanitary and Health Requirements; Workmen's Compensation, for Coverage of Employees; the Tax Office, for Income Tax; the Credit and Collection Branch, for Accounts Receivables; the Immigration Board, for Eligibility and Residency Status; and the Special Licensing Authority (in this case the US Coastguard). And all I wanted to do was take a sport fishing boat out with paying passengers for a day's fishing.

In that first month in Pago, so much happened. We moved into a house ashore and found work and friends, but it slowly crept up on us that settling in Pago Pago, doing what we were doing, wouldn't satisfy us for long. Furthermore, we began to suspect that it might be difficult to get a visa to stay beyond the six months we'd been granted, which would make building some sort of life or business a waste of time.

The Aegre was still propped up in the boatyard. I'd stripped her of everything, and now she was an empty hull awaiting repair to the planking. To sail on, we'd need to repair the planking, rebuild the rig, and replace all the equipment required for ocean cruising. I contemplated this, but was discouraged by Julie's 'I'm not getting back on that boat for anyone' attitude. She said she was finished with sailing, she just wanted an easy secure life, a family, a career related to education. I didn't feel finished with sailing at all, but I felt weary at the thought of a complete rebuild and re-fit of *The Aegre*. If I was going to put that much work in, I wanted to do it on a bigger boat. Julie didn't want any boat at all. What were we to do?

Amongst our many new friends was a New Zealander, Clare Hedgpeth, who told us one day about her brother, who had done a New Zealand outward bound school course. She knew all about it. I'd heard of outward bound schools when I was living in England. I vaguely knew them as very physically demanding outdoor pursuit centres in the hills or near the water, to which employers would send young apprentices to help them mature. Just a little bit like Ridgway's adventure school in Scotland.

Clare told us that the NZ Outward Bound School was situated in the beautiful Queen Charlotte Sound, in the north of South Island, and had a broad-based program of bushwalking, sailing and white-water kayaking. It sounded wonderful. We wondered if we could get work there. It seemed a long shot. We didn't even have passports at that time.

We wrote to the NZ Outward Bound School and quickly received an encouraging reply. An instructor vacancy was anticipated, but they would give us no guarantee of work without a personal interview in New Zealand. Nor were any plane tickets attached.

Should we persist in Pago Pago or abandon our efforts to make a living there, leave *The Aegre* and fly to New Zealand, on the off-chance of finding work at the outward bound school?

Julie was bored with her work at the bank and keen to go. My sport fishing business was picking up and clearly had potential, but it rained a lot, which didn't help. Despite the rain, I was now often out on the water with tourists, but that was having an unexpected effect. Some of the chiefs were not happy, I was quietly told. There were murmurings that this should be a Samoan business. Privately I agreed. There clearly wasn't any future in it for me.

All in all, everything pointed to New Zealand.

Then we heard back from Tonga that our replacement passports had been sent to the NZ High Commission in Apia, to be collected, except of course I couldn't leave Pago or enter Western Samoa without a passport. But in the South Pacific, these things can be arranged. Soon I was on the overnight ferry and back again with our new passports. Now we could travel.

But what about *The Aegre*? Ken Bailey stepped up and agreed to repair her planking, make a new mast and re-rig her as a day sailing boat over the next few months and then sell her on our behalf. So then, with *The Aegre*'s future decided, we made a bold decision. We emptied our bank account and, with an advance on the sale of boat loaned by Ken, bought two air tickets to Auckland, New Zealand.

I made one last visit to *The Aegre,* now rather forlorn in the boatyard and awaiting repair by Ken. But even in her distressed state, she was still the epitome of a small but extraordinarily seaworthy boat. Our trust in her had not been misplaced, her Viking heritage proven by her handling of the roughest seas. She had met our wildest expectations in every way, carrying us safely through the weeks of gales in the far North Atlantic, the mistrals off the coast of the Sahara, and the many long days becalmed halfway between Africa and the West Indies. She'd hosted the Barbados cruising fraternity's most memorable Christmas party, cruised the Grenadines, the playground of billionaires, averaged more than 100 nautical miles a day across the Caribbean, traversed the Panama Canal and taken us 4,200 nm non-stop across the Eastern Pacific. Aboard her, we'd cruised Melville's Marquesas and the Kon Tiki's Tuamotos. She'd lain on a beach in Tahiti under the brooding shadow of Moorea and the watchful eye of the great *Varua*. She'd survived the very worst the South Pacific could hurl at her and brought us safely to Samoa. What tales of the sea were embedded in her very body! What spirit she had! She had given us so much more than we had ever expected to ask of her.

I felt guilty abandoning her when she needed me most, but there seemed no other way. I was consoled by my confidence in shipwright Ken Bailey. She was in good hands. I knew he'd restore her. She'd sail again, proudly, as the only Shetland boat in the South Pacific. But still, after what we'd been through together, it was tough to turn and walk away. I knew I'd never see her again. She had brought us so far, both in miles and in life. I wanted to hug her, kiss her, thank her, and ask her forgiveness for being a poor master.

Thus it was that eighteen months after sailing from Scotland and a little over two months since we'd struggled onto the Pago Pago quay with our near wrecked boat, Julie and I got on a plane about midnight for the five-hour flight to New Zealand. It was 19ᵗʰ December 1974. We had everything we could carry in a faded green Avon dinghy bag. I felt well on the way to being physically and spiritually restored and deeply thankful to all the people who had helped us recover.

As the plane climbed to the south, I turned to peer out of the small porthole and watched as the tiny dots of light from Pago Pago sank below us to become mere pinpricks in the immense darkness of the Pacific. I thought of the past two months and all that had happened. From the relief of arriving safely, through the optimism about work and finding somewhere to live. And how it gradually faded.

The dream, the voyage of *The Aegre,* was over.

But at least we did better than Maugham's Sadie Thompson and got out before January, when the rain really came down.

Julie and I did find work with the NZ Outward Bound School in the Marlborough Sounds and stayed there for 18 months. Then we moved on to work in Auckland and later Invercargill, living together in NZ for five years. And then … and then … but that's another story.

Postscript — So what happened to *The Aegre*?

When Julie and I flew out of Pago for New Zealand at the end of 1974, *The Aegre* was in the hands of Ken Bailey who had taken on her repair and eventual sale. Subsequently from New Zealand I often corresponded with Ken explaining how to set up the rig, and other details. The restoration was eventually completed, and *The Aegre* sold to the only Scandinavian person living on the island, Hans Mose. Since then, I'd often wondered what became of her, but Ken and Jennifer Bailey had soon returned to the U.K. and I had no contact with Mose or anyone else in Pago Pago.

Thirty years later, in 2004, I received an unexpected email bringing me news of *The Aegre*. It was from a Gene Carl Feldman in the U.S., telling me that in early 1976, he had bought *The Aegre* in Pago from Hans Mose, and sailed her while living in Apia, Western Samoa and working as a young Peace Corps volunteer.

He'd tracked me down after seeing a short account of *The Aegre* voyage on a website. He told me how he had chanced across *The Aegre* in Pago harbour in March 1976. It was love at first sight; he'd graduated in biological sciences/oceanography, and his eye tuned by his time at sea had told him this was a very special boat. He soon met her owner, Hans Mose, and learned something of her ocean-spanning story. He persuaded Hans to sell *The Aegre* to him, and then despite having limited sailing experience, set off to sail her to Apia, in Western Samoa, a hundred miles to the west, including a 60-mile open ocean stretch.

The Aegre looked after Gene as well as she had us, but not without a few adventures, he safely arrived in Apia some days later.

The Aegre then became a resident of Apia harbour, often taking Gene and his friends for days sails, picnics and the occasional over-nighter. But Gene's volunteer role came to an end in October 1977. He wasn't game to try sailing her back to New York and instead passed her into the care of a small group of Japan Overseas Cooperation Volunteers (JOCV).

From there her story becomes murky. No-one seems to quite know what happened to her when these volunteers returned to Japan. And then a few years later a violent tropical cyclone swept over Samoa, and *The Aegre* is believed to have been lost. There is no further record of her.

I rather like to think that she became dissatisfied with her life rotting on a tropical mooring, and when the opportunity came, she took herself off to sea in the Viking way, never to be seen again.

Acknowledgements

I am indebted to Julie, without whom the voyage would surely never have happened. There could have been no more steadfast and supportive a partner and shipmate. Furthermore, I would like to thank her for allowing me to quote from her letters and diary, for reading early versions of the story and for her helpful suggestions.

I am most grateful to John and Marie Christine Ridgway for employing me when I barely knew a sheepshank from a bowline and then inspiring Julie and me to undertake the voyage. And furthermore for their introduction to David Burnett, a retired publisher, whose help has been critical to publishing the story.

Julie and I must also thank our parents for giving us the confidence to think such an adventure was possible.

Thanks should also go to Tom Edwardson from Yell, who built *The Aegre* and Bob Macinnes, the boatbuilder in Scourie, who decked her in. Their workmanship stood up to the fiercest the world's oceans could throw at it. Moreover, Bob's belief in the boat and us led to Mr and Mrs Hay at the Scourie Hotel employing us and the people of Scourie taking us in in mid-winter. Their generous and entertaining support made the preparatory months in Scourie worthy of its own book (yet to be written).

In the story I've written about some of the many ocean-cruising people and people ashore who helped us along the way. There are too many to thank individually here, but Julie and I were so grateful for your friendship and support. To mention a few, I want to thank again Pat Chilton in Madeira who taught me how to work out astro sights at 700 mph, Alex Bell in Grenada who gave us all his Pacific charts, the Canadian Navy for you know what, Tom Blackwell who took us through the Panama Canal lashed alongside his big ketch *Islander*, Pierre who employed me in Tahiti, Captain Ryohei Kikuchi and the crew of the *Hokko Maru* who saw our flare, and Ken and Jennifer Bailey and many others in Pago Pago whose generous help eased our transition back to life ashore immeasurably.

Fifty years later my young granddaughters, Maggie and Rania, unwittingly inspired me to write the story down before it was lost in the haze of old age, but I would never have completed it were it not for the insistence and tireless support of Dr Gene Carl Feldman, in Washington, DC. Gene had bought the rebuilt *Aegre* in Pago back in 1976 as described in the Postscript. Reading and giving me suggestions on every chapter as I wrote, and rewrote it over nearly three years and more than ninety teleconferences, finally saw it done. Then he created the front and back cover and prepared the photos, maps and diagrams.

Apart from the drawings Gene and I did ourselves, I'd like to thank Dr Adrian Osler for allowing me to reproduce some of his drawings of the construction of Shetland boats and John Quirk for his truly terrifying depiction of the capsize.

Writing the story, I greatly benefited from the comments, suggestions, questions, and encouragement of a number of intrepid readers in the UK, US, Australia and New Zealand and for this I would like to particularly thank Professor Judy McKay, Norman Kuring, Diana McLachlan, Neville Roberts, and Brigitte Sass.

Finding a publisher is surely always difficult, and I would like to thank Richard Wynne of Lodestar Books, who believed in the project when no big publisher did. However, in those anxious pre-publication days, I was greatly heartened to receive a commendation from the well-known all-rounder, TV presenter, successful writer and sailor, Paul Heiney, recently Commodore of the Royal Cruising Club in England. He'd read my manuscript, and his comments gave me a huge boost as a first-time author, so my warm thanks to him. It was with increased confidence that I decided that if I was to tell the story in the way I wanted, regardless of the market, I needed to publish the book myself. To do so, I am indebted to publisher David Burnett who came out of retirement to not only become an advisor to me on all publishing matters but a link to editor Chris Newton, page maker Dr Digby James, and further readers and advisors Jeremy Burnett and Sandra Bell. All gave invaluable help.

Finally, I must thank my two daughters, Erica and Mariko, and son-in-law Jevon, who keep my feet firmly on the ground, and my wife Tomoko, without whose support, encouragement, insight, and patience, the story would have missed much and possibly never been completed and published.

Nicholas Grainger,
Melbourne, Australia, 2023.

Map Credits

MAP 1A: Endpaper Map 'A new chart of the Atlantic 1797'
adapted from map found at: https://collections.leventhalmap.org/search/
commonwealth:kk91fr56g

MAP 1B: Endpaper Map 'A new chart of the South Pacific Ocean 1849'
adapted from map found at: https://www.digitalcommonwealth.org/search/
commonwealth:zk51wb060

MAP 2: Scotland
adapted from map found at: https://commons.wikimedia.org/wiki/
File:Scotland_map-en.svg
credit: Eric Gaba — Wikimedia Commons user: Sting

MAPS 3: North Atlantic, 4a: Barbados Grenada to St Vincent, 4b: Caribbean
Sea and 7b: Tahiti, adapted from maps found at: https://ian.macky.net/pat/
credit: Ian Macky

MAPS 5: Panama to French Polynesia and 8a: Tahiti to Samoa
adapted from GMT maps generated by Norman Kuring

MAP 6: Panama Canal
adapted from map found at: https://www.eia.gov/todayinenergy/detail.
php?id=26792
credit: U.S. Energy Information Administration

MAP 7a: French Polynesia
adapted from map found at: https://commons.wikimedia.org/wiki/
File:French_Polynesia_relief_map.svg
credit: L. Claudel

MAP 8b: Samoa Regional Map
adapted from map found at: https://npmaps.com/wp-content/uploads/
american-samoa-regional-map.jpg
credit: U.S. National Park Service